Understanding Quantitative Analysis

Understanding Quantitative Analysis

CHESTER R. WASSON

APPLETON-CENTURY-CROFTS
EDUCATIONAL DIVISION
MEREDITH CORPORATION
New York

(669-1)

Library of Congress Card Number: 76-93998

PRINTED IN THE UNITED STATES OF AMERICA

390-92780-5

Preface

As the title indicates, this is not intended as a text on mathematical techniques, nor is anyone likely to find it very useful as such. Rather it is aimed to impart that understanding of the quantitative side of all information which is needed to make a balanced judgment concerning the alternatives open to us in any decision situation. One of the major success stories of the Peace Corps is said to be that of a girl whose sole accomplishment in a year with an African tribe was to introduce the concept of counting and to teach them to count. The result was a doubling of their income and a boom in the local economy. Their sole major source of income was the harvesting and sale of palm nuts, and because their culture included no concept of counting, they had been regularly cheated by traders. If this book helps any substantial number of decision makers in our society to gain a parallel understanding of the more sophisticated and less certain process of measurement, estimation, and prediction, I feel certain (99% so, anyway) that a similar boom in their affairs and those of the nation will occur.

Most of the numbers we all must use to comprehend a mass economy are the results of the measurement process and are used to make predictions. However objective many of our measuring instruments may seem to be, measurement itself contains a large component of subjective judgment, and prediction is never an automatic, mathematical process. Compilation and calculation of the numbers must usually be delegated to specialists, but interpretation of the meaning of their results cannot be entrusted to them any more than could the count of the harvest to the traders in the African village. The problem lies not in cheating, in this case, but in the fact that the quantitative side is only half of the descriptive truth although nearly all of its objective side. The other half is the personal and unique qualitative side which come out of the objectives of those who must make use of the computed results. To be half-informed with full knowledge of either side of truth is usually to be fully uninformed. Real knowledge comes only with the interpretation of the qualitative side in the light of the objectives of a decision and of the personal and often unquantifiable insights into possibilities of the future.

Not everyone needs to be a mathematician. Once we know what our objectives for the use of information are and what tools might give us some help, we can usually delegate to others the relatively objective and routine operations of computation. But all of us who must make significant decisions of any kind need to understand the values and limitations of the techniques being used in the calculations, and the limits which must be put on the interpretations of the results. Furthermore, no one else can be trusted to make the final qualitative judgments about the meaning of the results for our own purposes.

In the discussion which follows, a minimum of mathematical symbolism is used, but not solely because many of those at whom this book is aimed have little regular practice in its use. Such symbolism adds little, if anything, to an understanding of any of the tools. (Sometimes, indeed, its use seems to cloud the meaning.) The value of the symbols is the convenience they provide for actual mathematical operations, and this work is not intended to teach the latter. The basic nature of modern decision tools is not best comprehended in terms of symbols, but needs the nuances of prose. Moreover, even actual computations must eventually be translated into prose when they become an input to decision. Even though symbolism is avoided whenever not really useful, this author hopes that even those adept in its use may pause to consider some of the truths summarized herein, if only to remind themselves of the real imprecision of their calculated results and the necessity for their clients to use a large dollop of judgment and imagination in application of the numbers they furnish.

The evaluation of uncertainty is the subject of much of this work. One of the uncertainties of life is knowing what others need to know that we can impart, and whether our attempts at communication are likely to succeed. I have been fortunate in getting help from two perceptive people in developing the final draft. Barbara Fox, formerly with Bell Laboratories performed a painstaking review of my presentation and made many substantial suggestions and corrections. Ralph Zaletal, of the U.S. Civil Service Training Division, and now with the Maxwell School of Public Administration, gave valuable guidance as to needed subject coverage as well as some very useful suggestions on approaches.

Grateful acknowledgement must also be given to my publisher, Appleton-Century-Crofts Co., for permission to include substantial excerpts of my previous books, The Strategy of Marketing Research, Research Analysis for Marketing Decision, and The Economics of Managerial Decision.

Chester R. Wasson

Contents

CHAPTER 1 INTRODUCTION: THE LANGUAGE OF QUANTITY

The Need for Understanding

This is a book about a language--a language which is, informally at least, a necessary part of the thinking of all civilized men. This language is that of numbers and other symbols of quantity. However, it is probably poorly understood by most of those who use it and often not clearly understood by many of those expert in its manipulation.

To a great many of us--probably even the overwhelming majority--the formal written language of quantitative expression and quantitative analysis seems to be a horribly complex, strange tongue. Conversely, fairly large numbers of people perceive quantitative expression as the most exact and beautiful essence of all truth, and in addition, a wonderfully fascinating game. Both extreme attitudes are far too unquestioning, both equally devoid of understanding of the meaning and intellectual purpose of mathematical expression. Both overlook the information that is lost in the simplification needed to translate the disorder of the natural world into the orderly language of mathematical symbols. Both result in the unquestioning acceptance of pure nonsense when put into mathematical form.

This mystical acceptance of mere figures was exemplified some years ago when an official of a teacher's organization wished to give impact to his theme that teachers should be paid more. Without authority of any sort and without any sound definitional basis for his figures, he asserted that "90,000 teachers are leaving the profession every year." His implication, of course, was that this condition was shocking. This was, indeed, the import of an article which appeared soon after in a popular national magazine, "Why Are 90,000 Teachers Leaving Every Year?" Yet even had his figure been based on some real count (which it was not) it could have actually been too low for a profession employing 1 million people. The number retiring or marrying and going to raise a family might alone have been greater than his 90,000 if he included them in his definition. The point is, neither he nor anybody else ever indicated what his figure included and what it omitted. It was an arbitrary figure, quoted without content, representing no definable set of facts. Nevertheless, because it was given in numerical form, apparently no one challenged either his statement or his interpretation of it. While such numerical trickery is not as rare as it should be, an even greater danger arises from lack of effort to understand quantities. The real, everyday danger is that we will lead ourselves, or let others lead us astray through faulty acceptance of half the answer. Quantity is never the whole answer to any problem, or even an adequate half answer. A more complete answer is clear only when we relate the quantity to those elements we define vaguely as quality, only when we arrive at an understanding of how the quantitative statement relates to the non-quantitative objectives we hope to achieve.

This book is an attempt to impart some of this understanding of quantitative methods, particularly those methods of greatest value in making decisions in the world of people and business. It is meant for all those who must apply the results of calculations to choose between courses of action, to help them find for themselves the true meaning of the calculated results and understand the limits on precision which result from purely quantitative analysis. Many if not most such choices cannot rest on the figures alone. The figures help spell out some of the limits, but they only aid, they do not replace human judgment. Indeed many of the tools which will be discussed use figures which come from judgmental sources, and are only as good as the judgment. In turn, the end results of the tabulations are quite usually devices to insure that rational human judgment will be the basis of the decision rather than arbitrary feeling.

THE NEED TO UNDERSTAND QUANTITATIVE LANGUAGE

It would be difficult to say which is the surer road to error: basing decision choices solely on the simplistic calculations of formal mathematics or ignoring the efficiencies of such formal calculations and relying mainly on qualitative judgment. The latter hides the quantitative aspect under cumbersome vague generalizations. The former ignores the important differences which numbers must disregard.

It is not hard to say, however, which is the less efficient. Every decision has some inescapable quantitative implications, and these must be dealt with in some manner. The action taken must deal in quantities, and the only usual feedback for evaluation of results is some form of quantitative measure. Relying on vague prose formulations makes consideration of alternatives much more cumbersome than the use of formal mathematics and can lead to gross misjudgment of results. Moreover, the basic language of mathematics is by far the easier side of the decision to comprehend and evaluate. Ignoring such efficiency sacrifices effort and time which need to be given to consideration of really important subjective appraisals of the qualitative side of every decision, a side not reducible to such a simplistic language. Avoiding the need for precise definition of the "how much" of the action inputs courts the dangers of too little or too much, too soon or too late.

Efficient decision-making thus depends on maximum formalization of the quantitative aspects and maximum interpretative attention to the qualitative aspects. Fortunately it is not necessary to be skilled in the intricate details of mathematical calculations in order to understand their meaning for decision. Indeed, there is some reason to suspect that those who devote the most time to gaining such manipulative skills are the least likely to take a balanced look at the less precise qualitative side which must enter all wise decisions. Moreover, the qualitative side of a decision necessarily involves highly subjective personal values which can be assessed only by those who hold responsibility for the decision and its results. Consider the simplified example of the choice between two investments each costing $10,000: (1) one which has a 90% probability of yielding a $20,000 return in five years, (2) one which has a 9% probability of yielding a $200,000 return in the same time. The mathematics says that the two opportunities are equal--both have an expected return of $18,000. (0.90 x 20,000 = 18,000 and 0.09 x 200,000 = 18,000). But few of us would view them as really equal from a personal standpoint.

THE REALITIES NUMBERS DO NOT MEASURE

Some of us would see as most important the actual return, if successful, of only $20,000 in one case and $200,000 in the other, and so would choose the riskier course. Others would put greater weight on the fact that the one is almost as close to being certain as is likely in practice, the other highly improbable, and decide on the safer one. Which we would choose would therefore be dependent in part on our resources, in part on our own objectives and a very personal attitude toward risk. No mathematics yet invented can make such a decision for us. It can, however, tell us that they have the same (risk x return) product. Similar calculations would tell us that if the probability of the $200,000 return were to drop to 6%, for example, its expected return would be less than that of the more certain choice, and therefore not a rational alternative whatever our attitude toward risk.

The illustration illuminates both the values of quantitative language and the limitations which require every decision maker to be his own interpreter of meaning. Numbers help us to cut through the many details in which, for a given purpose, two phenomena or two alternatives differ, to bring into focus those attributes in which they can be compared--for that one purpose. Given the purpose, such comparisons can be objective. They are nonpersonal, since anyone with the competence to understand the situation and the language of quantity would arrive at the same ordering of value--in the example above, that the two $20,000 investments yielded comparable returns, relative to risk.

However, even the numerical description of the example indicates that the two investment alternatives do differ, both in actual return and in accompanying risk. In the quantitative statement, the two inequalities balance out, but in any personal assessment, two equally competent executives of differing temperaments would make different choices because their risk aversion values resulted in a different qualitative ranking.

In other words, quantitative language helps us to measure the nonpersonal similarities in our universe by ignoring matters in which, for a given purpose, even a nonpersonal view can detect dissimilarities. The decision process is thus freed to concentrate on the much less easily measured qualitative attributes whose relative ordering of importance depends on the personal objectives and insights of he who makes the decision. Since every decision involves both halves of reality--both the quantitative and the qualitative--neither the choice of alternatives nor the evaluation of results can rest solely on either the quantitative side or the qualitative sides. The calculations of the quantitative sides can often be delegated to skilled technicians, and often should be, since these are nonpersonal.

But the choices of alternatives and evaluation of results rest on criteria so personal in value that the technician's results by themselves are meaningless. The decision maker must therefore understand the language of quantity in order to know what quantities are important to his ends, and which results of highest value.

In the example above we have assumed that the figures we are using are quite solid and known, unvarying in meaning. This however, is not an inherent characteristic of numbers. Indeed, the truth is quite the opposite. Numbers have no meaning at all by themselves, and their very use requires us to ignore some of the facts. As already indicated whatever significance they have is relative to the circumstances of their uses.

Thus, it is important that we understand just how simple and incomplete numerical information, and indeed all mathematical language is, and how dependent it is on nonmathematical information for meaning.

THE MEANING OF A NUMBER

Numbers, we all must recognize, are not natural realities. Indeed, they are not reality at all, but artificial constructs of the human mind which have been invented, paradoxically, to help us understand part of reality. A number represents a count, and we can count nothing until we are willing to shut our eyes to a basic reality of nature. That reality is that no two things in existence are exactly alike in every possible respect. Yet whenever we say there are two of anything, or two million, we are stating that each of the units in our count--people, apples, pies, dollars, or whatever--can be substituted for any other unit. We can do this wisely and honestly only when we define the limits of substitutability, when we state the purpose, time, place, or other conditions under which we are willing to substitute one for the other. Thus, if the bank teller offers us the choice of ten dimes or a dollar bill in exchange for our check for $1, he may be perfectly correct in saying that he is offering us one dollar in each case. But if our purpose in cashing that check was to get some coins to make a telephone call, the dollar bill is not, for us, equal to the ten dimes, however equal they may be in the bank's bookkeeping. At the moment, the dollar bill is worth nothing to us because it does not fit our need for dimes.

To take a more complicated example, let us consider the population of the state of Arkennessee which the Census Bureau defines by the rather definite-looking figure of 5,397,836 people listed as of April 1, 1975. To the grocers of this fictional state, this probably represents the number of mouths they can sell to, and while each person does not consume the same amount of food, the approximation is close enough. To the state's two political parties, the Republicrats and the Demopublicans, every member of that count is important in determining the state's representation in the United States House of Representatives. At election time, however, their focus of interest shifts and both parties regard as consequential only 2,195,410 people, the number of registered voters. For the makers of hair-coloring compounds, the number is less than that - possibly the 1,090,119 teen-age girls and adult women who are not natural blondes, but dream of the romance they might have if they were. To the makers of Pepsi-Cola, the 5 million number probably does represent the number of mouths in the state that are able to formulate a request for their product. Their advertising salvos, however, must be aimed at the million and a quarter teen-agers, the important one-fourth of the total which consumes well over three-fourths of their output. To a harassed presidential administration seeking to pry an important bill out of Congress, Arkennessee has at the moment only ten people: its congressional delegation of 7 Demopublicans who will probably vote favorably, another who is on the fence and must be brought into line, and the 2 Republicrats who are sure to oppose the measure. In addition, the fence-straddling Demopublican happens to be heading the committee handling the legislation and counts more in the president's estimation than the other 9 members.

Obviously, any decision maker must question and analyze the measurement quality of all the figures he needs and intends to use: Where did they come from, and how measured? For what purpose were they gathered? What are they worth for his own particular purpose? After appraising the quality of his figures as obtained and analyzing their meaning in terms of the decision he must make, he asks further questions: What are the precise objectives he seeks as a result of that decision? What are his own capabilities and risk affordability? In addition, since the structure of the future is certain to differ from the structure of that past from which the figures were of necessity drawn: what is the best estimate of those differences? Finally, he must ask how must the figures be modified, how must they be tailored to fit best into the composite sketch of the future resulting from the answers to all his previous questions?

The Instability of Numerical Meaning

The meaning of a figure used for decision changes with the passage of time. The height of our year-old baby yesterday, however precise the measurement, will not be the correct measure of his height next year, and the clothes we buy for him must take into account the probable growth. Similarly, any measure we have of the popularity of dress or automobile styles today is unlikely to be an accurate guide to production schedules for those to be sold next year.

In the world of decision, we must always recognize that accuracy of meaning is highly perishable. Whatever was precisely true yesterday of customer choices, competitors strengths, or prices, may still be approximately true tomorrow, and may be quite incorrect twelve months hence. Unfortunately, whatever figures we possess must always be out of the past, must always refer to a specific time and place which have vanished. Our decisions can only deal with the future, a different time, usually a different place, and always with people who are no longer the same or have the same structure of desires. Such information from the past can be applied to a somewhat different present by development of generalizations which apply to the similarities of past with present and future. Foresight about the future requires us to also recognize those aspects in which the specific situation is likely to differ from those sketched by the past and the effect on events of those differences. For this reason, all of us who seek to apply calculations must interpret for ourselves their applicability and meaning. Every decision of any consequence concerns specific, individual situation which no generalization is likely to fit exactly. The unique aspects of decision are beyond mathematical illumination.

Indeed the tendency for measurements to change with time, place, and use is one reason for the use of the symbols which repel so many of us, rather than numbers. This repelling quality is hardly mysterious. It is our usual reaction to the strange and misunderstood--a reaction which evaporates with understanding and familiarity.

The validity of the mathematical relationships we can use depends upon their appropriateness, their accuracy depends upon the precision of the data. The meaning of the results depends on the purpose for which we use them. Thus we need to be able to learn the meaning of those results in the context of the decisions we seek to make. Fortunately, no language is so simple as that of mathematics. The strangeness of its appearance, and the apparent mystery of what it says may well be due to a natural tendency to impute to the strange and unfamiliar complexity and depth of meaning which does not exist.

Alegbraic symbols probably pose the strangest and most awe-inspiring aspects of mathematics both for the nonusers and those inclined to arcane expression in order to give the semblance of precision to imprecise knowledge. Such symbolism should be understood as the simplest of all shorthands, as a representation of the ultimate in imprecise meaning--the abstraction of general categories. Only three types of abbreviations are used: operating symbols which really are abbreviations for ordinary active verbs, letter abbreviations standing for generalized categories of things, and symbols denoting relationships between things. All of them are mere abbreviations which carry no more meaning than the ordinary language we all use. In many ways, they carry less solid meaning because they are abstractions intended to eliminate attention to the coloring and nuances which every living language communicates.

However little we may think in mathematical terms, all of us constantly use similar abstractions and later retranslate them into specifics. The only difference is that we do much of such thinking in terms of ordinary words, a small part in the language of mathematics. We thus deprive ourselves of the manipulative convenience of algebraic abbreviation. This is a foolish procedure, since no other language has a vocabulary as small and simple as mathematics.

THE SHORTHAND OF MATHEMATICAL EXPRESSION

Figures, Counting, and the Process of Generalization

Most of us use figures all of the time without much thought that they are abbreviations representing a very high degree of abstraction. They present counts of things, treating as equals items which we know do differ in substantial detail. If asked how many fingers we have, we may say "10." or else "8 fingers and 2 thumbs." We do not list them separately nor indicate the unique characteristics of size, shape, position, and utility for differing tasks each of these digits has. Yet we all are fully aware of these differences, and use the actual fingers in different ways. In making our reply, therefore, we have chosen to ignore divergencies which are important in <u>some other contexts</u>. We have also demonstrated our complete comprehension of the foundation of all mathematical expression--the abstract generalization, the expression which deals only with the aspects of any phenomena which <u>can, for a single purpose, be treated as the same</u>, however much they differ in other contexts. Such a comprehension of the utility of a count is the universal building block out of which all mathematics is constructed. Every other mathematical operation is an extension and abbreviation of the counting process.

Operations and Operating Symbols

When we say that "we" have \$18 between us, I have \$8 and you have \$10, we have performed a second shorthand of abstraction. Instead of starting our count all over again, we have piled a single figure representing one count--the count of your money, on top of the count of my money. Addition is thus just another shorthand for the counting process.

Similarly, subtraction is a form of counting backward. If I hand \$3 of my \$8 to the cashier to pay for my dinner, I can say I have "subtracted" \$3 from my \$8, and have only \$5 left. I have actually taken dollars number 8, number 7, and number 6 out of my wallet, and know that number 5 is the highest count I have left. To most of us, I am sure, these examples seem so elementary as to appear trivial. But how many of us think of multiplication as repeated addition, and division as repeated subtraction? Yet that is precisely what they are, and they thus involve a third order of abstraction.

Consider a relatively trivial example--computing the floor area of a room to determine how many parquet blocks each 1 foot square are needed to cover it. Few of us would have any trouble with this problem. We would simply say "multiply the length in feet by the width in feet. The product you get is the number of square feet in the room. Since each block is one foot square, that is the number of parquet blocks you need." This is right, of course. But what we have done is to say to ourselves: This room is a rectangle, one row will contain as many blocks as there are feet in the width of the room. I will have to add as many successive rows to this first row as there are feet in the length of the room. Since each row is the same length, this means I will have to add as many rows as the room is long, in feet. I can express this process by taking the width, in 1-foot square blocks, as many <u>times</u> as the room is long. The quickest way to say this is "The number of foot square blocks is the same as the length <u>times</u> the width in feet."

All of the other operating symbols form a further layer of shorthand abstractions, derived from the initial abstraction of a count. One that bothers some people is merely another simple shorthand expression for a long series of additions--the summation sign represented by the Greek letter sigma(Σ). Just as a figure enables us to avoid listing all of the individual items to which we have reference, so the Σ permits us to avoid listing all of the counts we have made by indicating that we are adding all of a whole series of values. For example, suppose we were planning a cross-country trip with an ordinary road map having only distances between towns, and wanted a formula for the distance between Pittsburgh and Chicago. We could say: Add the recorded distance from Pittsburgh to East Liverpool to the distance from East Liverpool to Mansfield, etc. But it would be much quicker to write it as $\sum_{\text{Pittsburgh}}^{\text{Chicago}}$(all intercity mileages). Anyone familiar with mathematical notation would understand this to be shorthand for "add all of the map readings for intercity distances on the road between Pittsburgh and Chicago." This, in turn, would be understood as shorthand for an actual listing of each of the intervening mileages to be found on the map and then summing them.

A simple extension of Σ is the integral sign $\int$--a kind of elongated s. The meaning is the same as sigma, but covers more complicated cases. $\int$ also is a shorthand for a series of summations but is used where what is being summed is an infinite series of values, such as the area under a continuous irregular curve.

Other cases of mathematical "active verbs," or operational symbols of importance are those of powers and roots. These, of course, are simply special cases of multiplication and division, cases in which the multiplier or divider are the same number as the one multiplied originally.

Thus the active verbs in the language of mathematics are not only few (plus, minus, times, divided by, and their derivatives) but they are all derived from the same one--count. We use the symbols of +, -, x, and ÷ simply because they are quicker to write than the words "add" or "plus," "take the sum of" etc.

Similarly, the items which are the subject of these operations are usually represented by single symbols for convenience. The actualities behind these symbols are of two types: variables and constants.

Mathematical Symbols for Quantities

Probably the most confusing aspect of mathematical language is the fact that only actual figures and operating symbols have any real meaning. The rest are place-markers which are merely empty labels intended to tell us what kinds of figures we need if we are to carry out the operations and what to do with them when we get them.

Most of us can understand specific numbers, and the errors we make in arithmetic are usually just mistakes, not the result of confusion. It is easy enough for most of us to undertand that if we multiply 20 feet--the length of our living room--by 16 feet, the width, that we will get the product, 320 square feet, and that this will represent its area. Even the generalized formula put into words gives most of us little trouble: "multiply the length by the width, in feet, to get the area in square feet." Some of us begin to get a little confused, however, when the mathematician starts using single letter abbreviations as convenient substitutes for our words. His choice is arbitrary, and he always clearly defines the meaning of his abbreviations, such as:

Let l be the length of the room in feet

w be the width of the room in feet

a be its area in square feet

Then, $l \times w = a$ will give the area of any rectangular room. Yet, this last says exactly the same as our earlier prose statement. We have simply made the formula easier to read and work with by substituting single letter abbreviations for the words, and a standard multiplication sign, x, for the verb "multiply." The single letter symbols chosen in this case were actual initial letters of the words, but this is not always convenient and never necessary--they can be any arbitrarily chosen letters or other symbols, provided they are carefully defined in advance. They might even be the same letter with subscript numbers, as

Let x_1 be one rectilinear dimension of a room,
x_2 by the other rectilinear dimension,
x_3 be its area

Then $x_1 \cdot x_2 = x_3$

Note that this formula is identical to the other except for a different arbitrary choice of symbols (abbreviations), and the use of a different multiplication sign--the dot--instead of the cross, to save confusion with the x's. Although x_1, x_2, and x_3 are not initial letters such as l, w, and h, they serve the same purpose of abbreviations, except they may seem to be more arbitrary.

The arbitrary choice of symbols often results in quite dissimilar notation by different authors discussing the same relationships and formulas. This tendency toward diversity of expression has no doubt contributed measurably to the fog through which many of us seem to peer when confronted with calculating instructions expressed in symbols instead of the words. The tendency toward such individual choice of symbols is unfortunate, but the confusion is partly due to the habit most of us have of reading specific meaning into something that is an abstraction--in this case a mere label. However, such abstractions serve a necessary purpose in communicating knowledge, in representing the generalized knowledge we have which while expressible in words, soon becomes too cumbersome to be readily understood.

Certain agreed-upon rules cover the general choice of symbols, although there is considerable latitude within these rules. Distinctions are nearly always made between the kinds of symbols chosen for phenomena we call <u>variables</u> and those which are <u>constants</u> in the context of a particular calculation.

Variables

It is important to remember that both word generalizations--such as length--and the symbols we use to represent them--such as x_1--are stand-ins for numbers which are necessary to complete any calculation. Under any specific set of circumstances, the solution of any given mathematical expression depends on substituting the number which the symbol represents in the specific instance, and then performing the actual operations (addition, multiplication, etc.) which the expression instructs us to make.

A variable is only a symbol which stands for values which change with the circumstances. It is simply an abbreviated label useful in conveying instructions to others about how to solve a problem if they have specific numbers of the sort designated by the label. We can use either the formula $l \times w = a$, or $x_1 \cdot x_2 = x_3$ (with corresponding definitions) to communicate how anyone can make his own calculations of floor area without any advance knowledge of our own as to the specific dimensions of the various sizes of rooms. Thus l and x_1 both are labels for a whole series of numbers. Each represents a specific value at any one time and place, but different values at different times and places, for different people.

Conventional usage has normally been to represent variables with letters from the tail end of the alphabet (x, y, or z), or to simplify notation when the variables are many, x with a numerical subscript--x_1, x_2, x_3, etc. Because x is the most commonly used, scientists have tended to use the dot ($x_1 \cdot x_2$) instead of the cross ($x_1 \times x_2$) to indicate algebraic multiplication.

Constants

Some of the symbols in some of the generalized calculations we wish to communicate are fixed for whole families of circumstances, even though the value may differ for different families. For an example, let us consider the calculations for the yearly cost of operating our automobile. The number of miles we drive is obviously a variable in this calculation. The dollar cost of fuel, tires, and lubrication, for any given automobile, is probably about the same for each mile driven. In this problem, operating cost per mile is a particular kind of constant if we know the car, but varies between the VW and the Cadillac, for instance. Certain other costs are fixed over time. The license, and the depreciation in sales value are yearly costs without regard to the miles driven, and the resale value depreciates inexorably with time. Thus the cost involves one value--mileage--which depends on how much we drive the car, and two values which remain relatively constant for any given car, but will differ between cars--operating costs and fixed annual costs. We can generalize the instruction which tells us how to determine automobile ownership costs for one year by a formula with four abbreviations, or symbols: one for total cost (the answer we seek), one for per-mile operating cost, one for mileage driven, and one for annual fixed costs.

Let x_1 = total annual cost of operation

x_2 = number of miles driven

a_1 = operating cost per mile--fuel, lubrication, tires, etc.

a_2 = annual fixed costs for license, depreciation, etc.

Then $x_1 = a_1x_2 + a_2$

Note that we have taken our symbols for the constants, a_1 and a_2, from the first end of the alphabet. This is the standard convention. Some writers might indeed have written the formula thus, using different first-of-the-alphabet letters for each constant:

Let y = total annual cost of operation

x = number of miles driven

a = operating cost per mile

b = annual fixed cost

Then $y = ax + b$

In general, where the number of constants may be more than 2 or 3, it is simpler to use a with subscripts, but the two formulas are the same.

In both cases, the relationship is one which any mathematician would recognize as linear. That is, the value of the one variable (x_1 or y) bears a constant proportional relationship to the value of the second variable (x_2 or x). The convention which dictates that first-of-the-alphabet letters be used as arbitrary symbols for constants and last of the alphabet for all variables helps us recognize the nature of this relationship immediately.

Some constants and other values have such wide importance that they are assigned special universally-used symbols never employed to represent anything else. The most widely recognized of these constants is the relationship between the diameter of a circle and its circumference, always represented by the Greek letter π. This relationship is constant--the value of π is identical whether the circle is the size of the earth or as small as the ring on your finger. In a case such as this, π is simply a convenient way of indicating a single irrational number--approximately 3.1416. The symbol π is a constant which represents the end calculation of a very simple mathematical relationship, the equation, or equality, $\frac{x_1}{x_2} = \pi$

x_1 = circumference of any circle
x_2 = diameter of the same circle

Equalities are one of the more important mathematical relationships.

Mathematical Expressions

By itself, any individual symbol is an unnecessarily awkward substitute for the more meaningful word for which it stands. Its value lies in the compactness given to visualization and communication of mathematical relationships, mainly those of identities, expressed equalities, and of inequalities.

Most of us are familiar with equations--expressions which state that the items on either side of equals sign are identical, can be substituted for each other. Any such identity or equation can be viewed as a set of instructions.

"a = l x w" is really shorthand for "to find the areas of a room, multiply the length by the width."

or

$s = \frac{d}{t}$, where s is average speed
d is distance traveled
t is the time taken

can be read as "to find the average speed, divide the distance traveled by the time."

All such expressions permit a definite solution in any one given set of circumstances. That is, we get the desired numerical answer when we replace each variable label with the figure which applies, and carry out the actual arithmetic which the generalized instruction (equation) tells us to perform.

However, not all of the knowledge we need to use is in such clearly defined form. Quite often, it is in the form of a limitation on the value of one item, set by the values of other items in the expression. To get down to concrete cases, we may observe that we "do not really know the size of John's room, but we know it is larger than ours, and this room is 12 x 15." In a case such as this, we cannot make any statement (formulate any equation) which gives a precise statement of the size of John's room, but we can make a statement about the lower limit of size which it exceeds. We can say it is "more than 12 feet by 15 feet."

We designate such an unequal relationship by a v lying on its side: The point of this inequality sign indicates the lesser of the two values, the mouth the greater one. Translating the original statement that John's room is larger than ours, which is 12 x 15 feet," we would write it in mathematical shorthand thus: Let x_1 = size of John's room, then $x_1 > 12 \times 15$ or $12 \times 15 < x_1$. This limits the value on the down side, but leaves it wide open in the other direction. At first blush, this may not seem a very useful kind of knowledge. A little reflection will show that we often use inequalities in our everyday decision-making. If our wife asks, when we start a trip, "How is the gas?" we are likely to glance at the fuel gauge and answer "We have enough to get there and to spare," without trying to estimate our exact tank level. We probably do so by some such mental arithmetic as "We usually burn a gallon in 18 miles. The map indicates that the distance is 90 miles. 90 divided by 18 is 5 gallons, and with the fuel gauge needle at the half-way mark, I know we have far more than 5 gallons."

If we were inclined to think in mathematical language, we would have thought.

Let f = our fuel supply

Then $f > \frac{90}{18}$

This may be enough to complete the planned trip, and thus our statement is adequate for the decision as to whether or not to purchase more fuel before we start out.

On the other hand, we may note the possibility that the return trip will be made late at night, with few stations open. We know that with the fuel gauge at the 1/2 point, we have less than 10 gallons, and therefore we decide to stop first for gas after all. In this case, also, we have made and need no precise measurement. Our inequality in this case gives us enough limiting information in both directions to arrive at a decision. In this case, our inequality would read

$$2\frac{(90)}{(18)} > f > \frac{90}{18}$$

which reads "f is between 90/18 and twice 90/18. Note that it is equal to neither of these quantities, and, for our current purpose, we don't need to know its exact value.

The knowledge of merely one or two limiting values is clearly enough for decision at times. Clearly, also, the more limiting values we have, the closer we are to learning the exact value. In a nonmathematical context, we all are familiar with this principle as the basic solution of parlor charades. The answer to the standard "is it vegetable, animal, or mineral?" is enough to narrow the search a great deal. An astute questioner stands better than an even chance of pinpointing the object, without other clues, in less than 20 such limiting questions.

In business, we may know only that a price response is less than unitary elasticity or greater than unitary elasticity. This is sufficient information to enable us to decide on the proper direction for a price move predicated on that response. A best, or optimal answer can often be calculated from knowledge of a few limiting conditions. Linear programming, a useful decision tool which is discussed in Chapter V, is based on this process.

Inequalities can be in terms of "more than" or "less than," or in terms of "at least," or "no more than." This last implies, of course, the possibility of an identity, and the operating symbol is $\leq$ ("less than or equal to") or $\geq$ ("equal to or greater than"). Notice that this does not mean that the quantity is actually equal to, only that it may be.

Indefinite Relationships

Sometimes we have no real knowledge of the operating nature of a relationship or of the limits. We may know only that some definite relationship does or may exist. We may have reason to believe, for example, that the flavor and other quality factors in apples depend on variety, climate, soil, and method of cultivation. However, we are not certain of the exact nature of any of these relationships. We could simple state that "apple quality is some kind of resultant of the effect of climate, apple variety, soil, and method of cultivation." Or we might make use of the mathematical abbreviation f (for "some kind of function of") and express the same vague statement in more precise-appearing terms, such as:

Let x_1 = apple qualities
x_2 = climate factors
x_3 = soil factors
x_5 = method of cultivation

Then $x_1 = f(a_1x_2, a_2x_3, a_3x_4, a_4x_5)$

We may not even be certain that we know all of the significant factors which affect apple quality. In such a case, those with a taste for mathematical expression would write it thus:

$$x_1 = f(a_1x_1, a_2x_2 \cdot \cdot \cdot a_kx_k)$$

The dots indicate simply that there the expression represents a series, up to $\underline{k}$ in number. $\underline{k}$ is used instead of an actual number to indicate that the writer himself is ignorant of the number of factors.

The meaning of such statements of indefinite relationships is identical whether put in prose formulation or in mathematical language. In both instances that meaning is simply that "quality varies with a number of factors, but I really don't know how it varies, nor what all the factors are." Whether the mathematical expression is even as convenient as the prose in such cases is a matter of taste. A symbolic presentation undoubtedly appeals to some individuals on occasion because of the aura of precision with which it seems to clothe their ignorance. They have obligingly forgotten the concomitant need to give meaning to all such expressions in light of a specific decision context.

The use of indefinite statements of relationships has none of the main value of the symbolic statement of relationships--the advantage this second order of abstraction gives us in identifying the class of relationship we are dealing with, helping us to compare relationships just as figures help us to compare the similarities in counts or measurements.

Symbolic Expression as a Means of Revealing Similarities in Relationships

The use of numbers suppresses the real dissimilarities in items to help us understand the similarities. The use of symbolic expression carries the suppression of real differences one step further by suppressing the real dissimilarities in count to reveal the real similarities in relationships. A great many of the relationships in the world fall into definite families which are easily recognized when put into symbolic form, and knowledge of the family characteristics tells us immediately a great deal about the relationship. Thus all straight lines have the family relationship $y = ax + b$. Since the mathematician realizes that either of the constants $\underline{a}$ and $\underline{b}$ can be 0, he also recognizes the form $y = b$ as a member of this family. When $\underline{x}$ is a variable, the actual values of $\underline{a}$, when known, tell him something more often worth knowing. The constant $\underline{a}$ is the proportion of y/x, and in the graph of the equation is the slope of the straight line, that is the angle the line makes with the base of the graph. Whatever the value of b, then, all lines with the same value of a are parallel. If b is not 0, we also know where the line intercepts the 2 axes of the graph. Other forms of equations identify circles of whatever size, ellipses, parabolas, sine curves, and many other families of relationships of numbers and other quantitative formulations which involve no substantial degree of personal judgment in their development. it is obviously even more true when the data itself is, as is most of that needed for business decision, of a highly subjective nature. The judgmental character of much such knowledge is no reason to ignore the value of attempting to place numerical values on personal insights and experience. Just such quantification of subjective estimates is the basis of Bayesian and other newly developed tools for the mathematical comparison of decision alternatives discussed later. Judgment, however, is not the sole source of inexactness in figures. Although figures themselves arose out of the counting process, most of them represent a different process--that of measurement, and the measurement process introduces both distortions and some degree of approximation.

SUMMARY

1. The utility of the language of mathematics lies in its very limited vocabulary and the limited meanings that vocabulary attempts to convey.

2. Any form of mathematical expression ignores a large part of reality--the part which describes the unique aspects of every element of what we know. By concentrating solely on the similarities, mathematical calculations help us focus on those elements in our experience which aid in understanding of new experiences and new situations. It abstracts from the complexity of actuality those simpler aspects which are common to many phenomena.

3. The very abstracting process, however, limits the validity and the accuracy of any results. The user of the calculations must always weigh their meaning for the decision he is to make in terms of those qualitative values of which no mathematics can take full account. He must understand both that numbers cannot represent personal and subjective values and that the objective meaning itself differs with time, place, and circumstances. He needs to realize, also, that the degree of precision expressed by numbers is quite variable--that numbers present an appearance of precision which is often false.

4. Any decision-maker must therefore have a reasonably good reading knowledge of the language of mathematics. That language is a very simple and limited one, consisting of fewer active verbs than we have fingers, ordinary figures, and the place-card markers for the latter called symbols. The latter can help us to construct abstract instructions on how to use whatever figures we may be able to furnish. The whole of the language is not really a strange one, but a series of abbreviations for words and ideas we all work with every day.

5. The basic element of mathematics is the number, a shorthand for the result of a count. Nature knows no numbers--only individuals which are all unique in some aspect of time, place, and physical dimensions. Any number ignores the uniqueness in order to help us grasp the similarities. The validity of any figure thus depends on the validity of the assumptions we are making about the identical value, for a given decision, of each of the units in the counts.

6. The operational verbs of mathematics--add, subtract, multiply, etc.--are all variants of one--to add. Addition itself is merely a shorthand extension of counting.

7. Arbitrary symbols are chosen by each writer to serve as abbreviated labels. Such label symbols enable him to convey instructions about how a given calculation can be carried out _if_ we can get figures of the sort designated by the labels. These instructions could just as easily be expressed in ordinary words.

8. Such symbolic labels are of two general types, variables and constants. Variables, usually represented by _x_ or some other letter from the end of the alphabet, denote figures which can vary with every different set of conditions. Constants, usually represented by _a_ or other letters from the beginning of the alphabet, indicate that the figure used is one which may be the same for a whole family of solutions.

9. The principal reason for use of symbolic language is to render compact the statement of mathematical operations and relationships, and permit ease in manipulation, handling and comparison of relationship. The principal basic relationships are equations, inequalities, and indefinite relationships.

10. Equations are basically instructions concerning the method by which a definite solution can be obtained once the actual numbers referred to are available.

11. Inequalities tell us the limits to the solution we seek, but not its exact value.

12. Indefinite relationships--generalizations of the function--simply indicate that the solution requires certain types of figures, but give no guidance as to how these shape the solution.

13. The greatest values of symbolic statements are to enable us to identify the family to which a relationship belongs and to see how the statement of the relationship can be simplified for calculation by means of substitution and other devices.

14. The assumptions of similarity, significance, and relevance upon which any number or symbol rests are matters of subjective judgment and thus all quantification is to some degree subjective. Some of the most useful tools, moreover, make use of quantities which are themselves subjective in origin as well as measurement. The process of measurement introduces another source of inexactness and distortion.

1 + 1 = 2

(or does it?)

"The hardware store didn't have a two-inch wrench, so I got two one-inch wrenches."

(Adapted from the Wall Street Journal of November 5, 1968, p. 5 by permission of Cartoon Features Syndicate)

CHAPTER 2: MEASUREMENT, ITS PROBLEMS, COMPLICATIONS, AND PITFALLS

All numbers originated in the need to make a tally, or count, but the simple "how many" of a count meets too few of our needs for quantitative expression. Usually we need to know "how much" rather than how many, and the latter is seldom an answer to the former. That is, most of the numbers we seek are intended as forms of measurements of phenomena which are not natural numbers, not integers--"how far," "how costly," "how much benefit," "how much effect," etc.

Measurement is a much more complicated process than mere counting. Although the process of tallying requires many of the same kinds of decisions as any other measurement system, the basis of those choices are quite intuitive and obvious. When we say "3 sheep," "3 girls," "300 people," the context and the purpose of our count is usually clear, the choice of unit no strain, and the definition of that unit not one likely to give rise to ambiguity or challenge. But when we measure the production cost as $3.5436 per 1000 pieces, we go through a process on which objective agreement between equally competent observers is far from likely. Furthermore, the number itself has a far more restricted significance than the count of 3 sheep. The same 3 sheep will always tally out at 3. The same production system which produced a cost of $3.5436 may cause the cost to be $7.0872 or $1.7718 tomorrow or in some other setting. Or even at a given time, a different objective for the measurement of that cost may change the calculation to indicate that true cost figure, for that given objective, is only $.5436.

Measurement is a process which has validity only in terms of its objective, is strongly colored by the fallibility of human observation, always involves some degree of approximation and inaccuracy, and never gives an answer free from the need for interpretation.

The most difficult problems in measurement usually involve the choice of criteria to be satisfied by measurement, and the development of the instrument or method of measuring the chosen criterion. The greatest mistake is to seek greater precision than necessary.

All measurement starts with an end use or purpose and has meaning in terms only of that purpose. Accomplishment of the end purpose, however, is frequently not directly measurable, and we have to be satisfied with measuring something judged to relate to this accomplishment. In eggs, for example, we are usually interested in measuring something designated as "freshness." If pushed, we would probably define freshness as the degree an egg approaches the quality of a just-laid egg. Time passage measurement alone is not adequate for this, and many factors of handling from the moment of laying can affect it. We do know, however, that at the moment of laying, the large end has a minute air cell which increases in size as staleness increases. There are tricks of storage and shell treatment which will retard this air cell growth, but if we rule out eggs over a certain age, or with treated shells, we can use this air cell as a criterion representing all the quality factors we associate with freshness--taste, odor, stiffness of white, etc.

Whenever we desire to measure a single dimension like freshness, we can, as with eggs, usually find some criterion which works and gives us a single scale value: AA, A, B, C, for example, as in eggs. However, various users of a measurement may need other dimensions. Eggs come in a range of size, for example, as well as in varying qualities. For some people, large eggs have more relative value than small ones. For such people we need to designate size, and we do so in terms of a size label designating a given weight per dozen. For some items, we may have to make many measurements to satisfy many users. What would an A grade automobile be? This would depend on what the purchaser sought. For some, it might be acceleration, for others, a quite incompatible item--low gas mileage. No single measure would satisfy even a majority of buyers, so those rating cars give a list of measured variables. We usually need as many criteria of measurement as we have purposes.

The Process of Measurement

A mere tally is adequate measurement in the case of few decisions in this world. A dairyman will build his barn to house exactly 100 cows and know that 100 cows will be accommodated. But a mere head count will not tell him how much milk production to plan for, even less the profit he can expect from these 100 head even with a guaranteed price. He needs measures of expected production from each head and of many factors involved in that production. Even in retrospect, the determination of profit achieved is a complicated measurement which differs with the objective for the measurement of that profit. Is the purpose to determine the wisdom of doubling the operation? Then every element of capital investment must be considered, every element of expected output benefit, direct and indirect, the value of every unit of labor and feed cost of any sort used estimated and included, every contingency of disease loss and price fluctuation discounted in some manner. In addition, the prospective profit from alternative uses of the same capital must be measured in the same manner. Obviously, this is a complicated process, and equally obviously will not be a really precise calculation. On the other hand, if the purpose is to report profit for tax purposes, the calculation will not and should not include the captive labor of the owner, the imputed value of fertility given to fields on which manure is spread, nor any alternative opportunity losses or profit, such as the value of home-raised feed. Still other purposes will lead to still other profit statements, each fully valid for its purpose.

The measurement process must thus start with a sharp focus on the purpose for which the resulting numbers will be used. The end result can have meaning only in terms of that one purpose and no other. Furthermore, the other steps in the process frequently result in a need for judgment as to the meaning of the resulting figure for the use intended, even when done as well as possible.

Measurement can be defined as a process which starts with some need for a quantitative comparison of alternate choices or of effects of an action relative to previous expectations. Obtaining the measurement requires:

An observer

A decision as to what kinds of factors will yield an acceptable comparison in terms of the objective

A determination of what key aspects of these factors are suitable for measurement

Selection and definition of a suitable unit of measurement

Development of apparatus for actual measurement using this unit

Application of measurement tool by observer

Analysis of the measurement result in reference to the original objective

Such a multistage process negates any possibility of absolute accuracy even if the constant interposition of the human element did not interfere. Nearly every stage also involves the risk--almost indeed, the certainty--of distortion between needs and results at every stage.

Purpose--The Crucial Element in Measurement

Formulation of a precise purpose to be served is easy enough in the case of many physical tasks, but sometimes extremely difficult in business, social, and governmental affairs. Few problems arise in developing a measurement for a clear-cut physical operation such as determining the volume of railroad freight-car capacity needed to bring a day's supplies of coke, ore, and limestone from the usual sources to the steel mill or to determine the amount of rolling mill capacity to furnish a given amount of steel of any one type to the market. However, measuring how much of each type and size of finished steel will constitute a profitable product mix over the larger run is not so simple, yet a measure must be used. And the right measure of the market share obtained by a product and price mix can be so far from obvious that the U. S. steel industry, to take one specific example among many possible, read its 1950's policies as successful during the very period its price and product policies were sacrificing profitable markets to aluminum, paper, concrete, plastics, and foreign producers.

Industry officials undoubtedly thought they had a measurement objective--to measure profit prospects. But they clearly had not completed even this first step of determining what they meant by a profit beyond the usual figure shown on current balance sheet. They certainly did not intend to sacrifice future sales volume in their most profitable categories for a temporary gain in a period of tight supply. Nevertheless, it seems clear that from the end of World War II to the late 1950's, the industry measured its success by the criterion of total tonnage sold. Little attention was paid to the inroads of aluminum on low tonnage, high profit margin products. ("Aluminum will never be a threat so long as output is in pounds. Steel can only be measured in tons," was the attitude.)

Even had the industry defined its profit ends more clearly, however, it still would have had the problem of deciding what market or industry events were relevant to attainment of a better profit structure. Was price important, and in what direction? The industry thought it was important--important that it be higher. The result was a price <u>per</u> <u>unit</u> <u>of</u> <u>user</u> <u>benefit</u> which brought aluminum in direct competition in casement windows, for example, and in cans. It also stimulated the use of prestressed concrete beams, and gave foreign producers a more profitable market in the U. S. Hindsight indicates that lower price should have been sought, that the industry should have set a lower-cost target to achieve profit at lower cost by improved technology (which was adopted later, when the markets were lost.) Should new product development have been a measure? If so, what kind of new product development spelled potential profits? Do newer, improved production facilities mean potential profits? The industry built newer and bigger blast furnaces--much more efficient than the older ones, at $300 per ton capacity, but neglected development of new types such as the oxygen converter, which took much less capital per ton.

In retrospect, it is always easy to see the missteps which led to trouble, either in the U. S. steel industry after World War II, or in such political quagmires as South Vietnam proved to be for the United States.

But the relationships assumed between measurement and effect desired were those which had seemed correct on many previous occasions. In other words, even when the objectives have been defined carefully and well, it is always necessary to make a fresh critical examination of the relationship between the factors thought to be criteria of accomplishment and actual attainment of that purpose.

Choice of Factors to Measure

All measurement involves simplification and compromise, but probably none more than the choice of what to measure. Some of the compromises are forced by the limits of what is possible. The user must measure what is observable and measurable. Other compromises are the result of judgment. Most items important to decision have innumerable aspects which might be measurable to some degree. Getting all such detail would court confusion, and much of the detail would have no relevance in the context of the given decision. The observer must choose what is simultaneously relevant, significant, and measurable. The resulting combination of judgmental choice and of choice constrained by the limits of measurability open up a number of pitfalls for the unwary. The more common problems are those of:

- Classification
- Indirect measures
- Incomplete measurement
- Problems of observation: the instrument, the unit, and the the observer

Problems of quality level

Time erosion

Improper interpretation of the precision necessary or that obtained.

Classification Problems

As already indicated, any use of quantitative expression involves a necessary assumption that somewhat unlike things are alike. Any measurement system involves classification, something not found in nature, which knows only infinite diversity. Such aggregation into classes requires judgment that the unique aspects of the various members of the class are not significant for the specific purpose sought and that the likenesses are relevant to that purpose. Put another way, the very process of classification assumes homogeneity, relevant to the purpose pursued, of all elements making up a single quantity. When the assumption is wrong, poor decisions can result and mistaken evaluations made of results.

As already noted, from 1946 to 1957 the U. S. steel industry predicated its plans on the assumption that its market position could be measured in terms of tonnage output, assuming that each ton was of equal importance. The industry measure ignored the detail of individual product (thousands of semi-fabricated forms, shapes, sizes, and qualities), and the profitability of individual items. Because output was measured in millions of tons, the industry foresaw no significant threat in the aggressive marketing of aluminum and other structural materials. Then the recession of 1957 revealed that while aluminum had taken a relatively low percentage of the tonnage market, it had captured a large part of the steel profit by invasion of the can market, once a monopoly for tin-plated steel, and of light structurals such as casement windows, and other important areas. Paper had taken over other segments of the can market, prestressed concrete structurals a substantial part of construction, and plastics many items into which steel had gone. Simple tonnage proved a poor measure of competition. The classification averaged together too many items needed to be considered separately, about which different decisions needed to be made.

Governmental economic and welfare policy long made the similar mistake of measuring employment only in terms of overall average. The disorders of the 1960's showed the need for several separate classifications of workers.

Few of the classifications used in business decisions cause greater confusion than those monetary quantities labelled as costs. Far too often, these are classified in terms of actual outlays and not in terms of the alternate opportunities open to decision.

Books of account usually carry only those costs resulting from actual cash outlays and include all such costs without regard to those directly attributable to some one decision. But many decisions involve real costs that do not show up as any kind of cash transaction, and some of the actual cash outlays incurred are not true economic costs, relative to a specific decision.

Depreciation reserves a firm has may be used in undertaking an expansion, for example. This money, although on hand and not borrowed, has a real cost. It costs whatever return it could bring in the next best alternate use. Or we could charge its use with the interest the firm would have to pay to borrow the money--the alternative source of funds. In deciding to use the funds on hand for this expansion, the firm is sacrificing--spending, in other words--income it would otherwise receive from this money in some other profit venture, or saving the cost of the borrowing for this purpose (and probably incurring an interest cost for some other purpose).

Similarly, the new plant may occupy land bought many years before, at perhaps $100 per acre, but could now be sold for $3, 000 per acre. The cost of the land for this project is no longer the original $100 per acre cost, but the $3, 000 per acre the land would bring if put on the market. If the firm did not already own the property, it would have to buy it at the current market price. The real cost is $3, 000 per acre even though the books may list it at $100.

Labor that would be kept on in any event to hold a skilled workforce intact obviously results in a cash payroll outlay. But this outlay is no part of the real cost of a job taken on simply to keep the force busy. Nor can any of the plant overhead outlays be charged against such a job. They would go on without reference to the decision to take or reject such an order. Only the difference in cost between doing and not doing is an economic cost.

In other words, the test of correct classification is always that of what would have happened under the alternate opportunities among which the decision maker had a choice. If a resource could have been used elsewhere, its cost value was the possible return in the highest valued alternate use. On the other hand, no decision alternative would have avoided the use of a resource, the expenditure is not, for the purpose of that decision, a cost. If any decision actually made misses making a profit which an alternative would have captured, the profit foregone will not appear on the books or on the tax report as a loss. Nevertheless, that opportunity loss is just as much a loss as though the better alternative had been chosen, the profit actually made, then stolen by some embezzler or other thief.

All classifications must therefore always be questioned in terms of their relevance and meaning for a given purpose of measurement.

The Distortions of Indirect Measurement

Many of the things we wish to measure are not directly observable and we must measure something else which is observable and can be assumed to be a criterion as to the measure of the phenomenon whose quantity is desired. This is a problem even in the measurement of stable physical realities such as temperature.

No one has ever seen temperature--all we ever see are results of the internal, unseen phenomenon of the energy form we call heat. Centuries of observation and experiment have, however, demonstrated a very close relationship between expansion of various physical materials and heat, and so we look at the height of a column of mercury, for example, and read the result as so many degrees of temperature. This reading has proved to be a very accurate measure of many physical phenomena associated with heat--for instance, the speed of a chemical reaction. Since the observed relationships have proved stable, we may even tend to think of our measurement as direct, but it is not in the sense of the measurement of length we make when we compare the length of a desk with a standard such as a foot rule or a meter stick.

The value of any indirect measurement rests on the correctness and the stability of the assumed relationship between the actual phenomenon being measured and the measurable effect which is taken as a criterion. Even in the physical world there can be problems, but they are simpler of solution than those facing decisions involving human reaction.

Sales trends, for example, are often used to measure the trend in profit because profit can only be estimated and then much later than desired and not always with ease. Yet sales are often pushed at the expense of profit, and frequently, a greater total profit can be had by seeking sales where the volume is low, but the margin higher.

The advertiser wants to know how much effect his advertising is having on his eventual total sales, but cannot measure this separately from the other factors of product quality, competition, distribution, publicity, sales effort, etc. So he looks at the readership of his ads, or the rating of his TV shows. The two do measure in part the attention-getting effect of his promotion, but experiments have indicated that the more attention some ads get, the less likely is the reader to buy the product. Even more confusing, a number of studies have shown that the relationship between purchase and advertising readership is reversed--that <u>those who already have purchased</u> are more likely to read the ads for a product than those who have not yet bought. The assumed cause-and-effect relationship is plausible but not true, at least universally.

For another example, the U. S. defense establishment long was led astray in evaluating its efforts in Vietnam because of reliance on the wrong indirect measures. Lacking the kind of direct measures of success available in normal warfare--land and objectives taken--it fell back on counting of enemy personnel losses, and on proportions of votes cast for the central government. Meanwhile, the enemy was building its strength in the country-side, and revealed in the Tet offensive of 1968 that it was far from defeated.

Even when measures are direct or a least valid, the impossibility of getting a complete measure causes measurement problems.

Incomplete Measurement: The Problems of Indexes

Measurement often has to be incomplete for one or more of a number of reasons:

--Complete measurement may be economically impractical because it is difficult to combine several dimensions in a single number

--the multitude of measurements needed to achieve completeness is too large to justify use of all of them, economically

--the concept whose measure is sought not only includes a lot of dimensions, but all of those dimensions are not clearly defined.

Most such uses also involve indirect measurements, and in any event, the measure we get is best distinguished as an index. The decision-maker needs to be especially wary in the use of indexes. He needs to keep alert to the real difference between the index values of the criteria he uses for data collection and the true values he is seeking to learn.

A good example of an incomplete measure from the physical world is the use of air temperature as an index of comfort. The physical comfort of human beings is related to temperature, but the air temperature alone does not measure probable comfort. An air temperature of well over 80 degrees F. can feel distinctly chilly if the surrounding wall surfaces are at 50 degrees F., for example. Conversely, an air temperature of 65 degrees, even at the same relative humidity, can feel confortably warm if the surrounding surfaces are at 85 degrees. The relative humidity is also an extremely important factor, as anyone who has lived in coastal regions knows. It is possible to construct some sort of comfort index, of course, by including some kind of weighting of each of these three factors, but human sensation is sufficiently variable that all human observers would not agree on the exact point of comfort, or the degree by which some other point missed this target.

Constructing a comfort index is a simple task in comparison with measuring changes in the general price level. Prices are notoriously independent of each other. At any point of time, some are going up, some are stationary, and some are going down, even in the wildest era of inflation. "The general price level" is shorthand for the purchasing power of the money we hold. This, unfortunately will differ according to what we wish to purchase. The purchase pattern, in turn, differs, from buyer to buyer, for one buyer from one week to the next and one year to another, and even differs with the shifting relative position of prices. In addition, any one average supermarket will have about 8,000 items on the shelves (some carry 15,000 or more) and a department store may carry 50,000 items. Moreover, the total market covers tens of thousands of other consumer and industrial items. Clearly, the measurement problem is formidable, and complete measurement not even definable. So we set up a few indexes of price movement.

The best known price movement index is the Consumer Price Index calculated monthly by the United States Bureau of Labor Statistics. The "market basket" priced covers only 400 items of consumption--not the tens of thousands of possible consumer items. The weights are based on average purchases made by wage-earners and clerical workers in each class of product as determined by survey in some base year. The weights do not change with the prices. Although meats are included, each kind and cut has a fixed weight. If the national supply of beef and thus actual consumption is short, the rise in price is recorded, but the index does not reflect either the drop in use of beef nor the corresponding rise in consumption of pork and poultry, also in the index as fixed weights.

Furthermore, the index represents only an average for a relatively young urban family of four (father, 38, nonworking mother, boy 13, girl 8), and thus does not correspond with the expenditures of many specific families of four even in this age and working class, nor among families of other classes with other cultural and expenditure patterns, or families with working mothers (over a third of the total), or any of the other real variations. Goods priced are very carefully and rigidly defined, but changes in design from year-to-year are not evaluated in terms of value/price relationships. Last year's Ford-Chevy-Plymouth average car of the selected model is considered the equivalent quality of this year's.

All of these limitations are well known to the BLS, and carefully publicized, of course. The index claims only to indicate the direction and a rough degree of the relative amount of movement in what is happening to purchasing power. It does not measure what happens to your dollar or to mine, and it is doubtful if any measure devised could. For what such a measure would seek is both too big a job, and one not objectively definable. Nothing objective could measure the changes in satisfaction obtained over time. This changes with the income itself, with changes in prices and in goods, with changes in the social structure affecting the individual, and with all the changes in inner drives and taste.

All that most of our indirect measures can do for us is to give a very rough measure of the general direction of changes, and the general order of value of those changes.

The quality is never up to the level of precision the actual figures seem to imply to the uninitiated.

The Problems of Observation: The Instrument and The Observer

In the final analysis, all measurement traces back to some human observer with all of his variability of judgment and of perception. All must be carried out with some kind of instrument, which can inflict mechanical defects of its own. All must be expressed in some kind of units, and these are not God-given, but defined by some very fallible humans. Finding a suitable and dependable instrument is often the most difficult part of measurement.

Humans can err and will always differ to some degree, even with themselves in such an objective process as the reading of a thermometer or a linear measure. In fact, the full name of the so-called normal curve is "normal curve of error." It is the random distribution of measurement variations obtained by a single competent observer, using the same instrument to measure the same phenomenon. Every scientist is aware of such variation and, whenever possible, averages several observations when making a measurement. In addition to such random variations, individual observers usually have their own biases--variations from the true value which are directional and thus do not cancel out.

One type of bias is that of point of observation--the phenomenon recognized as parallax in physical measurement. The unskilled observer, in particular, may look at an instrument from an angle, and thus line up the indicator with a different number from the one directly opposite.

A more important source of observer bias arises from differences in discrimination and perception. Experts, for example, often perceive quality differently than do laymen. Their training and experience enables them to perceive finer differences than the layman. The brewmaster can distinguish the taste differences between batches in his brewery imperceptible to most laymen. In addition, however, the expert may place more importance on some kinds of differences than do those without his interest, and thus he may measure value in a biased manner relative to the demand in the market.

Whoever does the measuring must do it in terms of some kind of instrument, and the means of measurement may itself give rise to bias and variation. For most organizational measures and decisions, money is the instrument by which inputs and outputs are usually reduced to measurable terms. Money is supposed to measure value, but it certainly does not do so in as objective and unvarying a manner as the international meter measures length. One dollar has quite a different value to two different men, to the same man under different circumstances or at two different periods of time. Moreover, what is expressed in dollars is often not money, but something whose value is simply estimated in monetary terms. As was indicated above, the cost data, always expressed in monetary terms, depends heavily on the judgment of those making the cost calculation.

Monetary value, moreover, is only a partial and biased measure of value. The price of any purchase can include varying amounts of time and convenience cost, not easily expressed in money, and of search effort.

One of the most difficult instruments to develop is one measuring "if not" characteristics. A firm with a maximum share of a convenience goods market (chewing gum or beer, for example) may feel certain that a relatively high level of advertising is necessary simply to maintain its market position. It may also know that a brief hiatus in its effort produces no measurable drop in market share. How does the president determine how much is needed, or justify a level such as $20 million for example? The Police Department may feel certain it is quite successful, and if right, all it will have to show is a low crime and arrest figure. Again, a short let-up will probably produce no noticeable effect. How can the department support the necessity of any given force level?

Two things are obvious: (a) the questions are not easy to answer, and (b) those making the budgeting decision must use some means of measuring value. Two approaches have some validity when used with eyes-open care. One that advertisers sometimes attempt is some indirect and partial effect measurements of attitude which have at least a logical relationship to functional results expected. The other method is to seek some parallel situation, one in which the forces being measured are weaker or absent, and use this as an index of the value of the force. Direct measurement of the value of the success of the Secret Service in suppressing counterfeiting, for example, is extremely difficult or impossible. But there are analog situations in industry which are not nearly as well policed--the pirating of designs in toys and garments, for instance. The incentives for such piracy are similar to those in counterfeiting money, the sanctions controlling the piracy not nearly so efficient. A little investigation of the extent of this problem would yield a rough measure of the effectiveness of the Secret Service's work.

Choosing The Unit of Measurement

Units of measurement are always largely a matter of arbitrary choice, but the wrong choice can impede comparison or comprehension. Whenever the observer has a choice, he should choose a unit which is:

1. large enough for convenient comparison--one which does not result in astronomical numbers (such as measuring the distance from earth to moon in inches).

2. one small enough to be sensitive to real differences in terms of integral quantities--in other words, one which minimizes the need to express results in fractions.
3. more than the usual range of uncertainty in measurement and thus expresses only those differences which are really significant.
4. homogeneous--does not include in one unit items which are, for the purpose of analysis, disparate. Thus in the analysis of markets, a county usually includes quite divergent smaller areas.
5. stable--a type of unit which does not shift in value because of extraneous forces. Generally, this means using physical measures in preference to monetary measures where there is a choice, since money values can change when no change takes place in the physical quantity represented.
6. expressed in terms of outputs and effects rather than inputs. Advertising impact is not a direct function of cost, for example, but of the change in attitude it causes. The efficiency of a labor operation is not measured by items worked on or degree of activity, but on useful or valuable outputs (which may often result in a visibly lower workload.)

Many of the figures we use for evaluation in particular raise problems of unit definition. How do we count the riders on the bus system? We can count the number of fares collected per day, for example, but this is merely a count of fares--not of riders. For some riders, one fare may mean one rider that day. For many more, two fares equals one rider. For some tourists, perhaps, one rider may have paid 8 fares in travelling about. The incidence of fares tells us nothing about how many people used the service.

Such incidence figures are easy to get, and therefore measurable. It is easy to count fares or admissions or employment service interviews. But none of these tell one important fact we often desire to measure: how many people have we been serving? For example, a sales promotion contest designed to promote sampling of the product, may have pulled in 1,000,000 entries. Did we get 1,000,000 families to try the product? Experience suggests the possibilities that the 1 million coupons may have come from only 200,000 families. This is harder to measure, but might be possible. But even families purchasing does not really tell us what we want to know. The promotion really was of value only to the extent that those entering the contest were first-time tryers. As a unit of measure for this, the contest entries is a valueless figure.

Incidence figures, such as attendance, employment interviews, or job placements are of questionable value because of the multiple counting and the lack of quality indications. But even a completed case count may lead to double counting. An organization which reported annually on number of individuals treated proved to have an average case endurance of 13 months. Their annual report was automatically reporting double the organization's throughput.

Effects of Time Period, Timing and Passage of Time on Measurement

Time is the greatest source of instability of measurement. The time period covered can itself result in differences in the very important details of composition of the total. Consider an attempt to measure the market served by a ski lodge, for instance. Some of the users visit for one day only and do not return. Some stay for a single visit, but remain for a week. Some come regularly, every weekend only. Each type of visitor has different distinguishing customer characteristics, and it could be important to know how important each type is to the success of the operation. Consider the differing effects of 3 different bases for counting customers: a one-day count, a one-week tabulation, and a full-season sample taken on 20 random days.

In the full-season sample, both the every weekend guests and the one-week guests would be counted more than once, and roughly in proportion to the intensity of their patronage. Such a sample would measure the relative business value of each public from which the lodge drew its trade. The one-week sample would give less weight to the weekender, who would be counted on three days only for a single trip, than to the one-visit customer. The one-day cross section would give the same weights to the one-day, one-trip visitor, the weekender, and the one-stay, week-long visitor, distorting the relative importance of the casual customer.

Totals used in comparisons can be affected by the point of time a measurement is taken. The differences can be quite obvious whenever a shift is made in the point of measurement, especially in accounting for costs. When is a cost incurred? Different bookkeeping systems may use any of seven points of time--the time of ordering (or of legislative authorization), the time of receipt into inventory, the date removed from inventory for use, the date of the billing, the date the check is used in payment, or the date the check is returned to the bank and debited against the account. A cash system uses one of the latter--usually the date of the check. An accrual system throws the measurement into an earlier time period. Whenever the accounting is changed from a cash to an accrual basis, expenses can jump without any change in the firms' obligations.

The passage of time can change the real length of our measuring sticks, particularly those related to money. The definition of a felony--a major crime, that is--is a monetary one. In most jurisdictions the dividing line between petty larceny and grand larceny has been $100 for many years and was $50 for generations previously. In quantity, this seems to be a relatively stable measure. But when a man stole $50 in 1910, he was taking as much as two months' wages for some skilled workers. When he steals $100 in 1968, his take is less than 3 days' pay for a hod carrier. Such a change in significance clearly could push up the apparent level of major crime in a period when it really is decreasing.

Similarly, the significance of income tax exemptions has changed drastically in the generation since World War II. The $2,400 exemption for a family of four once eliminated any significant tax obligation for many middle class families. By 1968, the $2,400 exemption meant that poverty level families ("below $3,300," officially) were paying a substantial income tax.

Thus time, in its many guises, erodes the quality level of our measurements.

The Differing Levels of Measurement Quality*

By this point it should be clear that not all numerical information is of the same level of quality. The specific numerical symbol denoting a measurement, such as 3.5436, can be an expression of the complete range of precision, from no meaning at all up to the one part in 100,000 level that the figures seem to indicate, depending both on how it was arrived at, and on the use to which it is to be put. Both the quality of the original measurement and the meaning of this measurement in terms of the future in which action is contemplated need to be assessed before it can be determined whether 3.5436 is a meaningful quantity at all for the current purpose, means something roughly between 3 and 4, or really is 3.5436

* Most of the material in this section has been adapted from Chester R. Wasson, Research Analysis for Marketing Decision, Appleton-Century-Crofts (New York, 1965) pp. 213-219.

in terms of that decision. Numbers of any kind, whether expressed in dollars, feet, or B. A. degrees granted, have to be evaluated by the user.

Meaningless and Ambiguous Quantities

The decision maker must ask himself what meaning and how much there is in any quantity given him as a basis for action. However precise it looks, a figure has no meaning if it is based on some purely arbitrary guess or on a ratio in which the numerator and the denominator come from different universes, or if it is to be applied to a different universe than that from which it is taken. The widespread circulation of figures of all kinds resulting from some purely arbitrary and even biased guess is greater than is commonly realized. Few business conventions go by without quotation in some speech of at least one of the more common meaningless statistics. Probably no harm is done in such an atmosphere, but no serious decision should be founded on figures whose source has not been carefully investigated.

Even more common, however, is the ambiguous statistic, the figure that looks like a careful and useful calculation, but actually has no meaning by itself and needs supplementing. Averages, including rates, are peculiarly susceptible to meaningless ambiguity. An excellent example familiar to those in academic life is the grade point average by which students are ranked, and which is not uncommonly calculated to the fifth significant figure (to the fourth decimal place). In this context, 3. 546 would mean an excellent course record for a graduating senior, one in which over half the student's grades were A. (A is valued at 4 points, B at 3, C at 2, etc.) But as a measure of the ability and diligence of two seniors being interviewed for a job, how good is this record? Do two students with this same score offer equally good prospects as employees?

One student attended a school in which the dean is interested in building up enrollments without regard for quality and exerts constant pressure on any teacher whose grades average low. In addition, this student has carefully detoured any electives with a reputation for difficulty and schedules instructors and courses on the basis of the instructor's reputation for grading. The other chose a school with a reputation for quality of instruction, chose courses which he felt would add most to his knowledge, including many with reputations for difficulty and volumes of work. Which would you hire, and how would you quantify the difference?

Obviously, schools must use some system of ranking students, and recruiters need some estimate of a student's achievement, but it is the height of nonsense to attach any meaning under any circumstances to digits beyond the first two (one decimal place), and even in the same school and with the same major specialization, even the first decimal place is no more than a very rough ranking for administrative convenience.

With academicians, who ought to know better, committing such obvious fallacies, it is not surprising to find similar uncritical worship of the ambiguous figure in the business world. The most notorious is probably the slavish acceptance of radio and television ratings. Much too frequently, sponsorship decisions are made after the first few showings, and shows are scuttled for lack of a few decimals of total audience tune-in, at a time when neither the content of that audience nor the impact nor compatibility of the program with the advertising can be known. Again, we do need some means of ranking shows as advertising buys, but the figures used cannot be an unambiguous measure of what we need to know. Ratings, at best, are a very rough ranking of total set tune-ins, and there are other factors of even greater importance at times. Without it, it does not even rate the significance of the lowest quality of measurement value, the nominal level.

<u>The four levels of measurement</u> Those accustomed to working with measurement recognize four general levels of measurement quality, divided into two main groups--parametric and nonparametric. The precision most of us attribute to numbers is true only of the two highest levels--the parametric levels designated as ratio measures and as other interval measures. Most of the figures we use in governmental and business decision do not meet the parametric test in the context of their use. They usually belong to the higher of the two nonparametric levels when they have any meaning at all--the ordinal level. The lowest level is the nominal level.

The simplest way to indicate the difference between parametric levels and nonparametric is to note that parametric numbers can be used in ordinary arithmetic computation--we can legitimately add them, subtract, divide, etc.--because the interval between any two adjacent numbers in the sequence equals any other. Similar nonparametric numbers look the same, but 2 plus 3 may not equal 5, but perhaps 21 or 2-1/2. They are essentially labels for relative positions, and do not indicate proportional scale lengths.

Parametric levels of measurement Measurement systems in which the scale intervals are really equal are called parametric, and there are two such types: interval systems and ratio systems. The only difference between the two is the location of the zero value, which is arbitrary in interval systems, such as our common Fahrenheit and Centigrade thermometers, and "real," (in the sense that there are no negative values) in ratio systems, such as the absolute temperature scale and the common foot rule. Most physical measurements today are of one or the other of these two forms, largely because of painstaking work on standardization and measurement research over the past five centuries. But there was a time when a "foot" meant literally that--the length of the measurer's pedal extremity, and other physical measurements had the same degree of vagueness we associate with most measurements we use for decision. It was only after such vague approximations were discarded that the physical sciences were able to make the wide use of mathematical manipulation characteristic of them today. Even so, it is not likely they could do so if they dealt with such changeable data as the human behavioral response. And even the engineer's calculations have to be treated as approximations when he deals with the future, with the problem of design.

At first glance, most of the financial data used in business and government might seem to meet the test of equal intervals. Certainly, any dollar in a total stack of money equals any other dollar. However, the tally of expenditures and receipts in a financial statement is not really a count of dollar bills, or of money, but of values which have been estimated in dollar terms. As already indicated, all dollars listed as spent are not properly classified as true costs, and some very real financial costs have been omitted from such tallies. Moreover, money costs are not the whole of the price paid in most transactions, nor is all of the value received accurately measured or even measureable in monetary terms. Furthermore, when the data given is actual, it records something out of past history. The only utility this history has is to indicate the need for some kind of management control action in the present or some plan for the future. The circumstances which gave rise to the figures will have changed by the time they are put to use, decreasing substantially whatever remaining degree of precision they may have had originally. Often, the quantities stated represent only a rough order of value, and must be treated as ordinal in value.

The Nonparametric Measures: Ordinal and Nominal

Although nonparametric measurements are most often designated with the same kind of numbers as parametric measures, the figures denoting such measurements are merely labels without any implication of proportionality. Ordinary arithmetic operations can be applied physically to such numbers of course, but the answer which results is meaningless.

Numbers or any other labels used merely for classification are designated as nominal measurement. Most nominal measures are so obvious that little temptation exists to treat them as quantities. Many such measures do not resort to numbers at all. The terms men, women, cost, profits, and loss are examples of verbal labels on nominal measurements. Like any other measurement, these terms need just as much scrutiny for the validity of the classification as any other, of course. The class labels frequently are numbers, as in catalog listings. Thus 3.5436 might be such a catalog number--a shorthand designation which enables the buyer to order exactly and the seller to recognize the item precisely, together with its warehouse location and the buying official or production department head responsible for its stocking. This is probably the only level of numerical measurement that occasions no confusion.

Ordinal or ranking measurement. The greatest confusion in the use of numerical information results from the lack of recognition of the difference between numbers that do indicate some differences in value, but only the general order or rank, and numbers, like those on our common foot rule and other measuring sticks, with known intervals. Any academic grading system is a ranking, or ordinal, system, no matter how expressed, and so, unfortunately is nearly all of the data we must use for business decision.

The nature and meaning of ordinal measurement is probably best observed in the academic grading system. Within any given classroom group, the instructor can usually do a pretty accurate job of ranking the students according to their level of understanding of the particular subject being taught and divide the students into at least the five groups designated by the commonly used letter system: A, B, C, D, and F. For administrative convenience, the university office assigns numerical values from four down through zero to these grades and makes up the average point value already referred to. But this is a mere convenience. Only a purblind instructor will insist that an A in one of his courses has exactly the same meaning as an A in a different course of his own, e.g., that an A in his Introduction to Economics has the same meaning (whatever that is) as an A in his graduate seminar on International Problems of Economic Growth. And the difference between instructors and subjects on any campus is well known. So is the difference between schools.

But not only does one A not equal another A. Beyond the point of ranking, we have no meaningful way of comparing the relative value of two ranks. For purposes of getting that sheepskin, an A is counted at twice the value of a C--four points as compared with two. But does the A student have twice the knowledge and understanding that the C student does? Most of us would say that depends on what sort of task you ask the student to apply his knowledge to. For relatively routine tasks putting insight, imagination, and judgment to little strain, there may be little or no difference between the A students as a whole and the C students. But if they were to be assigned to a critical piece of research analysis, the C student might not be able to produce at all, and there would be wide differences between the productivity of the A students, with some of them providing an extremely useful answer, and doing it in a fourth of the time of others with a similar grade ranking. Such ordinal values, in other words tell us only relative position, not distance between ranks.

Nearly all of the data we must use for business decision is of this ordinal level of quality. Television ratings are of this character. They do tell something of audience size, but not necessarily much about the relative quality of the program as an advertising medium for a particular product. One of the most effective programs for one particular kind of advertising the author has ever seen was a very low-rated Saturday evening program which appeared on a local Chicago station. It was a gardening information program built around films produced by the narrator who pursued the hobby of time-lapse photography of plants and flowers. The rating of this show was abysmally low by any normal standards. But garden shops soon learned to stock heavily any item featured, for there was always a heavy run the following Sunday morning. Similarly, price data, sales potential estimates, and most other data on which decision output must be estimated is largely a matter of relative rank, not interval measurement.

Well-managed purchasing departments have long since learned, for example, that even for the same commodity, relative price is not equivalent to relative cost, and have developed vendor rating systems to attempt to take into account other elements of value important to the particular firm. Even for standardized commodities, price is at best an ordinal measure of value, must be supplemented with information on delivery, dependability of source, uniformity of grading and other factors. Similarly, the best estimate of relative sales potentials makes assumptions about relative strength of competition, habits of consumption, and other crucial factors that are quite unlikely to be accurate. Even cost information that is meticulously accurate historically can be at best only an approximate projection of future costs.

Indeed, the fact that decision must anticipate a future that is somewhat different is one reason why little decision data will ever be more than a rough approximation. Tastes, technology, population and its distribution, and the identity and aggressiveness of competitors change with time, and sometimes overnight. Financial figures which are accurate historically become rough approximations of the future costs and receipts relationships which need to be measured. Major policy decisions, which inevitably deal with nonrepetitive events, will nearly always have to make use of quantitative information that indicates little more than a rough ordinal level of relative value. Such data cannot be fit into neat mathematical equations.

As with every other aspect of measurement, the origin of quantitative data does not tell us its quality. The quality as well as the meaning is completely relative to the purpose to which the measurement result is to be applied. The cost accountant, for example, may have done a completely perfect job of evaluating the cost experience of several alternative products or programs. For the purpose of historical comparison, the data may be completely parametric. But if the same figures are used to predict probable future costs, his figures are approximations at best, and may even be maliciously misleading.

The most important element in all measurement is the user himself, and he has the task of adjudging the extent to which data made available to him serves his purpose and the degree of approximation the data has when used for that purpose.

Evaluating and Using Measurements: The Use of Approximation

Clearly all measurement involves a considerable degree of approximation. That degree of approximation, moreover, is definable only in terms of the purpose, in terms of what the measurement is going to be used to represent. For purposes of executive decision, the use of any quantitative data carries an implicit assumption that the data is a sample, representing more information than it explicitly contains. Otherwise, the process would not be that of decision but the application of a known policy by a reasonably intelligent clerk. Indeed, the job of any executive could be accurately defined as the application of judgment to interpret the meaning and degree of approximation in the combined qualitative and quantitative information he has available, in the light of objectives he himself has set. Others can carry out the calculations, but the executive must determine what figures go into the computation, and what the results mean.

Since no figure is more than an approximation, a very important first step in that process of evaluating data is to determine the degree of approximation by asking himself a series of questions:

How do we know? (Are the data real, or just some horseback guesses?)

What do I intend to use the data for?

For what purpose was it collected, and how did this distort the meaning, relative to my purpose for its use?

Does the data contain irrelevant material?

In terms of my use objectives, are the categories of classification really homogeneous? If not, how can the data be reorganized or interpreted to yield relatively homogeneous classifications which are truly relevant to my use?

Do the categories used include significant quantities which are irrelevant for my purpose--costs which are unavoidable in any case, for example?

Do any of the categories used omit substantial quantities which are significant for my purpose, such as imputed opportunity costs in money or effort which are quite real, but not recorded?

What is the degree of indirectness of the measurement? Are the assumed relationships between measures and the phenomena they represent valid, either originally, or in terms of my objective for their use?

How incomplete is the measurement and what is the probable significance of the omissions, relative to my need?

How precise is the job of measurement and how biased the observations?

What effect could time factors have had in creating differences I perceive, or in changing the scale or significance of the measurements?

In terms of my purpose, at what point of expression does approximation begin?

Evaluation of data in terms of level of approximation is important both to ease of handling and to understanding of significance. Physical scientists long ago learned that no data is truly parametric beyond some discoverable level of approximation. Unfortunately, much policy decision in business and government ignores this experience.

A well-trained scientist always indicates the degree of approximation in his data by the degree of precision in his statement. Asked to give the distance from earth to moon, he will state it as 92.8×10^6 miles, not 92,800,000 miles. By this he means that he does not know what the figures should be in the positions in which most of us write the 0's, at least until he knows the time, place, and purpose of the measurement (such as the spot on the moon and the exact time and date on which we hope to land a rocket there).

Most nonscientists probably dislike reading approximations in terms of powers of 10, and this form complicates the typing of a table. The same end is achieved by saying the distance is 92.8 million miles, or if in the form of a table, labeling the column or row as "distance in miles (000,000 omitted)" and entering the number as 92.8.

Such care in precision is not an academic exercise, but a method of (a) indicating the limit on the relevance and degree of certainty of the measurement and (b) focusing attention on those figures which are really significant. For this reason, the mode of expressing precision is known as "significant figures." The purpose of limiting attention to significant figures is to avoid cluttering comparisons with irrelevant detail. Thus if we desire to compare the costs of 4 programs, it is much easier to make the comparison in terms of a significant figure approximation than in a 7 figure presentation, as can be seen:

Costs	Costs (000,000 omitted)
$9,636,783	$9.6
7,187,336	7.2
3,007,996	3.0
4,998,655	5.0

The term "significant figure" relates to the number of figure symbols, <u>starting the count from the first nonzero symbol on the left</u>. After all, it is the difference in millions we need to give the most consideration, not the pennies and individual dollars at the right-hand side. Each significant figure added to our precision of statement implies accuracy to an added power of 10. Even engineers find estimates in the range of stable inanimate nature are not better than 1 in 1,000 (three significant figures equal 10 x 10 x 10). How much less meaningful is data in the world of human whimsy?*

Calculations expressed in greater precision than is justified by the measurements tend to hide meaningful differences under the spurious or redundant detail, making the data hard to analyze. Consider the following not untypical table, a disguised but precise paraphrase of one appearing in a serious and really well-planned experiment in advertising psychology (Table 2-1). In this experiment, carefully controlled small groups of subjects were exposed to visual and audio stimuli of each of three types, and each possible combination of the types (arbitrarily labeled L, M, and N in Table 2-1). From a larger group of stimuli submitted for test, each subject was asked to recall the original stimuli now presented in one of the possible combinations. (Blanks in the table indicate test-presentation situation pairs that were impossible due to physical absurdities such as recognition of an audio-only presentation from a pictorial test.) Because of the large number of test-presentation possibilities, the total of over 1,000 subjects split up into groups ranging only between 23 and 36 in number, as noted in the table.

Some significant differences were found, but note how hard it is to spot them by glancing at the table. This difficulty stems from the use of calculations going more than two significant figures beyond that justified by the data, thus burying the only significant differences in the middle of each percentage shown.

---

* The discussion which follows has been adapted from Chester R. Wasson, Research Analysis for Marketing Decision Appleton-Century-Crofts (New York, 1965) pp. 219-224.

Table 2-1
Average Percentage of Recall of 25 Similar Stimuli
for 3 Different Forms of Stimulus Presentation,
and Combinations of These Forms

(n = number of subjects cooperating in each version of the test.)

Method of Initial Presentation	Method of Presentation for Test of Recall:						
	L	M	N	L&M	L&N	M&N	L, M&N
L	49.35 (n = 23)	49.42 (n = 24)	---	50.54 (n = 23)	42.53 (n = 25)	46.81 (n = 23)	47.68 (n = 24)
M	48.38 (n = 24)	53.65 (n = 24)	---	52.16 (n = 24)	42.64 (n = 24)	47.04 (n = 23)	47.62 (n = 24)
N	---	---	45.63 (n = 23)	---	42.06 (n = 23)	42.17 (n = 25)	40.77 (n = 23)
L, M&N	46.08 (n = 34)	49.19 (n = 36)	41.26 (n = 34)	51.14 (n = 35)	48.05 (n = 35)	47.05 (n = 34)	52.08 (n = 35)
L&M	49.30 (n = 31)	49.57 (n = 31)	---	53.13 (n = 30)	43.58 (n = 30)	46.82 (n = 29)	45.84 (n = 36)
L&N	50.13 (n = 32)	51.21 (n = 28)	45.97 (n = 31)	51.82 (n = 24)	50.11 (n = 28)	49.27 (n = 31)	52.25 (n = 29)
M&N	46.88 (n = 28)	49.04 (n = 27)	43.25 (n = 26)	53.06 (n = 31)	47.87 (n = 28)	49.56 (n = 31)	51.81 (n = 31)

These calculations should not have been carried beyond even percentages, and even this detail strains the rules slightly for convenience of presentation. At this level, each integer represents a difference of one part in one hundred. But individual scores could only be as close as four parts in one hundred, since each subject had only twenty-five chances to be either right or wrong, i.e., 25 test pictures or other stimuli to recognize. The table percentages are to four significant figures, however, implying an accuracy to one part in ten thousand.

The table, however, is an average of scores, each possibly accurate to four parts in one hundred. If we could assume the individual's score could not vary, we might be justified in going one step further so that we would have an accuracy to about one part in six hundred (25 subjects times 25 stimuli). However, psychological measurement of this sort is almost never this precise. If we assume a normal measurement variation, the error in the group average has an even chance of being nearly 7 percent for groups of 25 subjects, assuming the average is correct at about 50 per cent recognition.

$$\text{(Standard deviation of the average} = \sqrt{\frac{.50 \times .50}{25}} = .10$$

Chances are equal at about two-thirds this value, or .07, i.e., 7 percent.) This difference is nearly as great as some of the differences in the table, as can be clearly seen from a revision of this table to even percentages. However, the consistence in the differences, when we eliminate the fictitious detail of fractional percentages, indicates that the differences are real.

Redundant and fictional detail has contributed to confusion in another way. For reasons with which any experienced investigator is familiar, the reseachers were unable to end up with equal-sized test groups. The variation, as noted, ran from 23 to 36. Thus some differences at even the straight percentage would have shown up even if, in fact, there had been no underlying difference in the probability of recognition, due simply to the vagaries of calculation from different group totals to get the percentages. Consider, for one example, the first two recall percentages in the first row of Table 2-1(the L-L and L-M pairs): 49.35 and 49.52. The first represents the average score for 23 subjects, the second for 24 subjects. The simple fact that these two totals differ yields a different percentage result. This can be seen if we assume that the scores for the first 23 subjects in each group are identical, giving us the average for the first group: 49.35. The 24th subject in the second group, let us assume, also, was just as likely to recall as the group average, or nearly even. But his actual score could not be closer than either 48 percent (12 recalled out 25) or 52 percent (13 remembered out of 25). Under these assumptions the score for the larger group would have to be either 49.29 or 49.46. In actuality, it was in between these two results and closer to that of the first group than would have occurred under our assumptions. Thus the calculation beyond the even percentage confused by showing differences where none exist in fact.

The source of the example used here has been disguised because the procedure was no worse than is the common practice in most of business figure usage. It demonstrates empirically what any mathematician or engineer would have seen from the mere numbers involved. The decimal values presented are meaningless and result in a presentation of spurious precision. For this reason alone, the calculations should not have been carried beyond even percentages.

Table 2-2

Average Percentage of Recall of 25 Similar Stimuli, for 3 Different Forms of Stimulus Presentation, and Combinations of These Forms

(Number of subjects in individual experiments ranges from 23 to 36.)

	Method of Presentation for Test of Recall:						
Presentation	L	M	N	L&M	L&N	M&N	L, M&N
L	49	49	-	51	43	47	48
M	48	54	-	52	43	47	48
N	-	-	46	-	42	42	41
L&M	49	50	-	53	44	47	46
L&N	50	51	46	52	50	49	52
M&N	47	49	43	53	48	50	52
L, M&N	46	49	41	51	48	47	52
	Number of Subjects in Each Individual Experiment						
L	23	24	-	23	25	23	24
M	24	24	-	24	24	23	24
N	-	-	23	-	23	25	23
L&M	31	31	-	30	30	29	36
L&N	32	28	31	24	28	31	29
M&N	28	29	26	31	28	31	31
L, M&N	34	36	34	35	35	34	35

The Rules for Evaluating the True Level of Approximation in the Original Measurements and any Resulting Computations are:

1. A measurement is meaningless past the first point of estimate available on a scale giving accurate, standardized values. If, for example, you have an accurate yardstick graduated to tenths of inches, you can measure the width of your desk with it, estimated to some simple fraction of a tenth of an inch, e.g., a third or a fifth of a tenth. If the width seems to be about a third of the way between 29.7 and 29.8 inches, you should mark it down for 29.73," not 29.73+." You do not know whether what you estimate to be about one third is actually more, or slightly less than .03."

2. Calculations based on counts must not be carried out to more significant figures than are contained in the total count of the base

population. Statements of proportion, for example must have the same degree of approximation as is involved in the sample size from which they are drawn (remembering that all counts are, for purposes of prognosis and prediction, samples.) If a survey of 30 men locates 10 that use electric razors, it is quite incorrect to say that 33.3 percent use electric razors, for by this you are stating that exactly 333 out of 1,000 would be found to shave with electricity. You do not know this to be so. If your sample, by the accidents of sampling, had turned up only 9 users of electric shavers, your calculation would have dropped to an even 30.0 percent; if 11 instead of 10, the proportion would have risen to 36.7 percent. Or if, by chance, you had simply conducted one more interview, for a total of 31 instead of 30, your discovered usage would have had to drop to 10/31 (32.3 percent) or rise to 11/31 (35.5 percent). All you really know is that about one third shave with electricity, and you will note that this form of the statement is correct for all of the variations cited.

3. In general, any other quantity derived from a count or measure must not go beyond the precision of statement made possible by the base figure. In practice, this means that:

a. Quantities derived by multiplication and division must be expressed in a lower level of precision than the base count, i.e., to the level that would be affected by the minimum increase or decrease in the base figures.

b. Quantities derived by taking powers or roots may be expressed to the level of precision involved when dividing the number of significant figures in the base data by the value of the power. Pearsonian r and regression coefficients, for example, are affected because they involve calculation of squares. To justify the calculation of a coefficient to the second significant figure, therefore, the sample population studied must be in the thousands, and the other measures with which they are correlated must also be truly accurate to the fourth significant figure (to one part in 10,000). Otherwise it is quite improper, indeed untrue, to say that you have found the correlation to be .79, for example. In fact, to justify a statement that the resulting correlation is .8 requires that the base figures be accurate to one part in 100.

If such rules make uncomfortable an executive used to accounting for appropriations to the cent, he might reflect that he is risking his neck every day driving over a bridge designed by an engineer satisfied with the 3-significant figure precision of his slide rule. The engineer long ago learned that even in his static world of physical measurements, his data must always be treated as sample information, and that samples vary. The rest of us would do well to benefit by his experience.

How Much Precision Do I Need?

This is the most useful question an observer can ask, and one which can ease many of the problems of getting a measure. Getting high precision is an expensive process, and the search is frequently a fruitless one. Quite often, we need no substantial degree of precision at all--only a rough order of value or a ranking. Almost always, a decision will be unchanged over differences of 10% or more. Indeed, many of our own human perceptions seem to recognize and respond only to differences of this general magitude or greater. Moreover, very few decisions of any sort are irreversible, nor are they made once for all. Most involve tentative action which can be modified with the receipt of planned feedback information. We should therefore seek to obtain only that level of precision which can affect the decision we must make.

If this is done, and if it leads to the choice of a very low level --say to the nearest 10%--we may often be able to choose criteria and measuring instruments much more easily than if it were necessary to meet a demand for greater precision, and we may be able to ignore many of the lesser problems of measurement. This is especially true of formal sampling.

SUMMARY

1. A count can tell us only "how many," but we are far more often interested in the answer to "how much?" This type of number comes from a measurement process, a quite different, far more complex, much less certain, and much less objective activity than that of counting.
2. The validity of any measurement must be evaluated in relation to the specific purpose of its use, and the criterion of accomplishment is seldom clear and simple.
3. Measurement is a many-sided decision process with real possibilities of bias and distortion at every stage: the decision on the purpose to be served,

the decision on which kinds of factors represent criteria of accomplishment of that purpose, decision on what aspects of the criteria are suitable for measurement, selection of a useful measurement unit, development of an effective measurement instrument, application of the instrument by an observer, analysis of the significance of the results in terms of the purpose. Errors in such choices have misled many a business and governmental decision.

4. The major pitfalls in measurement are those of classification, indirect measurement, choice of instrument, selection of the unit, bias in observation, evaluation of the measurement quality achieved, ignorance of the erosive effects of time, and improper interpretation of the level of precision obtained.

5. Any number implies a classification of items on the basis of similarity. Since no two items are identical in all respects, any classification can be valid only relevant to a specific use and must be scrutinized relative to that use.

6. Much measurement must be indirect, must be measurement of some available attribute thought to be related to variations in the item whose measure is sought. The relationship always needs validation.

7. Measurement is sometimes incomplete because some factors known to be important are not measurable, or because too many factors are involved for economical investigation, or the relative importance of substantive items is not definable and stable. In such cases, we must satisfy ourselves with indexes--indicators sketching the trends and only the rough order of value of those trends.

8. Finding an adequate instrument of measurement sometimes seems nearly impossible. Special care must be used in using monetary values as the meter, since the money value of most things can change with no change in the physical quantity involved.

9. The observer himself can introduce a bias into the observations.

10. Units must be chosen that are convenient, combine items which are homogeneous for the purpose of the measurement, and which are stable.

11. Time affects measurements in many ways. The choice of time period for observation can change the relative composition of a measurement. The point of time at which observation is made can affect the numbers. And the passage of time can change the significance of the classifications and the units.

12. Not all numbers have the same accuracy and precision of significance. Many quoted numbers turn out on examination to be ambiguous or meaningless, to relate to nothing definable. Only parametric measurements have the arithmetic meaning we associate with numbers in general--only measurements which, for the specific purpose on hand have truly equal intervals between the integers. Many forms of numerical measurement do not. Ordinal values, sometimes incorrectly treated arithmetically, simply denote a ranking without any implication as to the distance between the various ranks. To some degree, nearly all available data about economic and social events must be considered ordinal when used for prediction of the future with which decision deals. The lowest level of numerical quality is the nominal--the use of numbers purely as identifying labels. This last use is seldom a cause for confusion.

13. The precision of any measurement is limited, calculations should not be carried beyond this meaningful level of precision, and significance should not be attached to figures below this level. Moreover, few decisions require any great level of precision, and to seek more is to multiply the expense of measurement and to confuse the comparisons of decision alternatives.

CHAPTER 3: WHAT DO WE KNOW, HOW MUCH DO WE NEED TO KNOW?

Sampling and Probability Distributions

Relative to their intended use, all observations and all measurement data are samples. Certainty, full accuracy and complete measurement are illusions. No observation and no measurement encompasses more than a small fraction of the possible facets of any object, or event. Hence we cannot hope to know "all the facts" even about what has happened already. Since the future never exactly duplicates the past, we will always have less knowledge than we would like of those pertinent facts which may shape the results of any future action we plan for. We must, therefore, make the fullest correct use possible of those sample facts we have. To make sure that that use is justified, we need to understand some of the major concepts of traditional formal sampling theory and their meaning in both formal samples and the accidental ones responsible for much of our information. The two key concepts we must comprehend are those of a population or universe and of all measurement as part of a probability distribution within that population, universe, or sample set.

Measurement, Probability Distributions, and Populations

Physical scientists long ago discovered that a series of readings obtained even when a single person is working with a single accurate measuring instrument, tend to vary over some range of values when carried to the limits of the instrument's precision. If the values are plotted as a frequency distribution, the resulting plot normally assumes a characteristic bell-shaped graph-- a symmetrical plot with a heavy concentration of readings around the center known as the Gaussian normal curve of error, or more commonly, simply the normal curve, or normal curve of probability. The central value of the curve is the arithmetic average (and also, always in such a case, the median, or center item, and the mode or most common value). This curve has a definite mathematical form, such that when we calculate the standard deviation, (the square root of the average of the squares of the deviations from the mean) half of all observations will be in a zone approximately two-thirds of this value of σ from the average, 95% with 2σ , but 1 out of 100 observations will be outside the limits as defined as 3σ from the average.

The same kinds of distribution will normally be discovered in any situation in which all major factors effecting measurement do not change--such as the dimensions of all pieces coming from the same machine, with the same operator, using relatively uniform raw materials.

Since physical measurement is the most favorable condition for stability of observations, it should be obvious that measurements of any phenomena will vary, that all measurement, all quantitative observations of any kind, must be conceived of as probability distributions.

Not all of these distributions will be bell-shaped. Most quantitative distributions of social and economic data seem to have a lopsided, or skew distribution. But all will have some concentration of values around some modal point, and a diminishing percentage as we proceed outward from this mode, if they are really part of the same population. This population requirement holds whether our data comes from a formal sampling procedure or is the result of accidental or nonsystematic observations over a past period.

The statistician uses population, or the technical synonyms of universe and sample set, to indicate a body of phenomena which should, for the purpose of a given measurement, yield a probability distribution. A population or universe is the sum total of all possible elements that have in common the particular characteristic being studied, at one point in time, and only those individuals having the characteristic in common. The universe may be as in the Federal Census, all the people having residence in the United States on April 1, 1960. It may be all those who bought a red Austin Sprite sports car during 1963. It may not be people at all, as the term population seems to imply. It may be the total of all farms on which red soft winter wheat was grown in the crop year 1963, or it may be all of the acres from which soy beans were harvested in that year.

Whether or not a collection of objects or phenomena is really a universe depends on the nature of the later analysis to be performed on the data. For the application of statistical evaluations, the universe must contain every individual possessing the characteristic under investigation, and only those individuals. Further, the individuals must be alike in terms of this characteristic in order to be treated as statistical units. If we are sampling voters in a Department of Agriculture crop control proposal for wheat, all wheat growers would be units because they have one vote per farm. But if we wish to estimate the crop, we must count acres as the unit, even though the replies themselves must come from people. The statistician considers a set of phenomena a homogeneous universe when he believes one force, and only one, has any measurable influence on member events. The variations from this central value occur because an uncountable and unknowable multitude of minute factors, each of no individual consequence in the context of measurement sought, combine to cause variations in both directions.

The decision as to whether or not all measurements come from the same population is thus a judgment, although the statistician does have some negative checks. If he assumes that the central tendency of the values of a series of measurements is the result of a single influencing factor, then he assumes that, for the purpose of that one set of measurements, he is dealing with a single universe and can then make some kind of prediction concerning probable future measurement values in that universe. If he gets some anatomical measures from a sample of girls of age 12, he feels confident he can tell a garment manufacturer what sizes and what quantities of each size to make for girls of this age, in the cities and countries represented by his sample.

Since the identification of what constitutes a population is a matter of judgment, we can define any set of quantities as a probability distribution of values if we have a good reason to believe that all of the individual values represent the effect of the same basic forces, even when the statistical purist cannot see that they are technically part of the same universe as he would define one. We all know, for example, that the various dress styles on the market are quite different in their total composition in any one year, from any other year. But we may feel that the probability distribution of taste among women, for individual numbers available, is relatively constant, even if we cannot predict which number will be most popular and which least popular. We can thus take the past percentage distribution of sales by items during each season as an estimate of the kinds of distributions to expect in future seasons--as a probability distribution of what we believe that sales of any one number will be, in other words, in the population of women's styles coming out next.

This use of probability distribution of belief goes beyond the kinds of problems that traditional statistical methods deal with, but not beyond the basic significance of the terms. Many of the tools discussed in the chapters which follow depend on the use of a series of past observations as a basis for estimating the probability distribution of the next event. If we have a sound reason for believing that such past events represent the same population, we may have a sample useful for decision, but not necessarily one to which traditional statistics applies.

SAMPLES AND EVALUATION OF THEIR MEANING*

A sample is some part of a population--any part, however chosen and observed. A representative sample is one that yields closely approximate measures of those characteristics it was selected to represent. A useful sample is one giving enough information about these characteristics so that, when combined with what the analyst already knows, workable inferences that are useful for decision can be drawn.

Note that while a representative sample is by definition, useful, the experienced analyst can often make use of a nonrepresentative sample if he gets enough information about it to fit in what he learns with existent knowledge. For example, a really representative audit of movement of a drug brand through retail outlets--one directly projectible to all sales--is seldom, if ever, achieved. But the trend revealed by such audits is usually a good reflection of the trend in movement. If the analyst has an independent knowledge of the level of sales, he can add this trend information to get accurate projections of sales.

Most of us tend to apply the term sample only in relation to the formal sampling process--in relation to observations that are labelled "sample." But there is no other kind of observation or measurement except observation of samples. The informal and unconscious observations that we conduct all the time, on which we base all but a minute portion of our action, are not only samples but often the very smallest and knowingly biased of samples. Nevertheless, experience usually proves action growing out of such observations to be sound. Some of the most important decisions in our lives are made on the basis of relatively small samples and samples that we know to be biased.

Courtship is a sampling process. Girls and boys associate themselves with a small number of those of the opposite sex--a select few not chosen on some sort of random probability basis, but most likely on the basis of the accidents of propinquity. They seek each others' company during a few hours of each week under conditions in which both are quite aware that the behavior of the other is somewhat biased. Yet most marriages are reasonably successful. The expectations coming out of the courtship period are usually confirmed

---

* Parts of this section are adapted from Chester R. Wasson, Research Analysis for Marketing Decision, Appleton-Century-Crofts (New York, 1965) pp. 109-110, 113 and The Strategy of Marketing Research, Appleton-Century-Crofts (New York, 1964) pp. 210-211.

and many of the divorces that do arise come out of conditions that could not have been foreseen whatever the care taken in sampling the universe and the actions in that universe. We normally choose our restaurants on the basis of one or two meals taken there and make our recommendations to friends on the same slim sample evidence. We vote for our legislators upon the most cursory analysis of their record, opinions, and character, yet usually find these legislators worth reelecting the next time.

In all these cases, we not only act on incomplete knowledge, we are consciously aware that we are so doing, although we seldom recognize the information we have as sample information. We do so because we know it is impossible to get "all of the information" even if we could afford the time and effort involved.

When we sample informally, we realize unconsciously what we should consciously recognize whenever we draw a formal sample--that all information, all samples have not one but four dimensions: numbers, the breadth of observational detail, the quality of observation of this detail, and time. All knowledge has a time bias since we can only measure what has occurred in the past. Even within that past, we usually realize that there are many things about which the numbers are so great that we cannot observe all possible happenings. But even when it might be possible to make contact with all of the numbers or happenings involved, it is not possible to take account of all possible details concerning the events themselves and surrounding events. These are infinite. We therefore limit ourselves to those we consider to have the greatest relevance to whatever kind of decision it is we have to make.

The greater the number of details we sample, the greater the job of sampling itself since the size of the task is a product of both the numbers involved and the number of details involved in each item.

Beyond a minimum of observations, we gain more understanding of phenomena and higher accuracy of analysis by collecting more detail about each observation than by increasing the number of observations.

This has been one of the lessons of statistical quality control. With 100 percent inspection, attention is usually focused on one facet of information: which items are outside standard limits of acceptability, and how many (and even the quality of this measurement may not be good). To do this much for the entire production run is so costly that little more can be afforded in the way of useful details about the go and no-go items. If long runs are involved, 100 percent inspection is a mass-production operation and must be done with an eye to mass-production costs.

By contrast, statistical quality control is a small-batch process. Because the total number of observations is relatively small, time and care can be spent on measuring the degree of off-standard quality and determination whence the deviation arose--from what batch of raw material, what machine, which operator, etc. Data pinpointing any need for corrective action becomes available, and the number of future off-standard pieces is reduced. Cost per item inspected will always be markedly higher than under 100 percent inspection, but total inspection cost may, just incidentally, be less. The real saving, however, lies in the control over product uniformity achieved because of broader information and the better data quality made possible by higher quality inspection personnel and the lighter stress on quantity inspection production.

Data quality results from emphasis on care and precision of measurement and close supervision of observation. There is an inverse relationship between data quality and sample size. How dramatic is the gain in quality from the use of a formal small sample was illustrated in a mail-order tally experience. A small sample was devised to replace two 100 percent tallies of orders and customers, used in making sales plans. Prior to sampling, tally results had checked so poorly with later data that they proved of little value. Sample results proved so accurate that minor errors in order handling were revealed. Yet the only difference in the information came from the quality of the personnel, their close supervision, and release from pressure for quantity production--all made possible by the small size of the sample.

When analysis begins, breadth and quality determine its accuracy, not numbers. These are matters which must be assessed on the basis of personal knowledge and judgment, and the statistician has no means of aiding this judgment. He can, however, answer another kind of question for us, one worth asking: "How reliable is our data--how precise or repeatable is our measure?"* With a given sample size, i.e., the device used is that of "confidence

* Precision and accuracy are sometimes thought of as synonyms, but are not the same thing. Accuracy denotes the degree to which a measurement approaches the true value sought. Precision simply indicates the closeness with which repeated measurements replicate each other, regardless of bias. Thus the speedometer on my automobile dashboard may be so inaccurate that it regularly registers a speed 10 percent above my actual rate of travel. The

limits," a measure based on the estimate of the standard deviation. With the use of this device, we can get some guidance on how large the fraction of the total universe we need to get a given level of precision. The answer deals solely with the strictly numerical or quantitative dimensions--it does not evaluate such questions as to whether the fraction came from the whole we were seeking to know, or whether the quality and breadth of the data were adequate.

Confidence Levels: Calculation and Significance

When the statistician refers to "confidence levels," he is using the term confidence with a more restricted and more precise meaning than we are likely to understand on the basis of common usage. When making any statement as to the confidence level of an estimate, he assumes that

1. all possible sources of bias in the measurement have been taken account of first
2. all measurements used came from a universe that was homogenous for the purpose of the measurements
3. that measurements in that universe will vary, but that the variations are due solely to chance fluctuations caused by the sampling process, that for samples of reasonable size, the behavior of the estimate of the mean will be governed by the normal curve
4. that the measurements have been secured by a true random procedure
5. that our interest is in the long run, not in the accuracy of a single measurement.

If the assumed conditions are met, we can make a statement about the probability that the true value of some population characteristic such as the mean will lie within a stated range around the value estimated from our sample. If we calculate the confidence level is 95% that the mean of the height of the trucks on the highway is 13 feet ± 1 foot, for instance, we are saying that 95 times out of 100, we would expect that the average of a sample

---

bias may even vary as between different individual true speeds, the reading showing 70 miles/hours when I am only travelling at 60, but indicating 27 m.p.h. when the car is moving at 26 m.p.h. The speedometer, however, is probably fairly precise: always registering 27 m.p.h. instead of 26 m.p.h. and 70 m.p.h. instead of 60 m.p.h. A measurement may be highly inaccurate but very precise. If accurate, however, it must also be precise.

of the same size, secured by the same procedure, would fall in this range. The complement of the confidence level value, the error rate, can be used to express the same idea. In this case, we would say that our estimate for the average height of the trucks is 13 feet $\pm$ 1 foot with a 5% error rate.

As with all classical probability statements, our estimates are understood to refer only to the long run, in a static universe. The statement is not intended to apply to a single set of measurements. These latter are, from the traditional statistician's point of view, either wrong or right, and he cannot tell which from his confidence calculation. He does not mean that it is 95% right, nor does he consider such a condition possible. The basis for the confidence level statement is the estimate of the standard deviation, calculated from the sample data distribution. An extended discussion of these calculations can be found in any standard statistics text, so will be merely summarized to aid discussion.

Estimating the Standard Deviation and the Confidence Level

To estimate the confidence level, we need know only the distribution of the actual sample measurements made, or a summary of this distribution, and the number in the sample taken. The size of the total population which was sampled is irrelevant so long as it is large.

The arithmetic mean $\overline{x}$ is first calculated by adding all of the observed measurements and dividing by their total number:

$$\overline{x} = \Sigma \frac{x_i}{n},$$ when $\underline{n}$ represents the number in the sample

(meaning: divide the sum of all the individual measurements by their total number to get the average value)

The standard deviation of the sample, s, is then calculated as the estimate of the standard deviation for the universe. This estimated measure of the dispersion of the values around the mean value is determined by the formula:

$$s = \sqrt{\frac{\sum_{i=1}^{n} (x_i - x)^2}{n - 1}}$$

Although the standard deviation is defined as the square root of the average of the square of the deviations from the mean, the denominator (n-1) is used rather than n to take account of the fact that s is based on sample data.

If we express the spread (dispersion) of data around the mean in units of standard deviation instead of the original measurement units, we can talk about how much of the data lies within some given interval such as $\bar{x} \pm 1s$ or $\bar{x} \pm 3s$. Even if we knew nothing about the distribution of the measurements in the population from which the sample was drawn and had to assume it was quite irregular and did not follow the normal curve, we would still expect 75% of all items to lie in the range $\bar{x} \pm 2s$ (See Chebyshev's theorem in any standard statistical text.) However, if we can assume that the distribution of the population is normal, we can make more precise statements about our expectations concerning the portions of the data lying within any given number of standard deviation units from the mean. These statements of that population spread are what the statistician means by "confidence level." Figure 3-1 depicts the more commonly used values.

FIGURE 3-1. Normal Curve Probability Distribution Indicating Intervals of $\bar{x} \pm k\sigma$ (approximated as $\bar{x} \pm ks$)

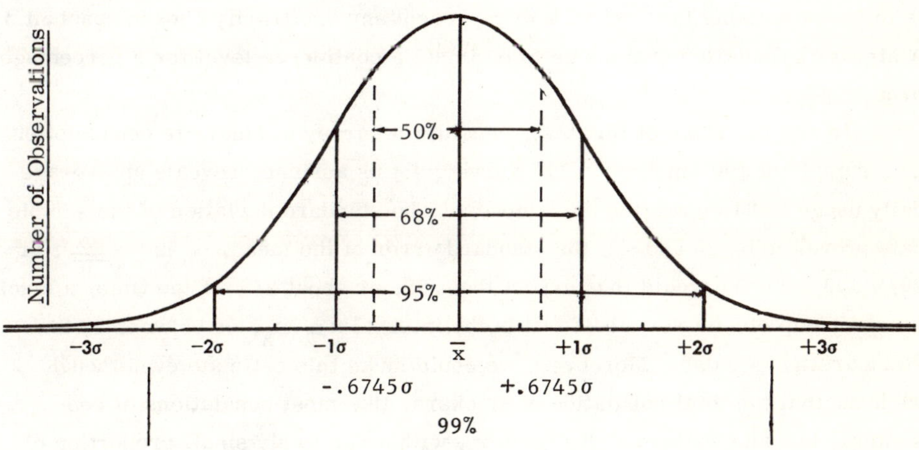

The estimate of the mean is also a variable whose range of value can be estimated in terms of $s_{\overline{x}}$, the standard deviation of the mean, also known as the standard error of the mean. The standard symbol so closely resembles that for the standard deviation of the observations (s) and is closely related to it, that the two are often confused. The formula and the resulting value differs, however:

$$s_{\overline{x}} = \frac{s}{\sqrt{n}}$$

Since n is always a positive value and a moderately large one, $s_{\overline{x}}$ clearly denotes a much narrower range of value than does s.

One important property of this term is the fact that as the size of the sample n increases, the distribution of the values of $\overline{x}$ approach those of a normal distribution regardless of the shape of the distribution of x. Because of this property, except for very small sample sizes--samples of less than 10, for instance--we can refer to tables of the area under the normal curve found in most statistics texts to get estimates of the distribution of the values of the mean in terms of multiples of $s_{\overline{x}}$. These indicate that the true mean is included within an interval of $\overline{x} \pm 1.96s_{\overline{x}}$, or roughly $2s_{\overline{x}}$, 95% of the time if the statistician's assumption of homogeneity and lack of bias can be accepted. The 95% estimate is called the confidence level for the estimate of the mean, and $\overline{x} \pm ks_{\overline{x}}$, the confidence interval. (In this formula, the usual convention is followed of using the symbol k to represent any arbitrarily chosen constant.) A similar calculation enables us to estimate a confidence level for a percentage or a proportion.

To see the value of this test, consider a survey of cigarette consumption by a sample of 100 smokers. The survey, let us assume, reveals an average daily usage of 24 cigarettes per smoker. The standard deviation of the sample data proves to be 20 and $s_{\overline{x}}$, the standard error of the mean, is $\frac{s}{\sqrt{n}}$, or $20/\sqrt{100} = 2$. We would thus expect that .68, or about 2/3 of the time, a much larger group of samples would fall in the interval $x \pm 1s_{\overline{x}}$, or between 22 and 26 cigarettes per day. Moreover, we could make this estimate even though we know that the total population of smokers, like most populations of consumers, has an unbalanced distribution, with a relatively small proportion of heavy smokers and a large number of moderate smokers. Nevertheless, the rather modest sample of 100 is large enough to allow us to use normal theory to estimate the variation in the mean. This example gives us a useful basis for looking at the influence of sample size, n, upon the precision of resulting measurements.

How Important Is Sample Size?

Probably no more widespread misconceptions about measurement practice exist than the distrust of small samples. Yet we saw from the above that a relatively modest sample--a mere 100--yielded a relatively precise estimate of a highly variable population. In fact, even if we seek a 95% level estimate, the calculations indicate that we could estimate that the true mean lies within a range between 22 and 28 ($2s_{\bar{x}} = 4$), and be wrong only 5% of the time. A larger sample, of course, would narrow the confidence interval, but not proportionately, and we might be satisfied this information were good enough for decision. Costs of data collection, never small, go up proportionately with the amount collected, but precision increases only in proportion to the square root of the increases in numbers. ($s_{\bar{x}}$, remember, equals $\frac{s}{\sqrt{n}}$.) To double our precision, we must quadruple our data collection cost.

This fact has an interesting corollary: whenever samples are small, additional information can be valuable in relation to cost, but as they increase in size, the incremental value of the same amount of added information decreases very sharply. If the initial sample is 25, adding another 25 narrows the confidence interval by the ratio of 5/7.1 ($\sqrt{25} = 5; \sqrt{50} = 7.1$) but adding the same number--25--to a sample of 100 decreases the error interval merely to $\frac{11.2}{12.2}$.

One of the greatest of "common sense" errors is to assume that the larger the population, the larger must be the sample. Both experience and the cold computations of traditional statistics refute this supposition. A review of the formulas listed will show that total population does not enter into the error calculation in any manner. The estimate of error does not depend on the size of the population from which the sample is drawn, only on the size of the sample. It makes no difference whether the population be 5,000 or 500 million, a sample of any given size will result in the same estimate of error, so long as the population is relatively large.

Since cost goes up in proportion to size of the sample, but its precision only increases with the square root of size, it costs us nine times as much to get 3 times the accuracy. We thus ought to weigh very carefully how much precision we really need in a sample result. This need is further reinforced by the practical fact, well known to those experienced in data collection, that as the size of the sample goes up, the quality of observation and measurement goes down, so that precision is lost through slipshod work. As taxpayers, we all have benefited from the increasing use of sampling by the United States Census over the last two decades. And as users of Census data (which nearly anyone in business is, directly or indirectly) we have profited by getting more kinds of data, and getting it quicker, and probably more accurately. Even the theoretical loss of precision occasioned by Census Bureau sampling is extremely small, for the 25% sample they commonly use. This means that much of the information we have about the 53 million households counted in 1960 really applies directly to only about 13.25 million households. Substituting in our formula, we see that

$$s_{\overline{x}} = \frac{s}{\sqrt{13,250,000}} = \frac{s}{3640}$$

Since the divisor of the standard deviation of each individual measurement distribution would also be approximately 3640, and the average per capita income, for example was estimated at $2250, the difference in estimate is certainly far less than the bias in measurement--a bias that extensive experience indicates is several per cent under the most careful conditions of reporting.

The "confidence" we can have in our results as measured by the concept of confidence level is thus simply a question of how consistent we could expect results to be if the only source of error were sample variation, and what we measure is free to vary, without restraints set by custom or other human forces.

However, most of the data we use for business policy decision and market strategy is the result of social forces which make for uniformity and destroy independence of reaction: social custom, educational systems, sales promotion activities, legal restraints, or the mere knowledge that what we do will affect our relationships with other people, or the actions of our competitors. The proportion of voters casting a Republican ballot in the upper class section of any city is much higher than in the labor wards. The kinds of music people listen to, the kinds of recreation they seek, the department stores they patronize, will all be different in the two class extremes, and relatively uniform within a district. Thus the s in the numerators of our formulas for $s_{\overline{x}}$ will be quite small within any population stratum, and the precision with which we estimate from actual data after sampling will be relatively high. The size of the interval for a given confidence level and a fixed sample size varies with 1/s (that is, with$\sqrt{n}$/s). The less the standard deviation of our population, the less our sample will vary and the smaller our confidence interval and necessary sample size. If we have some knowledge that some segments of our population can be expected to produce a relatively more uniform response, we can take advantage of this uniformity by stratifying our sample: that is, by taking a specified proportion from each segment, with reference to the segment's size in the population we are sampling. If we know in advance (which we seldom do) what the s is for each chosen stratum, we can estimate the approximate interval attained for a given confidence level since s for the whole sample will now be the weighted average of the s's for the individual strata. Actually, what we have in the case of a truly stratified universe statistically is not one population, but as many as there are strata, each with a very low dispersion around its own average. Since this is a relatively common condition for a large part of human activity, this means that for activities involving people, many calculated confidence intervals are conservative statements of the degree of consistency to be expected in our counts and measurements when the sampling plan makes use of what we know about social stratification.

Since the level of confidence we ask for can seriously affect costs, and getting too much data can affect its quality, the question should be raised as to how much precision we should shoot for.

What Confidence Level Should We Shoot For and Why?

Why not shoot for as high a confidence level as we can afford? Because we meet other costs beyond the monetary -- the cost of ignoring valid information for one. This is particularly likely to happen when a confidence level is used in conjunction with an acceptance criterion. The more confidence we wish to have that our criterion will ensure that the result will be true when we accept it, the less likely we are to recognize a significant deviation from the result when such occurs. Consider the problem in the context of statistical quality control (SQC).

In its simplest form, SQC consists of checking small batches of product and comparing the variation in the averages of the batches from an overall average or specification value. These averages, which frequently are plotted for clarity, are expected to vary within some predetermined limits, usually based on the standard deviation of previous samples of the same product. The limits most commonly used are based on 2 $\sigma_{\bar{x}}$ or 3 $\sigma_{\bar{x}}$. So long as the quality of the samples does not stray outside these preset limits, quality is considered to be under adequate control and the production run is accepted. But if one single sample batch strays outside the limits, it is assumed that something is causing too much variation, and the source of the variation must be traced down to determine whether it be the machine setting, the operator, the raw material, or some environmental factor.

Why is a particular standard chosen for the control limits--why 2 $s_{\bar{x}}$ or why 3 $s_{\bar{x}}$? If you set the limits at 2 $s_{\bar{x}}$ you are aiming for fairly tight quality control. You know that under normal conditions, a variation of just over 2 $s_{\bar{x}}$ will occur once in 20 batches, but you feel that the 19 to 1 chance that this variation is abnormal justifies looking into the reason for it. There is only a 5% chance that you are sounding a false alarm. There are very real risks, on the other hand, that the process average has shifted and that your sampling has not detected it. The probability that the latter has happened depends on where the average has moved <u>to</u> and changes with each possible new process level. An operating characteristic curve (O. C. Curve) can be plotted to evaluate your procedures against possible alternative levels of the process average. If 3 $s_{\bar{x}}$ is chosen as the control limit, your false alarm rate will have dropped to 1%, but the chances of a process shift going undetected will have increased in corresponding fashion.

In other words, the confidence level has two sides. Setting a high level causes you to reject differences as unimportant which may be really significant. Setting the standard too low causes you to accept differences as important which may not be at all. You must decide where the balance should be struck. An objective evaluation involves an estimate as to the costs of too much rejection versus the cost of too easy acceptance.

This is no academic question. Not infrequently a study may indicate a percentage probability for success of an alternative is only slightly over 50%, and yet successive tests reveal the finding to be consistent, indicating a low dispersion. And in business, profits are made only by taking risks. It is a rare business situation in which the low risk course is potentially profitable. To wait until our information is copper-riveted is usually to wait until competitors have gained an advantage.

Furthermore, the numbers dimension is only one of the important aspects of our sample. If this were not so, sampling would be a mere clerical operation, and interpretation of sample results safely left to the office boy. Unfortunately, all data has three other dimensions which cannot be evaluated by the simple logic of mathematics, but which are far more likely to affect the proper interpretation of the information than does mere sampling variation: the dimensions of time, data quality, and data breadth. Beyond this there is always the baffling question of the validity of the observations in relation to the decision to be made--whether we have, in fact, sampled the right population.

The Dimensions of Time, Quality and Breadth of the Sample

Business decisions always concern the shape of things in the future. By the time data has been gathered and analyzed, our samples tell us only the shape of things as they have been. This time element is relatively unimportant in the realm of physical measurements. But in the affairs of men, time means change. This season's favorite color will be less popular next. The sales strategy that is working so well now will meet counter moves from competition in a few months. The advertising appeal that is so fresh and has such impact today will be stale and too freely copied by the year's end. Even the physical dimensions of today's children may be a poor guide for the clothing maker 5 years hence. The only true probability is that what has been is unlikely to be. Hence, for many business and governmental decisions, there are no unbiased "probability" samples, and skilled judgment is needed to estimate the nature and extent of the time bias.

The quality dimension of our data is too often taken for granted, and, unluckily, is in inverse ratio to the volume of it we try to collect. Anyone with extensive experience in comparing "100% samples" with small sample results soon learns that the precision of the small sample is almost invariably greater than the mass measurement provided the sample truly covers the area of interest, without respect to the problem of data breadth discussed below. Mass measurement, like mass production of anything else, inevitably brings pressures for economy at the expense of care. Such pressure results in the use of the less skilled in measurement and observation, in part because skill is scarce as well as high paid. Nor are the differences between the mediocre quality of mass measurement and high quality small sample measurement always small. Indood, mass measurement can sometimes prove so inaccurate as to be of little value, whereas a small sample can produce quite reliable results. In one case, a one-thirtieth sample of mail order customers replaced two different complete tallies. The result was that for the first time in the company's history, the complex actual mailing results agreed with projections made on the basis of the tabulations. The only differences were the quality of the personnel assigned to the job, the tightness of the supervision, and the basis for evaluation of their work (care and precision, not quantity primarily)--all made possible by reducing the size of the job.

The advantage of sampling in cases like the above is the opportunity to minimize the human error in collection. Computers change the dimensions of the problem of 100% sampling of course. If the measurement involves no significant degree of judgment and no human intervention on the inputs, the problem of human error disappears as for example, when transistors are inspected by automatic test equipment and the data computer-processed directly without clerical intervention. Similarly, if the complete tally is a computer processing of prepunched tickets for all items sold in a department store, the results may be accurate. But where judgment is a factor in recording the measurement, or whenever recording of the result involves human intervention in any way, sampling is often the best answer to a data gathering problem, and the best sample is the smallest practical sample giving adequate answers for decision. Sample size is seldom as important as data breadth.

To talk of data breadth is to recognize that measurements do not occur in sterilized vacuo. They represent a picked few of the facets of reality which occur in a certain environment under specific conditions. If we are to make the most efficient use of the information gathered, we need to know some facts about that environment and those conditions. One of the most important superiorities of statistical quality control is its necessary emphasis on data breadth. With 100% inspection, we normally measure only one aspect of quality-- "go" or "no-go," for example. As a result we learn only after the fact what part of production is not meeting standards and must be scrapped. To do more than measure this one narrow aspect for every item produced would be clearly uneconomical. But with small batch sampling for statistical quality control, we can afford both to take careful measurements and to collect collateral detail as well: the raw material batch from which the item was fabricated, the machine on which produced, the operator, and any other details concerning matters which could bias quality. Knowing this, we can pinpoint signs of unfavorable change, identify those factors that are defect causing, and eliminate the defects before more occur. Similarly, when delving into the motivations of those who might buy from us or vote for our candidate, it is always more revealing to learn a great deal more about those responding, and the bases for their responses, than to collect a mass of limited responses.

Validity: Does the Sample Apply?

We are pretty clear as to the nature and boundaries of the population we are sampling in most of the problems of physical measurement with which traditional statistics has been designed to cope. The production run which the quality control inspector is sampling can be well and precisely defined. But the human population with which business decision must concern itself can only rarely be defined with any precision at all, especially when that universe will exist only in the future, as a result of the actions taken by the decision-maker, and shaped in unexpected ways by both these actions and the counteractions of competitors. The potential market for a new product, for example, is not a definite delimited entity. There can be no way of estimating the precision of our measurement if we cannot determine the degree of coincidence between the boundaries of our sample and those of the universe we intend to represent.

Fortunately, few decisions hinge on small differences, and the information from our samples, however vital, is a mere supplement needed to fill gaps in a much bigger store of accumulated experience, some of which can be taken into account by means of the subjective mathematics of Bayesian probability, other portions are of a qualitative nature not subject to mathematical manipulation, but can lead to positive judgments. In addition, most well-planned operating procedures contain provisions for a flexible response to the feedback of results from planned action, so that the really firm decisions are subject to revision in all but the very short run.

The purpose of data collection and observation of any sort is to reach some valid* conclusion as to our future course of action. Our concern is with the validity of those conclusions and our choice of action. Statistical tools can help us judge the reliability of data collection, but furnish no guidance as to the validity of the data gathered, even less of the judgments we make on the basis of that collected information. The judgments normally include a

---

* An extended discussion of the problem of validity can be found in Chester R. Wasson, Research Analysis for Marketing Decision, Appleton-Century-Crofts (New York, 1965) pp. 154-174.

mass of background and other knowledge which we must use to make our interpretations. Even the most picayune of samples is often enough to illumine that background and permit sound judgment. For example, a well-known firm we will designate as XYZ found that its major competition was pretesting a radical version of XYZ's key consumer product, one that might cripple its major market if successful. The XYZ analyst was able to obtain attitude information from 17 persons in the consumer panel being used by the competitor. Combining this limited information with knowledge he had gained from many other surveys and tests of quite different products, he concluded that the new version would enjoy only a limited and brief success. His recommendations to management forestalled a crash counterprogram which subsequent market events confirmed as unnecessary.

The background experience on which the XYZ analyst relied for his conclusions would not have met the test of homogeneity desired by the traditional statistician. His problem, however, was one which traditional objective statistics does not attempt to deal with--the results of a one-time decision. One of the more useful quantitative developments in recent years has been the renewed attention to the use of personalistic probability, of quantified judgments made on the basis of the kind of data which the XYZ analyst relied to come to his recommendation.

SUMMARY

1. All of the data we have is from some kind of sample and all measurements are truly represented only in terms of probability distributions.
2. Any single measurement is likely to be biased relative to the true value sought, and even the most careful measurements of a single phenomenon will vary. With physical attributes, the frequency distribution of careful measurements will generally follow the normal curve of error. Whatever is measured, when all measurements are from the same universe, there will always be a clustering around some central value and a diminution of the frequency the more the measurements deviate from this central value. In the case of most social and economic data, this distribution will tend to be lopsided, or skewed.
3. Sampling and deciding on the basis of very small samples is something we all do informally and often unconsciously all of the time. Despite this fact, many of us are suspicious of the utility of samples and tend to put too much stress on large quantities.

4. Primarily, most of us do not understand the purpose of sampling--to increase our knowledge and supplement it, not to limit it. In the search for the false security of numbers, we tend to overlook the importance of breadth and quality in samples, and to disregard the bias that time always introduces into their meaning.

5. Even the conservative tools of traditional statistics can help us gain a more balanced view of the requirements of sampling.

6. The most important of those tools involve confidence levels and confidence intervals. Confidence, in this context, does not mean faith, as it connotes in common usage. It simply measures the degree of repeatability of sample results under the same procedure, the precision of the measurement, but not its accuracy.

7. Confidence level calculations do tell us that although costs of data collection rise proportionately to the amount collected, the increase in precision is proportionate only to the square root of sample size.

8. As a practical matter, increase in sample size is not even as beneficial as this relationship indicates. As samples get large, the tendency is to cut down on the breadth of detail measured, and thus decrease the degree of useful knowledge. Generally, too, quality of measurement suffers in the attempt to control costs. For these reasons, small samples nearly always produce superior measurements to 100% samples.

9. The search for too much certainty--the requirement of too high a confidence level introduces error from the other direction: the error of assuming that some difference is not significant when it is.

10. Sampling theory cannot help us determine the validity of the sample, even less the validity of the interpretations we put on the results. These are matters of personal judgment and involve the skill of the user in supplementing informal knowledge he already has with the added information drawn from the sampling operation.

CHAPTER 4: BAYESIAN STATISTICS: MIXING JUDGMENT AND EXPERIENCE

The development of what has come to be called the Bayesian approach to decision provides a useful technique for the kinds of unique decisions needed in the dynamic economy of a mass industrial society. Back in the eighteenth century, the Reverend Thomas Bayes promulgated a simple theorem and a rather startling postulate. Bayes' theorem is a straight-forward conditional probability formula--a means by which the decision maker can modify his original estimate of a probability by using additional information on the conditions governing an outcome to modify his original calculation. But although this formula is applicable to ordinary traditional statistics, Bayes interpreted probability as a much more personalistic, that is, subjective phenomenon than statisticians did then or have since. To him, a probability could be a simple statement of the degree of belief in an outcome of an uncertain situation. Were he here today, the good pastor would hardly object to having his name attached, as it has been by some, to a rather broad extension of the formal use of subjective probabilities in making decisions amid the complex uncertainties of modern business and politics. Bayes Postulate goes so far as to propose that even in a situation of total ignorance, the decision maker should choose a prior estimate of probability before he gathers any information. Most neo-Bayesians would stop somewhat short of this point and seek some concrete basis for the prior probability estimate.

What has become known as the neo-Bayesian, or simply the Bayesian approach to decision making has been defined as the attitude that ". . .it is legitimate to quantify our feelings about uncertainty in terms of objectively assessed numerical probabilities, even when confronted by a single unique decision and when there is no extensive past history on which to base the assessment of probabilities."[1]

Two Kinds of Probabilities and Their Relationship To Decision

The need to make a decision implies some degree of uncertainty about the outcome of each of the proposed alternatives. Thus the decision itself must rest on some kind of assumption about the likelihood of success of the

---

[1] Harry V. Roberts, "Bayesian Statistics in Marketing," Journal of Marketing, Vol. 27, No. 1 (January 1963) pp. 1-4.

alternatives being considered. Traditional statistics was formulated to deal with decisions in situations which could be viewed as parts of a history and a future of similar events repeated over and over. The model was that of the gambling situation with honest dice or cards and an honest dealer. The expectation of future decisions with the same choices converts the short-run uncertainty of the individual outcome to a long-run certainty, expressible in terms of an objective probability statement. The latter can be defined as the limiting value approached by the ratio of occurrences of the given outcome to the total opportunities for its occurrence, as the chances for occurrence become extremely large. It is always a ratio, a fraction between 0 and 1, and is never a prediction applicable to a single event, only the long run.

Some of our most important decisions, however, are in the context of situations in which we lack any background of experiences which can be objectively described as similar enough to the current one to meet ordinary statistical standards of comparability. Faced with this kind of unknown outcome, we can make a reasoned choice between alternatives only when we make some judgment about the relative likelihood of occurrence of each outcome perceived as possible. Such a subjective probability is also expressible as a fraction between 0 and 1 which does not represent any kind of ratio but is a statement of our degree of belief in a specific outcome. Generally, too, this fraction derives from some kind of experience, but experience which cannot be described as objectively comparable to the current situation.

Thus we can have either of two kinds of probability fractions, both expressed as some value between 0 and 1: objective probability and subjective probability. To avoid confusion, subjective probabilities are often referred to as likelihood. The term personalistic probability is also often used to emphasize the judgmental character of subjective probabilities. Objective probability is so designated because competent observers analyzing the same information would normally arrive at the same probability statement, and would also generally agree on what evidence was admissable in its determination. By contrast, in the case of really unique decision situation, equally competent observers might well disagree as to both the admissability of the kinds of evidence being used and to the numerical value each would assign to the alternative outcomes. Objective and personalistic probabilities can be viewed either as different attitudes towards the admissability of evidence on the probability of an outcome, or as tools for different kinds of decisions.

The Viewpoint of The Objectivist

The objectivist views probability as the long run relative frequency of occurrence of an event, applicable only to a long series of events that can be repeated again and again under much the same describable set of circumstances. He would obtain the value of this frequency ratio either from an inference about an observable physical situation--such as the probable behavior of a six-sided die--or from observation of the actual number of times the event took place in a series of trials. He does not feel he should make predictions about unique events, situations which are not repeated and therefore can have no long run ratio. Nor does he like to bring to bear on his inference any evidence other than his original observations of repeated events or physical structure. To him, any single event is unknowable, there are no degrees of truth short of the absolute, and degrees of belief are not a subject for measurement.

The Viewpoint of The Personalist

The personalist, on the other hand, is interested less in what will happen in some kind of long run than in what will happen the next time, and thus views probability as a measure of his degree of belief in a particular proposition. To him, truth can be a variable, and the question of "how true is an event?" can have meaning. He will take into account all the problems and all of the evidence accepted by the objectivist, but much more besides. His main interest, however, is in unique events and those which may occur only a few times, or which have no prior history. He will therefore seek guidance from past experience of his own or of others with what seem to him to be similar but not identical situations. And he will use techniques such as Bayes Theorem which enable him to change his judgment by systematically taking experimental evidence into account. The objectivist and the personalist usually get similar answers when the amount of data is large. The two approaches may yield substantially different results, however, when dealing with small samples of data and short runs.

How The Different Viewpoints Lead to Different Decisions

At the beginning of a dice game, both types of probabilists are likely to use the same estimate of the chance of a 7 appearing on the first throw of two dice--6/36, based on an examination of the physical structure of the cubes and on experience with long series of throws of similar pairs. If no 7 has appeared by the end of the 15th pass, both men would agree that if the initial estimate was correct, something rather unusual has occurred. The probability of $(30/36)^{15}$, that is, the probability of no 7, is approximately .06. Each might then inspect the dice more closely, pay extra attention to the dice-handling, recheck his first presupposition that the dice were unbiased. Each might begin to question his original assumption that this one game was part of a long series of "fair" games. But the reactions of the objectivist and of the personalist would then tend to diverge. After considering the evidence, the objectivist would then either continue to estimate the probability of a 7 appearing as 6/36 or would conclude that, based on the collected evidence of the 15 throws, it is unlikely that this game is part of a long series of games where the probability of getting a 7 is 6/36. But he also considers the available evidence too slim for him to make a new estimate of the probability of a 7 on the 16th throw in this particular and unique game, and he lacks any tools for arriving at such a modified estimate. He would probably just quit the game.

The subjectivist, however, may feel that since this is the only game in town, it must continue, and the 16th roll must be evaluated. He simply sees a need to make a revised estimate of probability based upon the observed properties of this particular set of throws. He will therefore employ Bayes Theorem to calculate an estimate of the probability of a 7 on the 16th throw conditioned by the nonappearance of a 7 on the previous 15 throws.

Thus the subjectivist is prepared to address himself more directly to problems such as estimating defect rates in a new production process on which no manufacturing experience exists or projecting the sales of a new style appearing in a women's dress line for the first time. Since many such decisions cannot be avoided, he attempts to bring to them some form of systematic analysis and, in particular, a numerical evaluation of whatever he had available in the way of previous experience, business judgment, feelings, hunches and the like.

How The Problems Solvable by Each Approach Differ

The insurance business provides the classic illustration of the values of objective probability. If I desire to buy $10,000 worth of life insurance protection, the agent will quote the same firm rate to me as to any other applicant of the same sex, age, occupation and apparent condition of good health. His rate is based on a table summarizing the mortality experience for tens of thousands of men of the same general description. With enough policyholders, the insurance actuary can calculate how much premium to charge. This premium represents a financial risk in my individual case, but a virtually certain profit when spread over a large number of policyholders. This premium, however, is not based on any individual evaluation as to my own specific chance of survival during the next year but on the fraction of all policyholders presently living who may be expected to die during that year. Such an inability to pinpoint the survival chances of the next individual case is intrinsic to the definition of probability as a long-term relative frequency ratio.

The objective probabilities of the insurance actuary are obviously correct bases for the decisions about many of the activities of individuals, businesses, and other institutions, particularly at the routine operating level. Indeed one of the more useful developments in industrial production in this generation has been the adoption of statistical quality control to replace 100 percent inspection. This method of quality control is based on the recognition that each item produced is not a unique event but can be perceived of as one of a series of repeated events subject to minor chance variations. Without question, a great many of the routine operating aspects of business can be made more efficient and operational prediction can be improved by recognizing that the particular situation, for the purpose for which a decision must be made, can be perceived as one of a series of repeated events. Chapter 8 suggests some of these areas.

But at the policy level in particular, and at nearly every other phase of management at times, decisions must be made and the probability estimated for events that are truly unique because of the constant need to change competitive tactics and to innovate. To place an order for his beginning inventory, the fashion buyer must estimate the probability of a given volume of sales for a given dress of the newest fashion. To develop his production schedule, the factory superintendent must estimate the probable reject rate for a new part never before produced. The contractor must estimate the probability of landing a job with a specific bid. The Board of Directors must estimate the probability that the radical new plastic resin will sell profitably and in what quantity before approving the appropriation for the new plant. The bases for all such probability estimates can only be subjective, whether unconscious and intuitive or formalized and the result of some degree of calculation. The formal methods, called Bayesian analysis by some, permit a more thorough and more reasoned analysis of the assumptions and better integration of information sources.

The use of Bayes Theorem on conditional probabilities to modify subjective probability judgments makes possible an effective combination of experience with experimental data. The technique economizes in the use of available data, extracting the maximum amount of information from each bit. By making formal provision for the blending of past experience, seasoned subjective judgment, and empirical data, this approach to decision brings the executive, the practical experimenter, and the statistician into a closer working relationship than is likely with other methods.

Basic Bayesian Analytical Concepts

The term Bayesian analysis is frequently used to refer to the various procedures growing out of the use in decision making of subjective probabilities and Bayes Theorem. The use of this tool for dealing with economic decisions in the face of true uncertainty involves several basic component concepts. There is an underlying (random) process whose outcome is conceived of as a random variable--the percent defective in production runs of the new process or the actual number of dresses which will be sold if they are stocked. That is, although only one outcome will occur in actuality, this single outcome is conceived of as variable, whereas in objective probability, the single outcome is considered as fixed but unknown, only the frequency of occurrence thought of as variable. Second, for each value of the variable, there is a known set of decisions related to it. For example, if we knew we would sell exactly 100 dresses or other items, we would know exactly how many to order or to schedule for a production run. Third, a loss function can be constructed which gives the loss or gain which would follow from any difference between the quantity decided upon and the true values which result. Thus, if we estimate and prepare for a sale of 100 items, but experience a sale either greater or less than 100, we may incur out-of-pocket losses due to overstock or opportunity losses due to an inability to fill orders. Fourth, our knowledge about the random variable can be summarized in a probability distribution, a frequency distribution of possible values of the random variable. Such a probability distribution is constructed on the basis of some kind of previous experience or personal judgment deemed to be relevant to the specific problem at hand. This prior distribution is modified after the collection of experimental evidence and a new posterior probability distribution calculated, conditional upon the experimental data at hand. The result of weighting the losses by the probability of their occurrence (expected loss or expected profit) are summarized in pay off tables (or pay off matrices) which reveal the estimated profit positions of each proposed action or decision.

Human judgment being fallible, it is usually wise to test the importance of possible error. A sensitivity analysis can be conducted using several alternative possible prior probability distributions, or other parameters involved in the calculations, and observing the effect on the payoff matrices and profit positions. Such a step is particularly valuable whenever the amount of experimental data possible is severely limited and the prior probability estimates particularly important.

Expected value and profit position are both the result of the same kind of computation: the estimate of the payoff of a successful decision is multiplied by an estimate of the probability that such will be the outcome. Whenever the decision is one of a substantially repetitive long-run series under essentially the same type of circumstances, then the result is always called an expected value. Since the probability estimate is an objective one, such an expected value is an estimate of one kind of real outcome: it is the average payoff per decision of a long series of decisions.

Expected value is sometimes also used to denote what many refer to as a profit position--a very unreal but exceedingly useful management tool. Profit position is preferred by many to denote the estimate which results when the predicted event is unique and the probability estimate therefore subjective. Such an estimate is never a prediction of any recognizable real outcome. Since the situation is a one-time one, the only outcome is either failure or some anticipated degree of success. The payoff in the event of success will always be the total connected with that degree of success, not some fraction of it. The profit position (or the expected value of a unique event) is thus not a prediction but a means of discounting various alternative courses of action by the degree of the relative uncertainty of each.

A decision tree can be used to visualize the process of estimating profit positions if the number of possible choices and outcomes is small. Consider, for example, the buying decision being faced by (fictional) George Smilson, fur department buyer for a nationally famous Texas store.

Estimating the Payoff in a Fur-Buying Situation

George's customers include the wives of some very wealthy Texas cattle and oil men, and they always expect him to stock the latest in the most expensive and exotic furs, although, of course, the sales of the top-priced items are not in any real volume. One fur he knows he will have to stock for the coming winter season is a brand new mutation mink shade--pastel blue-green--made up into stoles he buys for $5500 and sells for $10,000 each. From past experience, George knows he must stock it and will be certain to sell at least one, perhaps as many as three, but no more. Thus his estimate of sales is a random variable between 1 and 3. Whether he sells 1, 2, or 3 depends partly on the prices of cattle and of oil and on the conditions of the high plains pastures, and also, when the season opens, on what the women choose as their current hair color and whether they feel that the new mutation will complement their choice. He also knows that he will sell to each customer only if he has the stole in stock. The customer must try it on and get a chance to fall in love with it enough to loosen her husband's bankroll. Thus an out-of-stock condition means a missed sale and with the missed sale a missed profit (opportunity loss) of $4500, the amount he realizes on each sale. All sales will be made early in the season. If he buys more than he is able to sell, however, he will have to unload any overstock to a jobber at a mere $1,000 at the season's end--a loss of $4500 on each one unsold. We can show the situation facing George in the graphic form of the act-event decision tree of Figure 4-1 (on the next page).

Any decision situation can be put in the form of a decision tree such as this, but the method is obviously too cumbersome if many alternatives are involved. A much more convenient way to represent the same situation is by means of a payoff table. Table 4-1 outlines both the calculations and the final summary payoff matrix in the case of George Smilson.

On the face of this, it might seem that if George were a cautious man, he would buy 2 stoles, because in this way he would, at worst, break even and might make as much as $9000. But the three possible outcomes of selling 1, 2, or 3 stoles may not be equally likely. For this reason, a question mark has been placed in the profit position blank for each act shown in the decision tree. Since this is a first time for this item, and there never really is a comparable second time for a fashion item, George has no identical experience that will tell him how many pastel blue-green mink stoles he may sell. But he has gone

FIGURE 4-1. Decision Paths Faced By George Smilson In The Purchase Of Mutation Mink Stoles

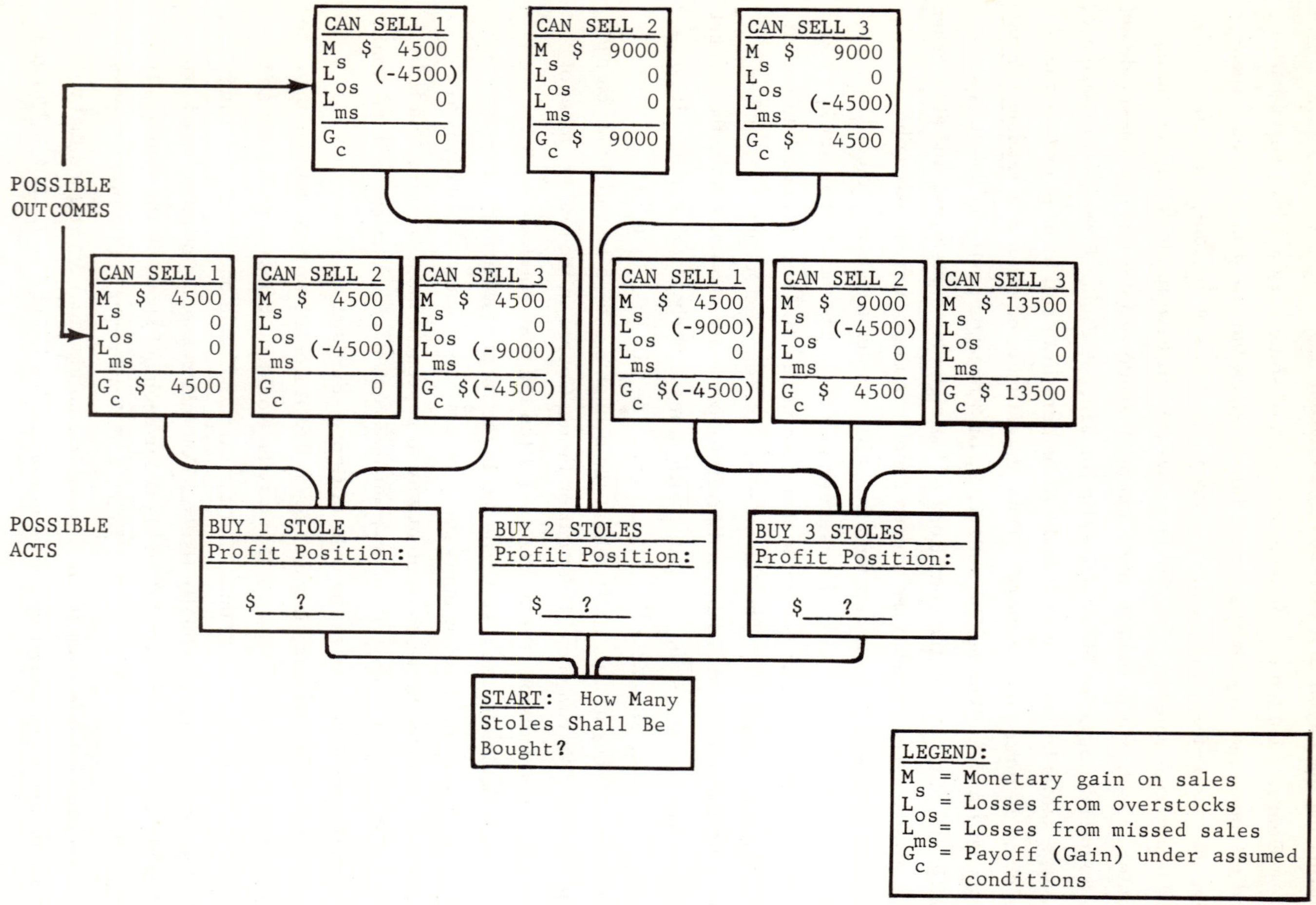

over his experience with other exotic purchases over the last 10 years and has come up with 40 situations where he feels the customer appeal was comparable. Only 10 of these were mink stoles--a different style and mutation in each case. The rest were fur capes and ultra-high-priced accessories of different kinds. In every case he sold at least 1, in no case more than 3. His tabulations are shown in Table 4-2.

TABLE 4-1. Payoff Calculations And Summary Matrix In The Mutation Mink Buying Problem

A. Payoff Calculations

Decision	Demand Condition, Could Sell:	Monetary Gain On Sales M_s	Possible Overstock Losses L_{os}	Missed Sale Opportunity Losses L_{ms}	Net Payoff Under Assumed Contingencies $G_c = M_s - L_{os} - L_{ms}$
Buy 1 stole	1 stole	$ 4500	$ 0	$	$ 4500
	2 stoles	4500	0	(-4500)	0
	3 stoles	4500	0	(-9000)	(-4500)
Buy 2 stoles	1 stole	4500	(-4500)	0	0
	2 stoles	9000	0	0	9000
	3 stoles	9000	0	(-4500)	4500
Buy 3 stoles	1 stole	4500	(-9000)	0	(-4500)
	2 stoles	9000	(-4500)	0	4500
	3 stoles	13500	0	0	13500

B. Summary Payoff Matrix

Decision	Net Payoff In The Situation In Which The Demand Is For:		
	1 Stole	2 Stoles	3 Stoles
Buy 1 stole	$ 4500	$ 0	$ (-4500)
Buy 2 stoles	0	9000	4500
Buy 3 stoles	(-4500)	4500	13500

Note: Net monetary gain on an individual sale = $4500
Actual Loss on each overstock item at season's end = $4500 (That is, it is the actual cost of $5500 less the realizable salvage of $1000)
Opportunity loss if sale is missed because item is not in stock = $4500 (That is, this is the amount of the profit opportunity which could not be realized.)

TABLE 4-2. Sales Experience With Presumably Analogous Items In The Mink Mutation Situation

Number Of Items Sold		Number Of Situations	Per Cent Of Total Experience	Corresponding Probability
Total		40	100	1.0
Sold	1	4	10	0.1
	2	16	40	0.4
	3	20	50	0.5

Using this experience as his best estimate of the probability distribution of the random variable (the number of stoles he could sell) he can complete his decision tree by computing the profit position (or expected value) for each alternative buying decision. These are calculated by taking each of the payoffs arrived at in the previous computation and multiplying them by the estimated probability of their occurrence. These are then summed to get the average or expected payoff for each of the alternative buying decisions (Figure 4-2).

By exactly the same process, we can apply these same probabilities to the payoff matrix of Table 4-1, but the calculations can be visualized more easily. For example, if George decided to buy only 1 stole and his subsequent sales demand was also for only 1 stole, then his gain would be $4500. But the past experience summarized in Table 4-2 indicates that he can expect a demand for only 1 just once in 10 times. In 4 out of 10 times, he can expect 2 customers to be ready to buy. Under these conditions, he will be out of stock when the second customer comes in and suffer an opportunity loss of $4500, offsetting a gain of the same amount on the first sale and thus breaking even on the decision to buy only 1 stole. Furthermore, half the time (probability 0.5) he estimates that he would be able to sell 3 stoles if he had them in stock, and the buy-only-1 decision would cost him an additional opportunity loss of $4500, for a net loss value for the decision of the same amount. To estimate the most likely effect of the decision to "buy 1" he must weight each of these possible outcomes by the estimated chance it will happen (payoff x probability). The algebraic sum of these three computations represents what the longrun effect of a series of similar conservative decisions would be. Table 4-3 summarizes the profit positions (expected profits) for each of the three possible decisions.

FIGURE 4-2. Profit Positions Of The Decision Paths In The Mutation Mink Stole Case

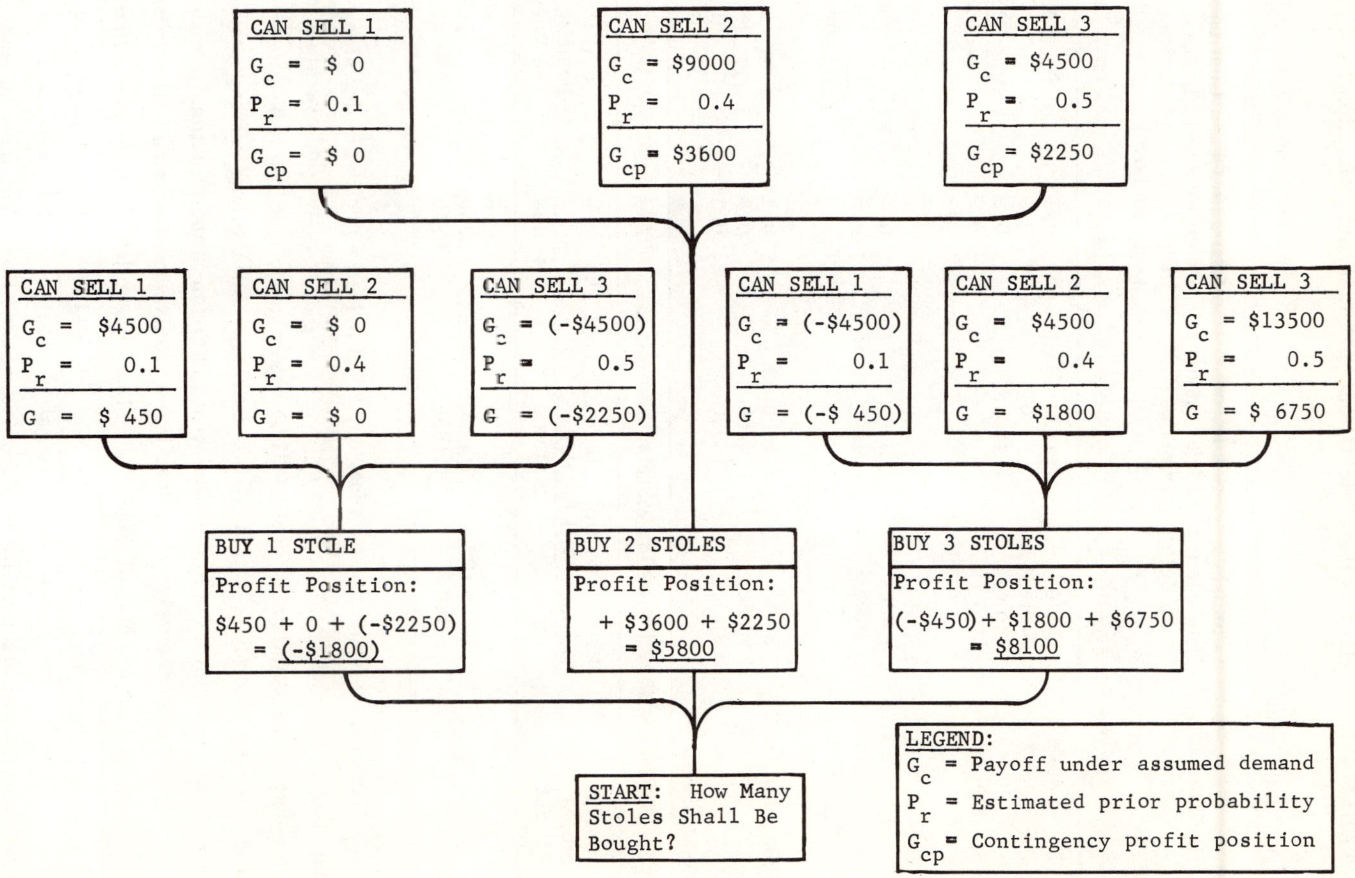

TABLE 4-3. Profit Position Calculations And Summary, Mutation Mink Purchase Decision

A. Calculations:

Decision	Demand Contingency, Could Sell:	Net Payoff Under Assumed Demand G_c	Estimate Of Prior Probability Of Demand Level P_r	Contingent Profit Position $G_{cp} = G_c \times P_r$
Buy 1 stole	1 stole	$4500	0.1	$ 450
	2 stoles	0	0.4	0
	3 stoles	(-4500)	0.5	(-2250)
Total				(-1800)
Buy 2 stoles	1 stole	0	0.1	0
	2 stoles	9000	0.4	3600
	3 stoles	4500	0.5	2250
Total				5850
Buy 3 stoles	1 stole	(-4500)	0.1	(- 450)
	2 stoles	4500	0.4	1800
	3 stoles	13500	0.5	6750
Total				8100

B. Summary Profit Position Matrix:

Number Of Stoles Bought	Profit Position Assuming That The Demand Will Be For: 1 stole	2 stoles	3 stoles	Total Profit Position For The Decision
1	$ 450	$ 0	(-$2250)	(-$1800)
2	0	3600	2250	5850
3	(-450)	1800	6750	8100

From this it would appear that "buy 2" is indeed a profitable decision, but that "buy 3" is much better. If his estimates of probabilities and overstock costs are correct, his department profit will be better in the long run if he consistently bases his decisions of this type of analysis. But the long run expectation does not protect him from making the wrong decision in the situation immediately before him. Unfortunately, if he does buy 3 stoles, he could still sell only one and sustain a real net loss of $4500. For this reason he certainly would like to have some reading on customer preference for this particular mutation shade so as to narrow the risk in both directions--from possible overstocks and from opportunity losses incurred by an out-of-stock condition. For such an exotic item with such limited demand, it is doubtful if any research could help him much. But there are many instances where data can be gathered about the situation at hand and incorporated into the analysis. The procedure for making use of such supporting data employs Bayes Theorem.

Using a Small Sample To Improve an Estimate of Probability

The economy in the collection of new information which Bayes Theorem makes possible can be illustrated by a typical production scheduling problem facing the production manager of Eastern Corporation who is set to start up a new production line for transistors. The layout includes provision for automatic testing of all completed product coming off the line, but if the percentage of defectives is high, other checks will be instituted earlier in the process to lower the percentage of poor product and to assist in pinpointing the causes. Such interim testing entails a substantial expense, however, and is resorted to only in the case of proven necessity. On the other hand, omitting it also involves risking delay in discovery of a higher than acceptable defect rate and thus in tracing its causes. The resulting scrap loss could be a substantial cost also. Since this is a new and untried production line, he has to base his decision on experience with prior production of other similar transistor types. Checking the extensive records of the Quality Control Department, he secures the following information thought to be applicable:

Process Defective Level		Portion Of
Group	Proportion defective	Past Production
A_1	.005	.30
A_2	.01	.30
A_3	.02	.20
A_4	.03	.13
A_5	.04	.06
A_6	.05	.01

This information is reasonably reassuring; since it indicates that if it is a good basis for estimate, he has an 80% chance that the rate of defectives will be less than 3% (.03), the level at which he would institute the additional inspections immediately. Even were the rate as high as .02, he would simply keep a close watch on the line initially in order to detect quickly any tendency toward an increase in the defective rate. However, he would prefer not to risk omission of the additional inspection if the probability of the .03 defect rate should really be estimated to be as high as the indicated 20%, and so he seeks a little information about the probability of the defect rate on this particular new production line. The PM therefore requests that a sample of 20 be taken and the test result reported as soon as it is felt that the line is "running." This done, it was found that none of the 20 samples were defective.

The PM now has two sets of information--a probability distribution of defects in a set of production processes (A_1, A_2, ... A_6) which he believes are similar to the new and untried one, and a single event indicating 0 defects in a run of 20 transistors in the new process, an event we shall designate as B for convenience. He does not know the probability of B (the probability that any run of 20 in the new process will have no defects), but he can estimate a new or posterior probability distribution by the use of Bayes Theorem, a formula which permits the calculation of the conditional probability Pr (A/B), which means the probability of the prior probability, A, given the new event or information B. The Theorem is stated in set notation, in which the expression Pr ($A1 \cap B$) is shorthand to mean "the probability that A and B will both occur," that is, in this case, the probability of obtaining an observation of 0 defective in a lot of 20 whose process level defective is A_1. Bayes Theorem would give us a new posterior probability distribution of six items--Pr (A_1/B), Pr (A_2/ B),... Pr (A_6/ B)--according to the following formula for Pr (A_1/ B):

$$\Pr (A_1/ B) = \frac{\Pr(A_1 \cap B)}{\Pr (A_1 \cap B) + \Pr (A_2 \cap B) + \ldots\ldots \Pr (A_6 \cap B)}$$

By means of 5 other similar calculations--from Pr(A_2/B) through Pr(A_6/B)--the PM will have his new, posterior probability distribution providing an amended estimate of the probable defect level in the new process. To make the estimate, the PM must have someone make four basic calculations for each of the six values Pr (A_i) in his prior probability distribution, illustrated below for the one value, Pr (A_1):

(1) The probability $Pr(B/A_1)$, the probability that if A_1 were the true process experience, he would have obtained 0 defects in a lot of 20. Since the probability of a single defect occurring was actually .005 for process A_1, the probability any given part would be perfect is the complement of this, or .995. From the usual rule for the repetition of any event, the probability of getting 20 perfect transistors in a row in process A_1 would then be $(.995)^{20}$, or approximately .905, calculated to the third significant figure, similarly for the other five values of $Pr(B/A_1)$.

(2) The combined probability $Pr(A_1 \cap B)$, the probability that both the process A_1 is the true experience to be expected and that 0 defects would occur in a lot of 20. This is obtained by multiplying the the prior estimate of probability, $Pr(A_1)$, which is .30, by $Pr(B/A_1)$, which is .905, as shown above. This multiplication, $(.905) \bullet (.3)$ gives us .272.

(3) The sum of the six values of $Pr(A_i)\ Pr(B/A_i)$ as obtained by five additional calculations similar to the two steps above, for each of the values A_2 through A_6, giving us a total estimate of $Pr(B)$, which is .753, as shown in Table 3-3.

(4) The dividend, $\frac{Pr(A_1 \cap B)}{.753}$, which is $\frac{.272}{.753} = .6$, the posterior probability estimate that our defect rate will be that of process A_1, or .005.

Table 4-4 outlines the complete calculation the PM has had someone do for him, giving him a new estimate of his probability distribution in the last column. Inspecting it, the PM finds that his posterior probability estimate of a really bad lot (4 to 5% defective) is now only 4% instead of the 7% estimated before he took his new sample, and his estimate of a defect rate of 3% or more has been reduced from 20% to 13% by use of the new information. He decides that this is an acceptable risk, and to start up the line on the assumption that the defect rate will actually be 2% or less. He orders inspection for the end of the line only, with instruction to watch the results very closely--just in case.

However, the objectivist statistician from the Quality Control Group, who carried out the calculations, protests. "How much information did you expect to get from a sample of merely 20?" The production manager admits that 20 is a pretty small sample, but points out that by using the information from prior processes and the Bayes Theorem, the new information did reduce his estimate

TABLE 4-4. Calculation Of New Estimate Of Probability Of Defectives In New Process To Be Used By Eastern Corporation

Process Defect Level Group	Proportion Defective	Prior Probability Estimate $Pr(A_i)$	Probability of 0 Defects Given This Estimate $Pr(B/A_i)$	Probability That Original Estimate Is Correct & That 0 Defects Would $Pr(A_i \cap B)^* = Pr(A_i) \cdot Pr(B/A_i)$	New Estimate, Given This I Information: Posterior** $Pr(A_i \cap B)/PR(B)$
A_1	.005	.30	$(.995)^{20} \simeq .905$	$(.905)(.3) = .272$	$.272/.753 = .36$
A_2	.01	.30	$(.99)^{20} \simeq .818$	$(.818)(.3) = .245$	$.245/.753 = .33$
A_3	.02	.20	$(.98)^{20} \simeq .668$	$(.668)(.2) = .134$	$.134/.753 = .18$
A_4	.03	.13	$(.97)^{20} \simeq .544$	$(.544)(.13) = .071$	$.071/.753 = .09$
A_5	.04	.06	$(.96)^{20} \simeq .442$	$(.442)(.06) = .027$	$.027/.753 = .035$
A_6	.05	.01	$(.95)^{20} \simeq .358$	$(.358)(.01) = .004$	$.004/.753 = .005$
				$Pr(B) = .753$	Total $= 1.00$

*$Pr(A_i \cap B)$ = the probability of observing 0 defects <u>AND</u> having the observation come from a lot whose process defective level was A_i

$$**Pr(A_1/B) = \frac{Pr(A_1 \cap B)}{Pr(A_1 \cap B) + Pr(A_2 \cap B) \ldots\ldots Pr(A_6 \cap B)} = \frac{Pr(A_1 \cap B)}{Pr(B)} = \text{the}$$

probability that the lot proportion defective is A_1, given that a particular sampling result B of a high defect rate substantially. The statistician, however, does like the use of information from these previous processes. They do not meet his standard of homogeneity, and he feels the estimate of probability rests on the sample of 20 only. On the basis of his reasoning, there is nearly a 1 in 10 chance that the defect rate will be as high as 10%. The PM, however, feels that the experience from these previous processes is valid information, although he conceded that he probably should use a slightly larger sample the next time in order to narrow still his posterior probability distribution. At least, he is going to base his sample size on an initial calculation as to the effect and value of added information.

Just how useful Bayes Theorem can be in estimating the value of added information before getting it can be seen in the case of Jim Walmer, the fashion buyer for Rural Mail Order, who has the problem of estimating the demand for each of 6 dresses he is stocking in his $19.98 line for the coming season.

How Much Is Additional Information Worth?

Jim has the complex problem of estimating in detail the demand for each size and each dress and each line of better dresses sold in volume by Rural Mail Order. The estimate for the proportion of each size to order is not difficult because past experience can be relied on to be reasonably well duplicated, although there has been a trend toward the larger sizes over the last decade. The proportion of orders received for each of the price lines has also proved reasonably stable. But total sales have varied from season to season, and the proportion sold of each dress in any given line has fluctuated widely from one season to the next. He needs to forecast his relative demand for each individual number: for example, dress 3923 in the 6-dress $19.98 line--rather well. Jim's estiminating problem is both simpler and more complex than that of George Smilson and his mutation mink stoles. It is simpler in that he buys--is in fact permitted to buy--only one-fourth of his total season's estimated requirements in advance, and then will make rebuys on the basis of initial sales. He thus has considerable latitude for error in his original estimate of demand--a situation typical of most business decisions. If his estimate is no more than 4 times too large, he can work off the excess initial purchase before the end of the season. Anything beyond that, of course, has to be jobbed off at a loss, usually for less than half his initial purchase cost. He has some latitude on the underestimate side, too, but not nearly as much, because any reorder during his six-month season takes 6 weeks to fill.

He can back order out-of-stock items, but house policy does not permit a back order period of more than 10 days. He can estimate sales of the total line fairly well in advance. In making his estimate of sales of 7500 for the line of 6 $19.98 dresses, he feels quite sure that, depending on general economic conditions, the total will not be less than 6000 or more than 9000.

But Jim's problem is complicated by the fact that the popularity of the 6 dresses in the line is interdependent: a heavy demand for any 1 number is at the expense of the demand for each of the other 5. On occasion, 1 or 2 of the numbers catalogued prove to be more than ordinarily popular. There have been times when a full half of the orders for the line have concentrated on a single number, with the result that 1 or 2 of the other numbers in the line had sold as few as 3 percent of the total. In those circumstances he sustained substantial end-of-season jobbing losses for unsold dresses of about $6.50 each plus excess inventory-carrying costs of $.50, a full loss of $7.00 for each dress in overstock. In the event of understocks, he has a direct out-of-pocket cost of $1.00 for the handling of any cancelled orders, plus the opportunity loss of the $5.00 profit he would have made on each one, for a total missed sale loss of $6.00.

Jim's real decision concerns the distribution of orders among the 6 dresses within the line, since his total order is limited by the 25% rule and his forecast for the line. To summarize his present knowledge:

<u>For the total line:</u>

Projected sales:
Minimum, 6000 — Maximum, 9000
Permissible initial order for the line:
Minimum, 6000/4 = 1500 — Maximum, 9000/4 = 2500

<u>For the single style, #3923:</u>

Permissible initial order if allocated equally among all 6 styles:
Minimum, 1500/6 = 250 — Maximum: 2250/6 = 375

<u>Knowledge of the extremes of demand for a single style:</u>

Minimum, 3% of the sales of the entire line. Would indicate a total demand of only 180 in a 6000-dress season (.03 x 6000 = 180) and an initial order of 180/4 = 45, in the poorest season.

Maximum, 50% of the sales of the line. Would indicate a total demand of .50 x 6600 = 3000, and a minimum initial order of 3000/4 = 750 in the poorest season, or a possible .50 x 9000 x 1/4 = 1125 if the season turns out to be one of the best.

Jim's range of choice between an initial order of 45 for the single style 3923 and 1125 is pretty wide, so he does some more figuring. He considers the range of various order choice and sales combinations for this one number, and gets the results shown in Table 4-5. By defining a period in which 25% of the

TABLE 4-5. Net Actual Profits On Sales Made. For Each Possible Sales Level And Each Initial Order Quantity. In The Period Before The Receipt Of The First Possible Reorder.

Number of Dresses Ordered	Profits On Sales If The Initial Orders Received Total: 50	100	200	400	600	800	1100
50	$250	$250	$250	$250	$250	$250	$250
100	250	500	500	500	500	500	500
200	250	500	1000	1000	1000	1000	1000
400	250	500	1000	2000	2000	2000	2000
600	250	500	1000	2000	3000	3000	3000
800	250	500	1000	2000	3000	4000	4000
1100	250	500	1000	2000	3000	4000	5500

TABLE 4-6. Losses Incurred By Unintended Overstocks And Through Stock Shortages As A Result Of Various Initial Order Quantities On Dress 3923

Initial Order Quantity (1/4 Of Season Estimate)	Seasonal Losses On Sales If Customers' Initial Orders Received Total: 50	100	200	400	600	800	1100
50	$0	$300	$900	$2100	$3300	$4500	$6300
100	*	0	600	1800	3000	4200	6000
200	*	*	0	1200	2400	3600	5400
400	1400	*	*	0	1200	2400	4200
600	2800	1400	*	*	0	1200	3000
800	4200	2800	*	*	*	0	1800
1100	6300	4900	2100	*	*	*	0

*Initial order will be in excess of enough for the initial period, but will be sold during the season.

TABLE 4-7. Net Contingency Payoff For The Initial Decision For Each Act-event Combination, Purchase Decision On Dress No. 3923

Initial Order Quantity (1/4 Of Estimated Sales)	50	100	200	400	600	800	1100
50	$250	-$50	-$650	-$1850	-$3050	-$4250	-$6050
100	250	500	-100	-1300	-2500	-3700	-5500
200	250	500	1000	-200	-1400	-2600	-4400
400	-1150	500	1000	2000	800	-400	-2200
600	-2550	-900	1000	2000	3000	1800	0
800	-3950	-2300	1000	2000	4000	4000	2200
1100	-6050	-4400	-1100	2000	3000	4000	5500

customer orders are received and matching it with his initial order period, Jim can calculate losses from overstocks or understocks which would be incurred for various initial order/sales combinations, as in Table 4-6. When the initial profits indicated in Table 4-5 are combined with the losses indicated by Table 4-6, Jim arrives at the contingent payoff matrix of Table 4-7 for the various combinations of initial sales and orders. In order to estimate the profit position for each decision quantity alternative, Jim needs a probability distribution of the various estimates of initial customer demand. He reviews his experience over the past several years and decides that, since style changes are no more radical than for any of the past 5 years, he can use the distribution of relative demand in the line for 60 similar types of dresses which have been sold over this period, as shown in Table 4-8.

Jim can now estimate his profit position for each of the decision quantity alternatives by weighting each contingency payoff as shown in Table 4-7 by the probability of its occurrence, as estimated in Table 4-8, multiplying each column in Table 4-7 by the appropriate value of P_i as estimated in Table 4-8. This yields an estimate of the average profit position for each alternative order decision as shown in Table 4-9.

Using the information available to him, Table 4-9 would indicate that Jim should purchase between 600 and 800 dresses for his initial order of 3923, provided the sales behave as have the average of similar styles in the past 5 years. But it gives him no assurance that 3923, or any of the other 5 numbers in the line, will have average sales experience. Furthermore, with no more information than is available to him, he must estimate the sales of all the numbers as equal. An initial purchase of 600 to 800 each would greatly exceed his maximum allowable initial order quantity of each. (600 x 6 = 3600, 800 x 6 = 4800). The potential demand for one of the 6 styles may well justify an order of this magnitude, but if so, he does not know which of the 6, and the potential for the full line definitely would not justify 6 such orders. Reviewing the frequency distribution, Jim can note that 30% of the styles had initial sales of 600 or more, but that 20% had sales of 100 or less, and the popularity of styles within the line, as noted in the beginning, is interdependent. What Jim needs is some indication of the probable popularity of each style within his current line, and past experience cannot give this to him. As did the Production Manager of Eastern, he feels he needs added information which applies to his current situation, but he cannot get it as simply as did the PM. Whatever he collects will cost substantially, and he needs to weigh carefully the kinds of information he will seek and its value to him.

TABLE 4-8. Estimated Probability Distribution Of Demand Per Number In The 6-Dress $19.98 Line, Based On Experience In The Last 5 Years

Total Seasonal Sales (Number of Dresses)	Average Sales Model	Corresponding Initial Period Order (Approx. 25% of Average)	Number Of Models	Per Cent Of Models	P_i (Probability)
180- 199	190	50	3	5	.05
200- 599	400	100	9	15	.15
600- 999	800	200	15	25	.25
1000-2199	1600	400	15	25	.25
2200-2500	2400	600	10	17	.17
2600-3799	3200	800	7	12	.12
3800-3799	4500	1100	1	2	.02

TABLE 4-9. Profit Position Values For Each Act-Event Combination In The Purchase Decision On Dress 3923

Jim's Initial Order Quantity	Profit Positions Of The Sales Returns If Customers' Initial Period Orders Are For:							Net Profit Position For All Sales Possibilities
	50	100	200	400	600	800	1100	
P_i =	.015	.15	.25	.25	.17	.12	.02	
50	$ 12.5	$ -7.5	$-162.5	$-462.5	$-518.5	$-510.5	$-121.0	$-1769.5
100	12.5	75.0	-25.0	-325.0	-425.0	-444.0	-110.0	-1241.5
200	12.5	75.0	250.0	-50.0	-238.0	-312.0	-88.0	-350.5
400	-57.5	75.0	250.0	500.0	136.0	-48.0	-44.0	811.5
600	-127.5	-135.0	250.0	500.0	510.0	216.0	.0	1213.5
800	-197.5	-345.0	250.0	500.0	510.0	480.0	44.0	1241.5
1100	-302.5	-660.0	-275.0	500.0	510.0	480.0	110.0	362.5

Jim reasons that the variations in his past sales and thus in his present estimates stemmed from two major sources: the effects of general economic affairs, and the relative attractiveness of each style as perceived by his regular customers. His estimating and planning ability would benefit by improved estimates concerning either. Which information would be the more valuable? While the influences of economic conditions and tastes are thoroughly mixed together and confounded, Jim reasons that the economic factors affect primarily the overall level of dress sales and that relative attractiveness is responsible for most of the variation in sales of individual numbers in each line, as measured in Table 4-8. The fluctuation in overall sales is between 6000 and 9000, a factor of about 1-1/2. By contrast, relative sales of individual numbers in the line have fluctuated between 3% and 50%, for a factor of nearly 17. It seems to him that style appeal is by far a more critical factor in his uncertainty than are economic conditions, and that it would be more valuable to try for information on relative appeal. So he approached the marketing research director to discuss with him the possibility of getting information about the relative demand within his current line of 6 dresses. The research director might well tell him something like the following:

"We can devise a small sample mailing to our customers that will cost you about $600 for this one line alone, if you can furnish us with advance copies of your catalog pages, just as they will appear in the catalog. From somewhat analogous tests we and others have run, we feel sure that sampling variation in cultural matters of taste such as fashion is minimal, so we will not need a very big sample so long as we know that our respondents are our own customers, drawn from our own files. A questionnaire return of 200 should be enough.

"But we can expect some considerable bias in the answers, whatever technique we use to obtain them. The expressed preferences will have some tendency to favor somewhat conservative styles. That is, acceptable models which lag slightly behind the coming style trend will be a little more popular, relatively, than they will be during the actual buying season. Likewise, styles which are in the vanguard of the coming trend will prove slightly less popular in the survey than they will be a few weeks later at the time of buying. The differences will not be great, but you will have to exercise some judgment in using the answers. On the other hand, we have always found in any study of this sort that an item earning a really low preference rating (which gets, for example only 6% of the choices in a line of 6 dresses) will be a dog and sales will not exceed the sample rating.

"Your problem will be in judging the accuracy of the high preference ratings. If dress 3923, for instance, should obtain a relative preference rating of 30%, and 3923 proves to be conservative in relation to the developing style trend, it will sell well, but may not get more than 20% of the volume of the entire line. If it proves to be right in the groove of the developing trend, however, it may actually garner 40% of the demand for your $19.98 line. There may also be some appreciable variation between ratings and sales for those with moderately good ratings--say those in the range between 10% and 20% of a 6-dress line--but the variation will not exceed the adjustments you automatically make when placing your reorders, within permissible back ordering policy."

Should Jim order the survey, at a cost of $600 for this one line alone? Let us look at what the new information could do to the two sides of the payoff table, and the net result, assuming Jim decides to order purely on the basis of the survey results without adjustment on the basis of his own expert knowledge of style trends, using his original estimate of total sales of 7500 for the line, and assuming the total could vary between 6000 and 9000.

First, sales in the two low brackets in our table can be predicted as certainties, if we interpret the research director correctly. A preference rating of 6% of the line translates into a seasonal sales estimate of 450, and an initial order period coverage of just over 100 dresses. Allowing for the economic forecast variation, this works out to a range of 90 to 135 dresses for the initial period, or quantities well within the buyer's ability to adjust. There should be no lost sales costs, since the research director has indicated that sales would not exceed the forecast percentage, and the 25% rule would prevent any overordering.

Similarly, preferences in the middle range would provide perfect information within the procedures open to the buyer--preferences up to 20%, or a total season demand of 1500, for example, on all of the brackets for initial orders up to 400. However, for this group, a surge of better-than-average total demand due to better-than-expected consumer demand could result in some underages at the level of initial orders of 400 or more, and thus some opportunity losses in the 400, 600, and 800 decision columns.

Initial orders of 600 and 800, and of course, of 1100, also presume a very high relative demand, under the 25 percent rule. In each case, however, any overestimate could be absorbed in diminished reorder quantities, since the error has been indicated by the research director as no more than a 50 percent overestimate. So the only possible losses for this group would be missed sales due to underestimate of both relative demand and economic influences together.

We can see in Table 4-10 that the loss function would be narrowed by this new information to the demand columns between 400 and 800 in the initial order period, and to a narrow diagonal band within this table. The loss table would include only missed-sale opportunities:

TABLE 4-10. Losses Possible Through Missed Sales As A Result Of Inaccurate Economic Forecasts And Biased Preference Ratings

Initial Order Quantity	Missed-Sales Losses If Initial Orders Are:			
	400	600	800	1100
400	0	$1200	*	*
600	0	0	$1200	$3000
800	*	0	0	$1800
1100	*	*	0	0

* Does not apply, since this combination is prevented by use of survey information.

The net payoff table now becomes:

TABLE 4-11. Net Contingent Payoff For The Initial Purchase Decision For Each Purchase-Actual-Sales Combination, If Survey Is Followed

Initial Order Quantity	Net Initial Period Payoff On Sales If Orders Received Total						
	50	100	200	400	600	800	1100
50	$250	*	*	*	*	*	*
100	250	$500	*	*	*	*	*
200	*	*	$1000	*	*	*	*
400	*	*	*	$2000	$800	*	*
600	*	*	*	2000	3000	$1800	*
800	*	*	*	*	3000	4000	$2200
1100	*	*	*	*	*	4000	5500

* Not a possible act-event combination.

The research director gave Jim no probabilities for the possible variations, although he might be interpreted to have meant that the possible losses are less than .5 probable. But Jim can evaluate the value of the survey information by assuming minimum accuracy, comparing the expected values of Table 4-12 with the minimum profit made when using the survey, as shown in Table 4-11 above, he calculates:

TABLE 4-12. Pessimistic Evaluation Of Survey Worth, Results For A Single Dress In The Line

Initial Order Quantity	Expected Value Without Survey	Minimum Profit Using Survey	Survey Contribution To Expected Profit
50	-$1769.5	$250	$2019.5
100	-1241.5	250	1491.5
200	-350.5	1000	1350.5
400	811.5	800	11.5
600	1213.5	1800	586.5
800	1241.5	2200	959.5
1100	362.5	4000	3637.5
			TOTAL $10,066.5

Since the $10,000 indicated savings applies to only one dress in the line of 6, and there will be comparable savings from use of the new information in ordering the other dresses in the line, Jim would have difficulty, in this instance, in finding a better investment for his funds.

Jim is fortunate, of course, in being able to get useful information at such a low cost, and in having knowledge of the kind of information which would be most helpful. Often, however, we do not know exactly which information needs are most crucial, nor can we always fill them when we know. Sensitivity analysis is a simple method for pinpointing our needs, and determining how critical the assumptions we are making about some of the parameters in our decision.

Sensivitity Analysis: Pinpointing The Crucial Decision Factors

Not every decision situation permits the collection of added information relevant to the choices to be made. Whether or not such information can be obtained we can learn, through sensitivity analysis, which of our assumptions and which information needs are most critical to our proper choice. We must still start out by carefully translating the inescapable judgments we make into the quantitative statement of a probability distribution. But once we have thus expressed our prior information in quantitative form, we may vary the values assigned to the prior distribution and observe the effect on our average profit position and optimal decision. By this means we obtain a measure of how much the best decision depends on the assumptions we are making about the values in this prior distribution.

Suppose we, as part of the Frantic Machine Works management team faced with a strike, have to decide whether to settle for the 25-cent-per-hour package the union is asking for, or let the men strike in the belief that we can thus get a better settlement. We have no way of taking a strike settlement "sample" of any sort, but we think we know everything any opinion poll could tell us about the temper of the men and about the politics inside the union. We believe we are as well in touch with worker sentiment as anyone ever is, and as a result of years of dealing with this union and its leadership we think we have a pretty good idea of the probabilities in the situation. We also have reason to feel that the estimated added cost of the 25¢ package, $1 million per year, will put us in an awkward competitive position.

We are convinced that the workers could be induced to settle for a 15¢ package after a relatively short strike, probably 4 to 5 weeks, possibly as short as 1 week, maybe as long as 8 weeks. We also believe that we could get a settlement for a 12-1/2¢ package if we let the strike go twice as long--our best estimate is 9 to 10 weeks. Because of our precarious market position, we feel we ought to rule out the 25¢ package with its $1 million cost and seriously consider taking a strike to get the 15¢ package (estimated cost $600 thousand, estimated savings in comparision with the 25¢ settlement, $400 thousand) or the 12-1/2¢ package (estimated cost $500 thousand, estimated savings $500 thousand). The strike itself, of course, will involve substantial costs offsetting some of the savings: $50 thousand per week in plant maintenance costs and lost markets. Also, we cannot be certain of the exact length of the strike in either case. Table 4-13 lists our best estimates of the probability distributions of each of the two packages, in the columns labelled $\underline{W}_{15}$ and $\underline{W}_{12.5}$, respectively.

These calculations--cost times the probability of incurring them--gives us an expected or average cost of $245 thousand for the 15¢ package and $475 thousand for the 12-1/2¢ package. When these are offset against the estimated savings, we obtain an expected profit position of $400 thousand <u>less</u> $245 thousand, or $155 thousand for the 15¢ package, and $500 thousand <u>less</u> $475 thousand, or $25 thousand for the 12-1/2¢ package. If we have sized up the temper of the men correctly, only the 15¢ package is worth trying for. We also note that a strike of 8 weeks duration for the 15¢ package would leave us no better off than an immediate settlement for 25¢ (cost of 8 weeks, $400 thousand, savings on 15¢ package, $400 thousand). Clearly, we should check carefully our assumptions about the temper of the men.

TABLE 4-13. Original Estimates Of The Expected Costs Of Taking A Strike For A 15¢ Package, And Of Taking One For A 12-1/2¢ Package

If Settled At End Of Week	Total Cost Of Settlement ($000)	Probability For 15¢: $\underline{W}_{15}$	$\underline{K} \times \underline{W}_{15}$ ($000)	Probability Of Settlement For 12.5¢: $\underline{W}_{12.5}$	$\underline{K} \times \underline{W}_{12.5}$ ($000)
1	50	.05	2.5	--	--
2	100	.10	19	--	--
3	150	.15	22.5	--	--
4	200	.20	40	--	--
5	250	.20	50	--	--
6	300	.15	45	.05	15
7	350	.10	35	.10	35
8	400	.05	20	.15	60
9	450	--	--	.20	90
10	500	--	--	.20	100
11	550	--	--	.15	82.5
12	600	--	--	.10	60
13	650	--	--	.05	32.5
Total expected cost			245		475

But first, what is the significance of this profit position value of $155 thousand? It is the long run average of a series of similar decisions, our best estimate of what might happen averaged over all similar likely events. Only by rare coincidence will this be the actual net effect of this particular strike, even if our cost and loss estimates are accurate, which is not likely. In addition, there is no long run of strikes--every one is different. Nor have we in any sense a prediction of the duration of the strike. We have only a means of ferreting out and analyzing the quantitative implications of all we think we foresee about the possibilities in the situation in order to be able to weigh the policy alternatives--to settle immediately, or to take a strike to force one of two alternate packages we think we might get, assuming we have judged the temper of the men correctly.

How sensitive is our calculation to this particular probability distribution as to the length of the strike? We can find out by using a series of other, less favorable probabilities as to the duration of the strike. (We might also do the same thing with our assumptions about strike costs.) Table 3-14 makes the calculation for one such set: the estimate that the strike will last at least 5 weeks before we can settle for 15¢, and would end not later than the 12th week. This calculation yields a profit position of minus $25 thousand ($400 thousand less $425 thousand), worse than if we settled immediately for the 25¢ package. Thus our position and our optimal decision are very sensitive to our assumptions about the length of the strike. We must be very confident of our probability distribution on the duration of this strike, and in particular of the assumption it will not last longer than 8 weeks.

TABLE 4-14. Expected Cost Of A Strike Lasting From 5 to 12 Weeks

If Settled At End Of Week Number	Total Cost K ($000)	Probability Of Settlement W	K x W ($000)
5	250	.05	12.5
6	300	.10	30
7	350	.15	52.5
8	400	.20	80
9	450	.20	90
10	500	.15	75
11	550	.10	55
12	600	.05	30
	Total expected cost		425

The Uses and Limitations of Subjective Probability

It should be clear from all of the above that the principal use and purpose of subjective probability analysis is in addition to prediction, which concerns objective probability. The individual event on which one focuses never, in actuality, has a fractional probability: it either is going to take place, with a probability of 1, or it will not, for a probability of 0. The additional uncertainty which subjective probability estimates, the imprecision it attempts to evaluate, is our foreknowledge of the given event, our degree of belief in its outcome. However imprecise that foreknowledge, we must nevertheless make a relatively precise commitment of resources to whatever action we decide upon, and we need some rational method of evaluating the worth of that commitment. Neo-Bayesian analysis forces us to analyze the quantitative significance of every kind of knowledge we bring to bear on the decision. It seeks to force all of this knowledge, plus all of our assumptions, out into the open and to make us put a hard quantitative tag on each bit rather than falling back on vague and sometimes unconscious formulations. The quantitative results are a means of comparison, not a set of predictions, and are, in fact, not likely to coincide with reality. The value of the process is in proportion to the care and thought which goes into the effort to arrive at the quantitative statement and the subsequent analysis. For once we have taken the initial quantifying step, we can and must proceed to apply careful logical analysis of these probabilities to the alternatives we face and find their implications in the light of the judgments we have made. In the process of the analysis, we can learn how important to our choice are each of the assumptions made and each of the bits of information fed into the calculations, pinpointing those assumptions and types of knowledge most crucial to correct decision.

No analysis can be any better than the information on which it is based. Faulty judgments about the relevance of information or incorrect assumptions about the relationships involved can only lead to inaccurate conclusions. But if we do a careful job, we have available a number of formal analytical tools to carry out the rest of the job.

The rather simplified examples we have given so far depict relatively common types of business situations which are often decided reasonably well without recourse to computations such as those indicated (although the latter might well lead to more efficient decisions at times). Even for such situations, formal use of the types of calculations illustrated can probably give substance to experience by creating a record of the judgments made, and their subsequent accuracy. However, many of the uncertainties faced in the complicated and dynamic modern business world contain more dimensions than do these simple illustrations, and the executive who can make really rational choices in such cases without use of subjective probability analysis is exceptional. The next chapter outlines four Bayesian decision models capable of handling complex situations.

SUMMARY

1. Neo-Bayesian statistics is designed to make use of subjective, or personal, probabilities: the conviction of the likelihood of unique events in the kind of real world situations in which all observable influences cannot be eliminated. Any such personal probability is a statement of opinion as to the likelihood of an individual event, subject to change with the addition of new information. It is an informed judgment, based on analogous experience, of the type every decision maker has to rely on in cases of true uncertainty.

2. The five central concepts of the Bayesian approach are the payoff table, the probability distribution of a random variable, profit position, opportunity loss, and conditional probability.

   a. The payoff table lists the estimated values for each possible act-event combination.

b. A random variable is any event which may be the outcome of a given action, subject to some estimated probability distribution of its value.

c. The profit position of any one act-event combination is estimated by multiplying the payoff profit from that combination by its estimated probability.

d. Opportunity losses are those profits that are missed as a result of that particular act-event combination.

e. The conditional probability of a compound event refers to the probability of a specific event, given the occurrence of some other event about which we are able to obtain sample information.

3. The Bayesian approach aims at sharpening our basis for judgment about the likelihood of different outcomes foreseen as possible, and thus assumes that the events flowing from any action can be viewed as variable--that is, can be viewed as uncertain.

4. For the Bayesian, a sample is not simply a measure of some characteristic of the universe, but is additional information against which to evaluate the prior probability distribution of this characteristic which had been arrived at on some judgment basis.

5. The calculations help us to appraise the profit position value of each possible alternative decision and thus furnish a solid basis for judging the value to us of added information that would narrow the range of the prior probability distribution.

6. Even when the situation is such as to preclude collection of new information, sensitivity analysis helps us make full use of subjective judgments about our expectations and facilitates the pinpointing of those factors most crucial to an accurate estimate of the outcome and thus in need of the most careful consideration.

GLOSSARY OF BAYESIAN STATISTICAL TERMS

BAYES: refers to the Rev. Thomas Bayes, an 18th century clergyman who formulated Bayes' Theorem and Bayes' Postulate

BAYES POSTULATE: a personal prior probability estimate should be made in any uncertainty situation before seeking new information, even in the case of complete ignorance

BAYES' THEOREM: an equation defining conditional probability:

$$P(A_1 / B) = \frac{P(A_1 \cap B)}{P(A_1 \cap B) + P(A_2 \cap B) + \ldots + P(A_i \cap B)}$$

This translates into the prose expression: The probability of event labeled A_1, given the knowledge that another event B has occurred, can be found as the ratio of the probability that both B and A_1 can occur jointly to the probability that B will occur jointly with all possible A_i events (that is, all of the possible variations of A in its prior probability distribution). A_1 might be the specific proportion of the season's sales--20%, for example. In this instance, B might then be a preseason survey preference of 20% among those surveyed.

Bayesian Statistics: The approach to evaluation and analysis of decision alternatives consisting of giving numerical value to the decision maker's personal judgment about the likelihood of possible decision outcomes, and of the payoffs associated with the possible outcomes attached to each act-event combination, then modifying this judgment on the basis of additional information collection if this is feasible.

PROBABILITY AND PROBABILITY DISTRIBUTION: in general, a probability is some statement of the relative likelihood of an event, expressed as a positive fractional value, a number between zero and 1 which represents the ratio of chances favoring the occurrence to the total of all chances for and against. A probability distribution is a statement of the probabilities of all of the expected outcomes of a given act. They must, therefore, add to 1, or certainty. Probabilities are classified as objective or subjective.

Objective probabilities are basically a prediction of the relative frequency with which an event will occur in a very long series of trials, as the number of trials approaches infinity. They are estimated on the basis of either a long history of trials under conditions believed to be the same, or *a priori* objective evidence of the structure of possibilities (the number of directions a rat has available for choice to move in a maze, and the like).

Subjective probabilities are expressed in the same kind of numbers, but they refer to the degree of belief the estimator has in the likelihood of a single event. Whoever makes the estimate may be using historical data in part, but even when he does, he will not insist that it be obtained from occurrences taking place under the identical conditions.

Conditional probability: the probability of A occurring, given the knowledge that the event B has already occurred.

Joint probability: the probability of events A and B occurring together.

Personalistic probability: the same as subjective probability.

Posterior probability: the new estimate of probability arrived at on the basis of additional information; often the prior probability conditioned by an observed outcome.

Prior probability: the initial probability estimate made on the basis of whatever belief the decision maker has about the factors favoring a given decision outcome.

PROFIT AND LOSS, PAYOFF

Contingent profit: an estimate of the actual profit to be realized if a given decision outcome materializes.

Contingent opportunity loss: an opportunity loss itself is a profit which might have been made but was not because the decision made resulted in a loss of the opportunity to realize that profit. A contingent opportunity loss is an estimate of the opportunity loss realized because of a specific decision outcome.

Payoff matrix: a table of values of profits and losses under every decision alternative being considered and every outcome foreseen as possible.

Profit position of a decision: the actual profit which would be realized if the outcome is favorable, discounted by the degree of likelihood estimated for that particular outcome.

SENSITIVITY ANALYSIS: an estimate of the importance of precision of the major assumptions about a decision outcome, carried out by recalculating estimated resulting profits and losses with different values attached to all important factors entering into the estimate.

VALUE OF INFORMATION: the total difference in the profit position values of the payoffs as estimated without the value of new information, and as they would be estimated given this additional information.

CHAPTER 5: FOUR BAYESIAN DECISION MODELS

The need to make a decision itself implies uncertainty about the outcome of the choices faced. The use of models built around the Bayesian probability concept can extend the utility of the kind of subjective and analogical information upon which the choice must be based.

Whatever the executive's approach, any rational decision hinges on use of some kind of objective or intuitive system of weighing whatever knowledge he considers pertinent to the problem. Gifted individuals have often achieved remarkable results through the use of intuitive approaches, and presumably not always by luck. But few modern large scale enterprises revolve around a single decision maker. When more than one man is involved in a decision, evaluations of alternatives based on the vague and unspecific, even subconscious, cannot easily be communicated and can lead to friction and fruitless argument. Some systematic method of conscious quantification of whatever the probabilities are felt to be can narrow down the area of disagreement, cool its ardor, and facilitate rational analysis of decision alternatives. Even for the individual, such a quantifying approach helps him sort out and take an objective analytical look at the bases of his decision and, as already indicated, can even help him discover which elements of judgment are really crucial for the choice to be made and thus require closer scrutiny. Where the structure of the decision is complex and multidimensional, such a quantification and subsequent analysis would even seem to be required.

Four types of more complex Bayesian decision models have an especially wide applicability: (1) the sequential decision model, (2) competitive bidding strategy, (3) inventory, and (4) production run and scrap loss.

As with many mathematical decision models, these last two have a wider applicability than the convenient labels given them seem to imply. The inventory model is useful in any situation in which a choice can lead to both underages and overages with cost proportional to size. Some production-scheduling situations have such characteristics as much as do most inventory situations. The production-run and scrap-loss model applies to any problem in which the costs of the overage are proportional to its size, but an underage of any size results in the same lump sum loss. In the case of some inventory decisions, this also applies (as, when a delayed delivery of any size could result in the loss of a major customer, or the shortage of a part cause the loss of a production run).

Sequential Decision Theory: When Decisions Chain Over Time

Not infrequently, some of the alternatives open to us lead not to some definite outcome, but to the probability that other sets of alternatives will have to be considered, some of which may in turn lead to a definite outcome, but others to a need for further decisions before the final end can be seen. *

It should be clear that in such a situation we need some way of calculating the values of the end result of all possible decision paths if our choice is to be a rational one. Let us consider a simplified example of such a situation. Suppose a man owns some land in the midst of a newly discovered oil field. A new value has now been added to this land; there is a possibility oil could be found under it, but not a certainty. He faces two choices immediately, if he desires to capitalize this new opportunity. He can sell a lease and get an immediate, certain profit. But the other alternative is to take some steps toward establishing the probability of oil, and even of drilling for himself. He can test for geological formation and, if the formation is favorable, sell the lease for a higher immediate return, or take a chance and drill. If he drills, he may find oil, for a greater return than the lease would have brought, or he may hit a dry hole and get nothing. In either case, the outcome is final. Let us look at Figure 5-1, a diagram of this sequence.

Which should the landowner do: sell the lease, test for formation, or drill? He has no means to arrive at a rational decision if this is the only information he has.

On the left hand side, he knows the payouts on the alternatives of selling the lease. But on the extreme right-hand path, the outcome of every decision has some degree of uncertainty. The test for formation may reveal a favorable formation, in which case the lease is worth more without going further, and the chance of getting oil if he himself drills is also better. But if the test is unfavorable, he has lost everything, including the added cost of the test. If he does drill himself, he adds another cost for drilling, and he may again lose everything, or get a big payoff. To know whether to test or to drill, he must somehow estimate the probability of finding a favorable formation, and the added probability of striking oil if he does. He thus needs some estimate of associated

---

* The illustration which follows has been borrowed from Chester R. Wasson, The Economics of Managerial Decision, (New York) Appleton-Century-Crofts, pp. 182-188.

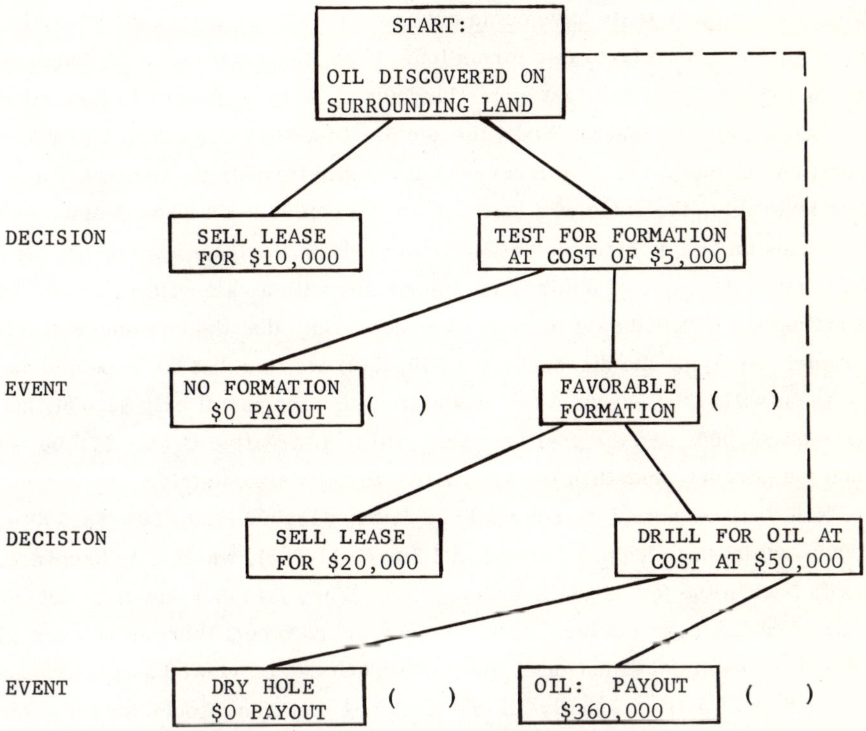

FIGURE 5-1. Possible Sequence of Decision and Event Alternatives in an Oil Lease Situation

probabilities to fill in the blank brackets shown on the diagram; the probabilities that a favorable formation will be found, and the probability that oil be struck if he does find formation.

He is not likely to find such information in any objective table. But he should have some data on which he can base a subjective estimate of both probabilities. If there has been any testing in the areas around him, he may be able to find out how these tests have come out and what percentage of the area, in each case, has shown favorable formation. If so, he can make some judgment as to the probability that a test on his land would reveal a favorable formation.

Let us suppose that he thinks these other tests indicate a 3 to 2 probability (p = .6) that a test would reveal a favorable formation, and that if the test is favorable, the value of a lease rises to $20,000. If he has decided that his finances and other circumstances dictate selling the lease eventually, he can now estimate the value of testing, in comparison with a sale without a test, by discounting the $20,000 sale price by the uncertainty that the outcome would be favorable. Applying the discount (.6 x $20,000), we find that the expected outcome is only $12,000. Thus a test would increase the payoff only $2,000, but would cost $5,000, and the position value of this alternative is only $7,000, or $3,000 (30 percent) less than the alternative to sell immediately.

Note that the actual payout would be either $15,000 ($20,000 - $5,000 = $15,000), which may happen 3 times in 5, or (- $5,000), which may happen 2 times in 5 when the formation is unfavorable. Since this is a one-time decision, as with most business matters, it will be one or the other; there is no averaging over several identical situations. But the $7,000 can be viewed as the average value of the test drill alternative if one imagines a series of decisions of similar nature, with similar information available and decided by similar rules. If a major oil operator were to make 100 such decisions--as he might well do--and we simplify by assuming that both payout values and costs would be the same in every case, he would receive $1,000,000 net if he sold all such leases before test. But if he chose to test first in every case, he would incur a cost of $500,-000 for a gross return of $1,200,000 (60 x $20,000), or a net of only $700,000.

Either before and after such a test, however, the landowner can decide to do the drilling himself, rather than sell the lease to someone else who would drill. Such a decision would commit him to a further cost of $50,000. Is this option worth the cost, even if he can afford the commitment? To find out, he must have some further information, and make some further judgments as to the probability of success. Since the initial decision arose because of oil strikes on surrounding property, it should be easy to find out how many struck paying quantities of oil. Assume that he finds that 1 out of 4 sunk into the favorable formation were paying wells, and that each such well had a capitalized value of $360,000.

If our landowner had made a test, and it was favorable, the value of a decision to drill rather than lease may then be estimated as:

(.25 x $360,000)	- $50,000	= $90,000 - $50,000 =	$40,000
(The payout discounted for its uncertainty)	(Cost of drilling)		(Position value of the alternative to drill, after a favorable test)

Once the test has been made and a favorable formation found, the position value of the alternative to drill is thus worth twice the certain payout of $20,000 from the sale of the lease at that time. Working back to the initial situation, however, we must discount this position value by the risk of an unfavorable test, and the cost of the test itself:

(.6 x $40,000) - $5,000 = $24,000 - $5,000 = $19,000

With all due allowance for risks and costs, this alternative has a higher position value than the certain $10,000 to be received from the immediate sale of the lease before a test.

To get to this point, however, he spent $5,000 simply to get some information, information on whether the formation was favorable for the presence of oil. As we discovered already, this information was not worth $5,000 if the owner had decided to sell the lease anyway. Would it be worth $5,000 if the ultimate choice would be to drill? After all, the chance of finding formation seems to be better than even, anyway 3 to 5. In this case, the position value of the decision to drill immediately is determined by discounting the value of a well by the product of the two probabilities of finding formation, then of finding a well in a favorable formation, and subtracting the cost of drilling:

(.6 x .25) x $360,000 - $50,000 = .15 x $360,000 - $50,000
= $54,000 - $50,000
= $4,000

clearly less than the position value of the path test-then-drill-information. The information gained from the test thus returns a value of $15,000 over its cost.

Note that in making these calculations, the sequence of calculations starts with the end point of a decision path, and works backward.

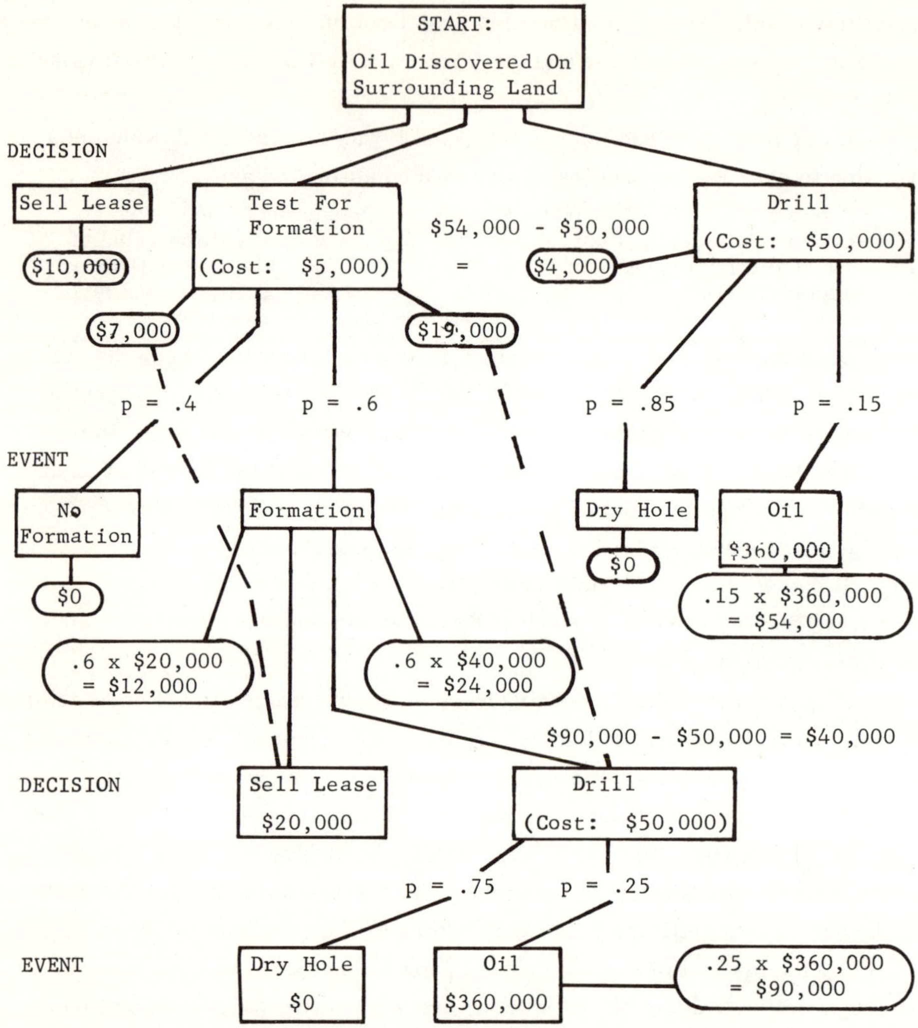

FIGURE 5-2. Completed Decision Tree, Showing all possible Decision Paths with Estimated Decision Costs, Events with Estimated Probabilities, Actual Payouts, and Expected Values of the Payout in Reference to the Preceding Decision (Circled values are expected values for the preceding decision; p is the probability of the event)

Figure 5-2 depicts graphically the three initial decision alternatives and the four decision paths which would result, together with costs and payouts. Comparing the four possible paths, we find that their position values are:

Path	Position Value (in Ms)	Probability of Success
Sell lease right away	$10	1.0
Drill immediately	4	.15
Test—then sell lease	7	.6
Test—then drill if favorable	19	.15

Clearly, the position value of test-then-drill is highest of the alternative decision paths. Is this the decision the landowner should make? Not necessarily. At this point, he must weigh some personal considerations not easily introduced into a mathematical formula (having used the latter to reveal the implications in his available objective information and subjective estimates translatable into reasonably objective form). The implications thus revealed are very helpful. They show that testing is not worth the cost if the end aim is to sell a lease anyway. On the other hand, the test is worth up to $20,000 in the information it gives, if the decision is to drill (the difference between the $24,000 gross position value of the test-then-drill alternative path, and the $4,000 position value of drill-immediately). They show that in choosing between the other two alternatives, we choose between a certain $10,000 for immediate sale of the lease, and $19,000, the expected position value for test-then-drill, not between $10,000 and $360,000 for a successful well. And they bring into focus the reason for the difference between the well value of $360,000 and the $19,000: the high risk of failure, and the financial resources committed.

Our landowner must now assess his own risk affordability, financial resources, and the utility of the relative returns to him. The question of financial resources is easily disposed of; either he has available $55,000 of risk capital needed to make a test and drill, or he does not. In the latter case, he must sell the lease immediately. If he does have it available, then more subjective considerations come into play, best illustrated in terms of three different landowners:

1. Alberts is a small landowner, with just this one lease to sell. The $10,000 from the sale of the lease would put him in a position to improve his own operations materially. The loss of the $55,000 in case of a dry hole would mean disaster. Since there is an 85 percent chance that he will lose all, the assured return of $10,000 has much higher utility for him than the $19,000

position value of an alternative with only a 15 percent chance of success, even though the $19,000 result is arrived at by taking objective account of the risk. His risk affordability is too low.

2. Baker is a wealthy neighbor, to whom the loss of $55,000 would be little more than an annoyance, even if the Internal Revenue Service did not bear most of the brunt of it. On the other hand, while the $360,000 from a successful well would probably have relatively low marginal value for him, the excitement of success, if he does bring it in, would probably have considerable personal utility. He would probably test-then-drill.

3. Charleston can scrape together the $55,000, if necessary, although it would take all of his resources. But he needs more than $10,000 or even $55,000; he needs nearly $90,000 to stave off some family disaster and pay for an operation needed if he is to live more than another year. The $10,000 would have little value to him. The $360,000 would salvage everything and give him a substantial stake in addition. Whatever the risk, he must go for broke. He probably would drill immediately.

Where Do the Figures Come From?

The mechanics of such a calculation are obviously not exotic. Given the numbers, the computation is elementary arithmetic. The essential problem is assigning something like the correct value to the payouts and their probabilities. (The costs can usually be estimated with adequate accuracy.)

The quantities in our equations will nearly always be rough approximations. They may be based on empirical observations of only somewhat similar or analogous situations, adjusted on the basis of the kind of personal feeling or hunch that grows out of the accumulation of minor, usually subconscious, experiences which give us a feel of the market. They may be inferences drawn from various kinds of available objective data--e.g., in our example, the experience of other testing and drilling operations in the neighborhood--such as census tabulations, trade statistics, or personal observations made by those familiar with the kind of situation with which a decision is concerned.

They should never be arbitrary guesses pulled out of the air, and all adjustments made on any objective base data used should have a supportable logic. Wherever we get our figures, we must check their credibility and their relevance to the kind of decision with which we are confronted.

Seldom will our figures have any high degree of precision; at most, they will usually express some sort of rough maximum or minimum. Our landowner thought that the probability of finding a favorable formation was .6 on the basis of the best information he could get. He probably meant "about .6," and did not imply the figure could not have been as low as .54, for example, or that it could not have been as high as .8. If such an initial statement leaves too high a range of uncertainty to permit a choice, the best decision is probably to seek additional information before acting. Otherwise, we are taking a gamble, not a calculated risk. We are permitting the outcome to be decided by the net effect of an infinity of minor factors that mathematicians sum up under the term random. In the long run, the true gambler always loses out to the certainty of the house percentage.

What Do The Results Tell Us?

Putting down some probability figures and performing the arithmetic confers no particular magic. The process can lead to false confidence if the figures alone are thought to be able to carry the weight of the decision. The real value of the process is often in trying to arrive at as accurate a representation as possible of the quantitative significance of all the data we have which we think pertinent to the decision, at a specific measure of the kinds of risks we think are involved, and at the size of the payouts we have a right to expect. When you must put down a specific figure and justify it, you are more likely to hone your thinking to a finer edge than when you are allowed to get away with some confortably vague generalizations.

Calculations carried out on figures furnished in this spirit can then reveal to us the relative monetary value of different decision sequences and thus help us choose a decision path that will optimize the kinds of results consonant with the firm's objectives, capabilities, and situation.

What Shall We Bid? — Competitive Bidding Strategy

The decision theory tool of competitive bidding strategy (CBS) can help us put the value of the alternatives in a bidding situation into clearer focus. Like all statistical decision theory techniques, CBS furnishes a means of extracting from normally available data, the best estimate possible of the expected value of a given estimated profit outcome. It helps sharpen our perceptions of the values of possible alternatives and the likelihood of profitable outcomes, if immediate profit is our objective. CBS does not, of course, tell us what our objective should be, but it can help us evaluate the profit position cost of some other objective, to help us decide whether it is worth the price.

Whenever the purchase or the sale is awarded on the basis of competitive bids, the final decision on the proposed price can be an ulcer-creating compromise. When the bid is on the sale side, the objective is presumably to quote a price just low enough to beat out competitors, yet one which, if successful, will lead to as much profit as possible. When the bid is to buy, the aim is the reverse, of course--one just high enough to land the purchase on terms which allow a profit on eventual realization.* The purpose of competitive bidding strategy is to quantify information normally used in arriving at such bids.

The process of bid preparation is usually built on appraisal of:

1. The number and identity of competitors and some idea of their degree of eagerness to win.

2. Some past history on the bidding performance of each competitor.

3. Some knowledge of the costs of past projects on which competitors' bids are known.

4. The bidder's own cost estimate for the project in the case of sales bids, or the buyer's own estimate of his expected later sales realization in the case of purchase bids.

5. The direct or indirect profit objective sought by the bidder.

CBS is thus a means of getting fuller use of the kind of evaluations commonly made in the usual bidding process. No change is made in the normal bid preparation procedure itself, which might be outlined as follows:

1. Make a careful estimate of the probable cost of doing the job.

2. Evaluate what special abilities or advantages we have for carrying out the task.

3. Take a look at the importance, to us, of landing this bid: judge its significance in terms of getting profitable jobs in the future or of holding together an organization.

4. Decide how anxious possible competitors may be for success in this competition, in the light of what we know about the current and near future activity of each and of the industry.

---

* An interesting discussion of purchase bidding will be found in Norman E. Taylor, "A Look at Competitive Bidding," Montana Business Quarterly, Spring, 1964, pp. 22-36.

5. In the light of these appraisals, redefine what we consider the elements of real cost to be.

6. Decide what information on past bids of probable competitors is relevant: which bids and bid situations represent similar circumstances. When chosen, tabulate the past bids of each competitor, and estimate how each competitor may be expected to bid this time.

7. Decide what our objective is to be if we submit a bid: choose whether or not, why, and under what circumstances we would like to win the bid. On this basis, select a specific profit target, usually in terms of a specific percentage of cost.

CBS mainly improves the operation in point 6 above: the estimate of what each competitor may be expected to bid. It consists essentially of four steps:

1. Make an estimate of our cost and of the range of bids we might make, based on this cost, as usual.

2. Construct a probability distribution of the percentage profit targets of each competitor who will be in the competition.

3. Calculate a combined probability distribution of our chance of winning for each bid within the range we are considering.

4. Calculate the profit position distribution of bids in this range.

The heart of CBS is a logical process for making full use of normally available information to develop a probability distribution for the bids of each competitor. This distribution, in turn, permits a quantitative evaluation of the profit position of a bid.

Calculating The Profit Position of a Bid

The calculations do not directly indicate exactly what bid the firm should enter. This follows from the firm's purpose in making the bid. What competitive bidding strategy comparisons accomplish is to make clear the relative effect of all of the possible bids under consideration on the long term profit position of the firm, as nearly as this can be determined from the available information and judgments entering into the computations. The technique does this by producing a set of numbers which combine the estimated profit of each bid if successful with the odds that each particular bid can be successful. The figure calculated for each bid--the profit position of that bid--is the simple product of the estimated actual profit times the odds that it can win. The estimated actual profit, of course, is merely the difference between the proposed bid and the firm's own computations of the project cost. The likelihood of winning is developed through a simple statistical analysis of past bidding strategy, based on several necessary assumptions:

1. Each bidder tends to follow a consistent pattern in his cost estimating procedure.

2. Cost estimates made by competing bidders will be similar and reasonably parallel over time.

3. If only winning bids are directly known, the competition was probably keen enough that the losers' bids were close to those of the winner.

4. As a result, the profit objective of each bidder can be approximated for any of his past bids if we have either knowledge of or a close estimate of his bid and our own estimate of the project cost. While such an estimate will contain some degree of error, the error in a series of such estimates will be small and consistent.

5. Each bidder makes his own bid without knowledge of the action of others and competitors' bids are therefore independent of each other. Thus the chance that each will enter a given bid is of the odds that others will enter that bid.

These assumptions would be familiar to anyone who has been making bids, just as the procedure cited earlier would be. All that competitive bidding strategy contributes, therefore, is a quantification of the inferences drawn about competitor behavior, in terms of a distribution of profit position values for all possible bids.

The profit position value of any given bid is merely the estimated profit <u>times</u> the likelihood of winning <u>successively</u> against each and all competitors likely to enter. (This follows from the assumption of independence of bidders.) Expressed in mathematical symbolism:

Let V_i = the value of the profit position of a given individual bid
M_i = the estimated value of the actual profit margin of that bid
$L_1, L_2, L_3, \ldots. L_k$ = the individual likelihoods that the given bid will be better than that of the competing bidders, 1, 2, 3, ... k.

Then $V_i = M_i (L_1 \times L_2 \times L_3 \times \ldots\ldots L_k)$ for <u>k</u> number of bidders.

Since M_i is a known figure, this formula is simple arithmetic once we have an estimate of the L's. To take a concrete example, assume a bid for $275,000 estimated to yield a profit of $25,000. Assume further that our estimate of the likelihoods that each of the three known competitors will bid higher than $275,000 are 0.5, 0.4, and 0.3, respectively. Then:

$$V_{\$275,000} = \$25,000\ (.5 \times .4 \times .3) = 25,000(.06) = \$1,500$$

Taken alone, this profit position figure of $1500 has little tangible meaning. It is not an estimate of the actual profit which might be realized. If a bid of $275,000 secures the contract, the firm will get the actual difference between its bid price and the actual cost--a profit already estimated at $25,000. If the bid is not a winner, the firm gets nothing. The profit position values simply permit a rational comparison of the best estimated consequences for the long run financial health of the firm of proposed bidding procedures and immediate objectives--the effect on average earnings of a series of similar bids, taking into account the number of times the bids might lose.

Clearly, the computation hinges on obtaining as good a distribution of likelihood values as possible for each competitor. How such distributions might be estimated is probably best illustrated in terms of the hypothetical case of STL Fabricators, Inc. This general structural steel fabricating firm has been asked to bid on construction of a set of special purpose Inland Waterways barges whose cost STL estimates at $250,000 each. STL executives are aware that three other familiar contractors (B&R, C&T, and D&Y) will be entering serious bids. STL men are also aware that all 3 competitors have had considerable slack capacity over the last 37 months. During that period, the competitors have been quite eager to land jobs and there is little reason to believe that this attitude has changed. The STL executives have therefore asked for the files on all bids made by STL and these 3 others during the 37 month period, excluding earlier bids made during a more prosperous period. Of the 24 files on hand, they judge 19 to be bids made under circumstances similar to those of the present job. In the other 5 cases, they believe that either special facilities of a competitor or special relationships between some one competitor and the awarding authority made the bidding circumstances noncomparable, even noncompetitive.

Of the 19 cases under review, only 4 had been for barges or other vessels of any design, and all of these for quite different designs and different kinds of programs. Other projects had been for a variety of other types of construction normal for the industry--for TV towers and microwave installations, for tank farms, pipelines, and other fabrication projects. But all of them were within the competence of all four competitors and all had entered serious bids.

Table 5-1 lists the information yielded by STL's files for the 19 projects considered comparable. In terms of total project value and dollar profit, the 19 were far from alike. However, the important data is not these totals but the estimated profit objectives of the winners, given in the last column. Except when STL won, these estimates are not precise, of course. It is rather unlikely that STL and its competitor arrived at identical cost estimates much of the time. But the difference cannot be substantial, and the figure listed is the best information available. In any event, the main problem is not the accuracy of the known figures, but the size of the missing ones--the bids of the losers in each case. About such bids, STL has one solid bit of knowledge: the losers had bid higher than the winner. How much higher? This, too, can be estimated from past experience. Looking at the difference between STL's bids and those of a winning competitor when STL lost, it appears that the difference has tended to oscillate around 1 per cent. The random distribution of the winners seems to indicate that bids, in general, have been close to each other, and STL officials believe they have done as well as any.

The loser's bid then is estimated by adding a nominal amount, in line with experience, to the winner's profit objective. Proceeding thus, STL has arrived at the profit objective values shown in Table 5-2. It is now ready to develop an estimate of the likelihood distribution of the profit objective of each competing contractor for the barge job.

To apply the likelihood objective estimate to the next contract, STL makes two additional assumptions: (1) for any contractor, each of his past bid objectives is as likely as any other at this point, (2) one additionally likely condition exists--the possibility that any contractor may bid just outside the range of past experience, might set a profit objective either just above or just below any of the 19 previous ones. STL then must consider each past bid objective as equal to the fractional likelihood of $\frac{1}{19+1}$, or $\frac{1}{20}$ of the possible bids. Table 5-3 gives the initial raw estimates of the cumulative likelihood distribution for each of the three competitors, and Figure 5-3 graphs these with a hand-fitted line for each contractor. By interpolating convenient values from each of these smoothed distributions, we can get an estimate of the cumulative likelihood that all three competitors combined will enter a bid higher than any given value, that is, the cumulative joint probability that STL will not be underbid. Table 5-4 shows the calculated values based on Figure 5-4. These calculated values are plotted in Figure 5-5 and again smoothed to yield the final estimate.

TABLE 5-1. STL's Information On 19 Contract Lettings In The Last 37 Months

Item No.	Bid Winner	STL Estimate Of Cost (C_s)	Winning Bid (B)	STL Bid	Difference: ($B - C_s$) Amount	Per cent of C_s
1	STL	$ 97,300	$105,110	$105,110	$ 7,710	+8%
2	B&R	121,500	129,030	131,000	8,530	+7
3	D&Y	190,300	196,015	196,700	5,715	+3
4	C&T	75,700	80,248	81,050	4,548	+6
5	B&R	253,200	240,550	243,100	-12,650	-5
6	D&Y	211,800	190,595	192,500	-21,205	-9
7	D&Y	495,600	455,970	460,100	-39,630	-8
8	C&T	136,500	146,055	147,490	9,555	+7
9	C&T	97,400	100,320	101,250	2,920	+3
10	B&R	157,100	136,251	137,600	-18,849	-12
11	STL	64,500	71,560	71,560	7,060	+11
12	C&T	77,900	84,920	85,670	7,020	+9
13	B&R	176,200	193,825	194,494	17,265	+10
14	D&Y	246,700	254,195	256,950	7,395	+3
15	STL	195,100	199,005	199,005	3,905	+2
16	STL	117,400	122,090	122,090	4,690	+4
17	D&Y	195,800	193,950	194,900	-1,950	-1
18	C&T	147,300	142,875	144,300	-4,425	-3
19	B&R	99,475	97,565	98,389	-1,910	-2

TABLE 5-2. STL'S Best Estimate Of The Bid Objective Distribution For Each Of Its Three Competitors In 19 Contract Lettings In The Last 37 Months

Item No.	Estimated Bid Objective As Per Cent Of Cost, For: B&R	C&T	D&Y
1	9	9	9
2	7	8	8
3	4	4	3
4	7	6	7
5	-5	-4	-4
6	-9	-10	-9
7	-7	-7	-8
8	8	7	8
9	4	3	4
10	-12	-11	-11
11	12	12	12
12	10	9	10
13	10	11	11
14	4	4	3
15	3	3	3
16	5	5	5
17	0	0	-1
18	-2	-3	-2
19	-2	-1	-1

TABLE 5-3. STL's Initial Estimate of the Cumulative Bid Objective Likelihood Distribution for Each of the 3 Competitors (Each single bid = 1/20 of total)

B&R Bid Objective (% profit)	L (cum.)		C&T Bid Objective (% profit)	L (cum.)		D&Y Bid Objective (% profit)	L (cum.)	
12	.05		12	.05		12	.05	
10	.10	.125	11	.10		11	.10	
10	.15		9	.15	.175	10	.15	
9	.20		9	.20		9	.20	
8	.25		8	.25		8	.25	.275
7	.30	.325	7	.30		8	.30	
7	.35		6	.35		7	.35	
5	.40		5	.40		5	.40	
4	.45		4	.45	.475	4	.45	
4	.50	.50	4	.50		3	.50	
4	.55		3	.55	.575	3	.55	.55
3	.60		3	.60		3	.60	
0	.65		0	.65		-1	.65	.675
-2	.70	.725	-1	.70		-1	.70	
-2	.75		-3	.75		-2	.75	
-5	.80		-4	.80		-4	.80	
-7	.85		-7	.85		-8	.85	
-9	.90		-10	.90		-9	.90	
-12	.95		-11	.95		-11	.95	

TABLE 5-4. Computation of Profit Position Estimates for a Selected List of Percentage Profit Objectives, Based on Figure 5-3

Profit Objective (per cent)	Estimated likelihood that a higher bid will be entered by: B&R	C&T	D&Y	All three		Estimate of actual		Estimated profit
+12	.05	.05	.05	.000125	x	$30,000	=	$ 4
10	.14	.125	.15	.0025		25,000		16
8	.27	.24	.275	.018		20,000		360
6	.38	.35	.40	.0533		15,000		800
5	.435	.45	.45	.08		12,000		1,000
4	.49	.465	.5	.114		10,000		1,140
3.5	.515	.495	.525	.134		8,750		1,170
3	.535	.52	.55	.154		7,500		1,155
2	.575	.57	.59	.193		5,000		965
0	.655	.66	.67	.29		0		0
-1	.695	.7	.71	.344		-2,500		-860
-4	.78	.795	.8	.495		-10,000		-4,950
-8	.88	.885	.89	.695		-20,000		-13,900
-12	.95	.95	.95	.862		-30,000		-25,960

FIGURE 5-3

SMOOTHED DISTRIBUTIONS OF THE ORIGINAL ESTIMATE OF THE LIKELIHOOD THAT EACH OF THE 3 COMPETITORS WILL ENTER A HIGHER BID

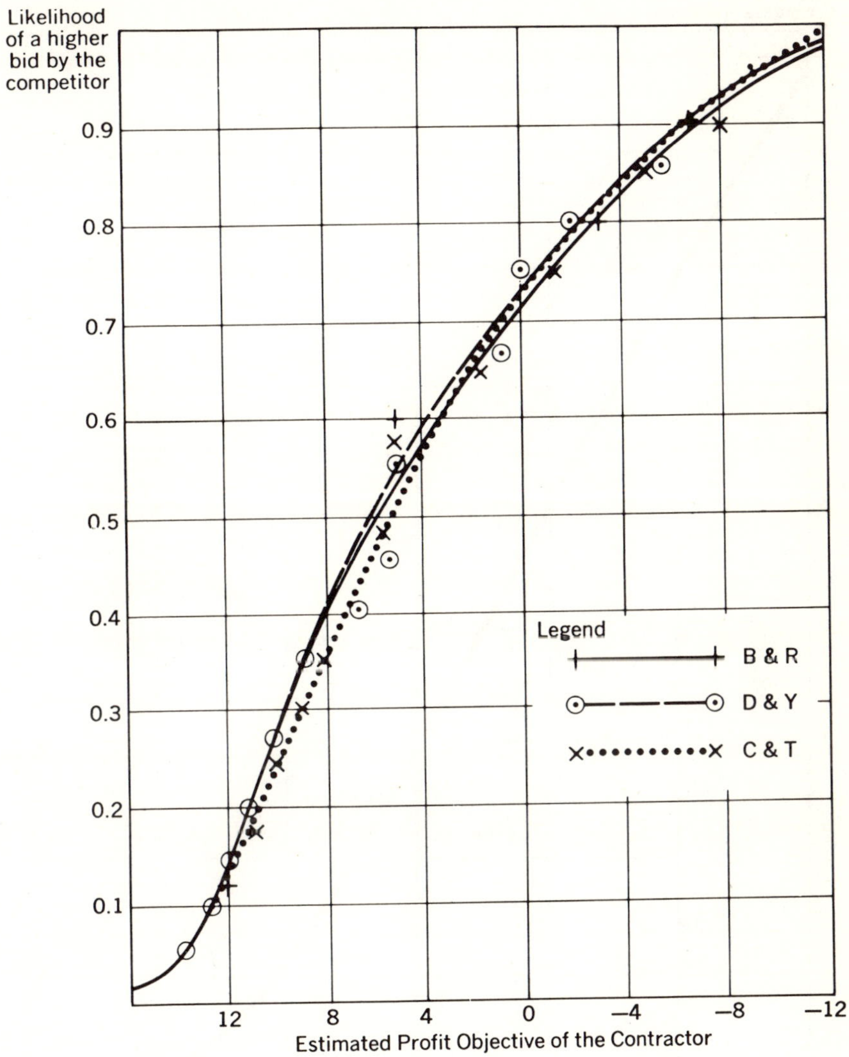

FIGURE 5-4

SMOOTHED ESTIMATE OF THE DISTRIBUTION OF THE LIKELIHOOD THAT ALL THREE CONTRACTORS WILL SUBMIT A HIGHER BID

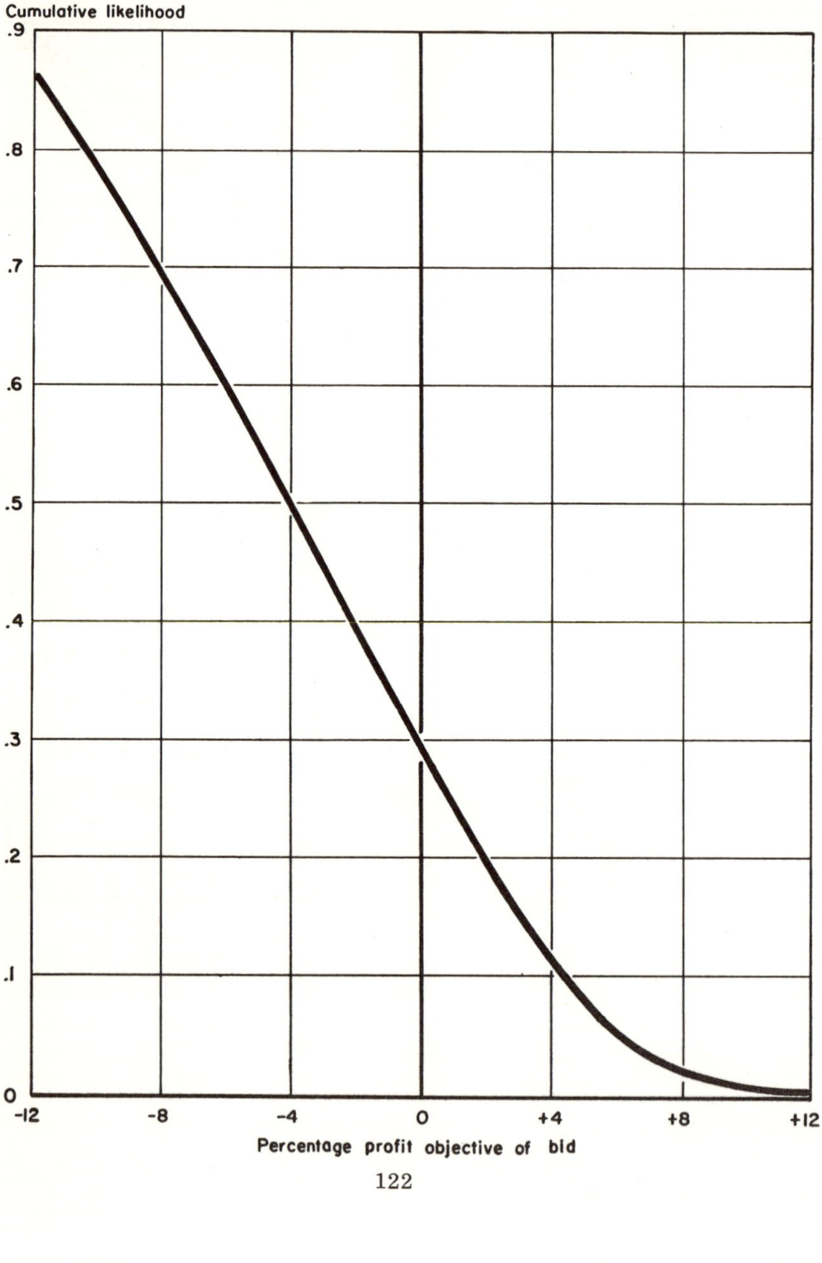

FIGURE 5-5

FINAL ESTIMATE OF THE PROFIT POSITION DISTRIBUTION FOR ALL BIDS YIELDING EITHER A POSITIVE PROFIT OR A VERY SMALL LOSS

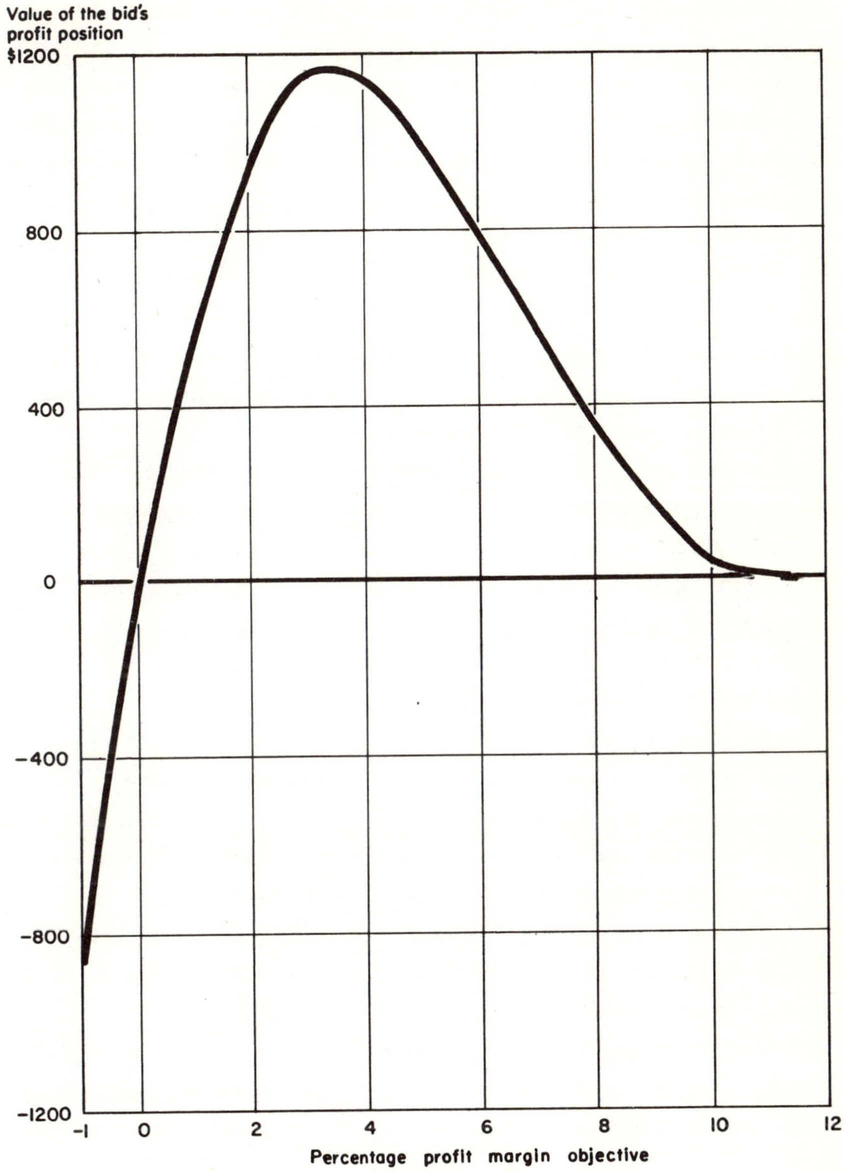

Given this final estimate curve, what should STL bid? The curve does not tell directly, only in conjunction with a decision as to the immediate objective of STL officials in trying for the contract. If that immediate objective is the best profit position, then the answer is approximately $258,750 ($250,000 cost + $8,750 profit), corresponding to the optimum profit position value of $1,170.

But the objective of STL and of its competitors is not always optimum immediate profit as is evident from the numerous loss bids submitted in the recent past. Some contracts were for prototype structures where the winner was sure of considerable advantage in bidding on a series of contracts that would follow. In such cases, the objective was frequently to maximize the chances of winning the prototype award. If such were STL's objective in the current job, it would bid with a lower profit objective than any previously submitted by anyone--lower than the -12% with which B&R landed the contract for item number 10. If, on the other hand, STL decides that it would undertake the project only for significant profit, it might bid $260,000, a little less than the optimum profit position, if willing to accept 4% as reasonable profit in the circumstances, or even $270,000 for an 8% profit but only a 2% chance of winning.

By contrast, STL may realize that in any case, no bid it can make has a very good chance of winning because one of the others--perhaps C&T--has an inside track with the awarding authorities and will be given an opportunity to change its bid to meet that of any other competitor. STL then ponders whether to submit a bid so low as to entail a considerable loss if the "second look" relationship C&T has is broken and would otherwise penalize C&T by forcing it to underbid at a much lower price than intended.

The judgmental computations of competitive bidding strategy are therefore only part of the whole--they simple furnish the prospective bidder with a reasonably objective measure of the likely long run consequences of any proposed bid. Like all Bayesian calculations, those of competitive bidding strategy are only as good as the judgments made as to what past experience is applicable--no better. While they furnish the semblance of objectivity, they are not objective in the sense that traditional statistical measures are. The basic data is derived from merely analogical information, not demonstrable similarities. In competitive bidding strategy, for example, the past bids used to estimate the likelihood distributions are chosen on the basis of a highly personal judgment as to which ones occurred in similar situations. They were for projects so varied that they would not meet traditional statistical tests for homogeneity. Every quantity used contains a large component of judgment.

But the purpose of any such Bayesian approach is to obtain optimum value from the kind of information available, information which will be used in any case, since nothing better can be obtained. By so doing the executive can learn the full import of the information for the decision he must make.

The Inventory Model

The inventory model takes its name from an early and still important use, but its applicability is far broader than the logistics of material movement. Any problem is an "inventory" problem which has the following characteristics:

1. There is an appreciable lead-time between an input action and useful output, which lead-time may or may not vary within a predictable range but in a random fashion. (In the case of an actual inventory problem, this is the lag between placing an order and getting it into stock.)

2. Potential usage of the items during any period of time can vary in a predictable range, but in an unpredictable random fashion. (In an actual inventory situation, potential usage means demands for withdrawal from stock.) Whether or not the actual lead-time varies significantly, then, this means that demand in any given lead-time is not fully predictable, and there will be shortages during some lead-times, overages during others, that is some old items still available when the new inputs arrive.

3. The input timing, or the amount, or both, can be varied at will. (Order quantity or the timing of orders can be varied at will.)

4. There is an associated fixed cost for each act of input or start-up. (The cost of acquisition--ordering, receiving and placing in stock--is relatively constant regardless of the size of order.)

5. The cost of shortages--items not available when demanded--is proportional to the number of items short. The cost of overages is variable and proportional to the number of old items left on hand. (There is a cost associated with any item not in stock when demanded, proportionate to the unsatisfied demand, and another variable cost associated with any stock left in inventory at the time a new order is put in stock.)

Many kinds of business situations will prove to have these characteristics, if we interpret the conditions above into the proper language. Systematic personnel recruitment and training programs would often fit, for example. The fixed costs of "acquisition" would become the fixed costs of the recruitment and training system; lead-time, the lag between attempt to hire or otherwise recruit and the end of the training period; demand, the positions which needed to be filled with trainees during any given period. Shortages would be any jobs which had to be left unfilled until the new training class graduated, and the shortage cost those costs incurred because of the lack of adequate trainees. Overages would be the excess of trainees at the end of a training period who were not immediately needed to fill the positions which opened before a new class was available, the costs the difference between their pay and the productivity expected from a trainee.

If the inventory is produced in intermittent batches within the firm, rather than purchased, cost of acquisition becomes the start-up costs for the production of each batch. The costs themselves do not have to be expressible directly in money, just so long as some kind of alternative to these costs can be so expressed.

The uncertainty of the demand during the lead-time is, of course, the reason we have a problem at all, whether that uncertainty arises from an uncertainty in the length of the lead-time itself, or results from the variability of the demand during a given period of time, or both. Any order clerk would need only a simple arithmetic calculation if total demand and the demand pattern are known and the lead-time to restock is predictable. In such pleasant circumstances, the minimum order quantity is just enough to carry the demand volume during the lead-time period. The most economical order quantity (Q) will be that which minimizes the total of two costs:

1. the annual cost of carrying inventory such as financing, storage, and deterioration (which increases as the order quantity, and thus the average size of stock, increases).

2. the annual cost of acquisition of stock such as the costs of processing an order (or making a machine setup), receiving, payment of invoices (which goes down as the lot size increases).

In the cost of predictable demand flow and lead-time, the reorder point (R) which will trigger the new order is just the amount of residual stock needed to cover demand during this lead-time. Under such ideal circumstances, of course, inventory is no management problem, but routine clerical work.

In most real life, inventory is a management concern because demand can fluctuate in an unpredictable pattern within reasonably predictable ranges and lead-time between order and receipt cannot always be considered constant. With either demand pattern or lead-time a probability variable, no single values of either the order quantity Q or the reorder point R, and no single combination can simultaneously prevent both occasional stock shortages (stock-outs) and occasional overages of residual stock at the time of new order receipt. Both stock-outs and overages add to inventory cost. Stock-outs can result in lost business, particularly if backordering is not possible or practical. Even with backordering, some customer goodwill is probably lost, and order cancellations are certain as the length of the backorder period is increased. Any stock overage results in an average inventory level higher than under certainty, and thus additional inventory costs.

Minimizing inventory costs thus requires determination of a procedure for routine calculation of two quantities (or parameters): Q, the quantity to be ordered, and R, the stock level at which a reorder will be triggered.

Whatever the form of inventory system, determination of the best procedure and rules for these parameters is a cut-and-try process, aimed at minimizing the net total of three conflicting costs:

1. the cost of carrying inventory
2. stock-out costs
3. the costs of ordering and acquisition.

The mathematical model that is needed is thus some systematic trial-and-error procedure such that each succeeding step gets a better solution until the optimum solution is reached and can be recognized. The mathematician calls such a model or rule an algorithm. There are two main types of inventory systems:

1. The fixed reorder point system, which seeks the best (Q, R) combination in which Q is held constant and the date of reorder is variable, being triggered by R, the level of inventory at which a reorder is to be placed

2. the system with fixed ordering dates, set once and for all, the quantity, Q, being determined by the stock on hand at the time of ordering.

The latter system has some important applications in cases in which delivery has to be scheduled on the basis of some kind of routine (as with bakery goods on the grocery shelves), or in which recent experience is a valid guide to near future demand. But the fixed reorder point system has more general applicability and will be discussed below. It is the preferable system whenever all of the following hold:

1. lead-time is relatively constant regardless of the order date

2. recent history is not a reliable indicator of demand

3. the cost of placing orders is not significantly affected by irregularity of their dating.

Even when lead-time is variable, it is still usually the better system, and it may be preferable when one of the other conditions is violated. The ability to use recent history to partially predict near future demand adds a minor complication in that it requires that we have a family of (Q, R) solutions, rather then one. Such would be the case of the dress reorder situation used as an example earlier. Seasonal demand patterns of known conformation would also require such a family of solutions. Furthermore, when recent history really is a valid guide to future demand, demand patterns are quite likely to approach a definite known pattern, and inventory control is dealing with a narrower range of uncertainty.

Fixed Order Point Inventory Control: Estimating The Probability Distributions

Let us visualize the problem of real-world inventory control in terms of Hectic Fishing Supply a commercial fisheries distributor that sells, among other items, kippered sardine nets costing Hectic $500 each. Hectic can count on selling close to 365 nets nearly every year, an average of one per day, with no perceptible seasonal variation. But on some days, none are sold at all, and on some, as many as 3. Hectic's experience on getting delivery for stock replacement has been that this can vary from 1 to 3 days. In setting up an inventory system for its nets, then, Hectic starts with the following knowledge:

1. Per item cost to Hectic is $500.

2. The cost of holding inventory is 20% of the average value, per year.

3. Order cost is $20 per order for placement, handling, and receiving, without regard to the number of nets ordered.

4. Hectic can expect to sell 365 nets per year.

In addition, Hectic has a policy of backordering all nets demanded but not available in stock and filling all backorders immediately when stock is received.

Looking over its past experience, Hectic decides that last year's demand and supply patterns were quite typical, and would be as good an estimate of the probability distribution for next year as could be made. Tabulation of the daily demand during last year shows volume fluctuating from no nets to 3 in one day and lead-time to refill stock from one to three days (Tables 5-5 and 5-6).

TABLE 5-5. Daily Demand of Kippered Herring Nets During The Past Year

Nets Demanded During One Day	Percentage of Days
None	40%
1	30
2	20
3	10
	100%

TABLE 5-6. Lead-Time for Restocking Nets During The Past Year

Lead-time Per Order (Days)	Percentage of Orders
1	25%
2	50
3	25
	100%

Careful analysis can detect no predictable pattern of any sort in either the daily demand or the order lead-time; they appear to be purely random variations. Hence there were times when no nets were needed to fill orders from the time stock was exhausted until a new stock was received, and there could have been times when 9 nets were demanded between the time stock was exhausted and a new shipment was received (a DDLT, demand during lead-time, of 9 nets). Hence, if Hectic were really to pursue a policy of never risking an inventory shortage, it would have to set a minimum reorder levels in excess of 9 nets. Such a policy would inevitably result in an excess stock on order receipt most of the time, however. Unless stock-out cost was inordinately high, this policy is unlikely to be as profitable as one which risked an occasional shortage. Hence, Hectic's officials must make the best estimate they can of the cost to them of a stock-out. After calculating the cost of keeping the necessary back-order records and adding to this their best appraisal of the cost of occasional customer ill will caused by backordering and delayed deliveries, these officials put the cost of a stock-out at $40 per item/time. Hectic now has enough information on which to determine a possible inventory policy, first constructing a table of probabilities for each possible demand level during the lead-time, from 0 through 9 nets per lead-time period.

If the demand and lead-time patterns are as simple as those we have assumed for Hectic, we can simply enumerate all of the combinations of demand and lead-time variations that could occur and compute directly the probabilities of each possible combination. One of these combinations would be a lead-time of 3 days and a demand for 7 nets during those 3 days. Such would be the case if the demand on the first day were for 3 nets and on each of the succeeding 2 days was for 2 nets, or any other permutation of 3, 2, 2. This combination of 7 nets and 3 days could also result from a 3 day lead-time and any permutation of demand per day of 3, 3, 1. Table 5-7 lists the 6 possible combinations resulting in a demand of 7 nets per day during a 3 day lead-time.

TABLE 5-7. Probability That Seven Nets Will Be a DDLT of 3 Days

Possible Pattern of Demand on Successive Days	Probability (P) That This Will Be The Total Demand-Lead-Time Pattern = P(lead-time of 3 days)	x	P(daily demands)	=	P(this combination)
3, 2, 2	.25	x	(.10x.20x.20)	=	.001
2, 3, 2	.25	x	(.20x.10x.20)	=	.001
2, 2, 3	.25	x	(.20x.20x.10)	=	.001
3, 3, 1	.25	x	(.10x.10x.30)	=	.00075
3, 1, 3	.25	x	(.10x.30x.10)	=	.00075
1, 3, 3	.25	x	(.30x.10x.10)	=	.00075
			TOTAL P (DDLT = 7)		.00525

We could thus proceed to count all the ways in which the various demand and lead-time combinations could occur and to compute their probabilities. The result would be as in Table 5-8.

TABLE 5-8. Probability Distribution of <u>DDLT</u> for Hectic Fishing Supplys Kippered Herring Nets

DDLT No. of Nets	Probability of This Demand	Cumulative Probability (Probability That The Demand Will Be Greater Than This)
0	.1960	.8040
1	.2310	.5730
2	.2260	.3470
3	.1797	.1673
4	.0935	.0738
5	.0477	.0261
6	.0190	.0071
7	.0053	.0018
8	.0015	.0003
9	.0003	.0000

The quantities in the last column are simply the sum of the probabilities of all the demands for a quantity greater than the number listed. The value of this at the <u>DDLT</u> level of 9 nets is zero, since Hectic does not anticipate any day with a demand greater than 3 nets, nor any lead-time for restocking of more than 3 days. This cumulative figure is the probability that a reorder level <u>**R**</u> of the number of nets listed in column 1 will result in a stock-out of at least 1 net. Thus if <u>**R**</u> is set at 5 nets, Hectic can expect a stock-out during about one reorder period out of 40 (261/10,000). The expected value of the stock-out for each lead-time period using a reorder level of 5-nets can be calculated as:

Probability of a shortage of 4 nets, <u>DDLT</u>:	(9 - 5) x .0003 = .0012
" " " " " 3 " " :	(8 - 5) x .0015 = .0045
" " " " " 2 " " :	(7 - 5) x .0053 = .0106
" " " " " 1 " " :	(6 - 5) x .0190 = .0190
<u>Total expected unit shortage when **R** = 5</u>	.0353

Now, obviously, there is no such thing as .0353 fractional part of a net, but this is the average risk expectation of a shortage over a long period, if the past year's experience can be used as a close approximation of <u>DDLT</u> probability. We shall label all quantities like this value, .0353, as <u>E</u>(<u>DDLT</u> > <u>**R**</u>), to be translated as "the expected amount by which <u>DDLT</u> exceeds **R** (the reorder point)," or the expected average stock-out risk per lead-time, in number of nets short. Multiplied by the estimated cost of a stock-out of $40, this tells us what the stock-out cost of an <u>**R**</u> would be for Hectic; in this case of <u>**R**</u> = 5, $1,412, per reorder period.

Fixed Order Point Control: Calculating The Optimum Order Quantity and Reorder Point

Our Hectic example chose a very simple case in which the demand quantities and lead-time values were very small. Even here, as can be seen, the total calculation would be rather cumbersome when done by hand. Where total quantities are much larger, as is usual, this system would be too much work to use if we did not have access to a computer and a convenient technique for using it. The technique, in this case, is to use Monte Carlo simulation (discussed later) to construct tables of probability based on known experience.

The starting point and general procedure would remain the same, however: First, an estimate of the probability distributions of unit-time demand and of lead-time variations on the basis of some kind of experience considered to be a valid approximation of the pattern that lies ahead and then construction of the total DDLT probability distribution this experience implies. From this we can use some procedure to calculate the total annual cost (TAC) for each plausible combination of Q and R, on the basis of this experience, starting with the minimum reorder value R needed to cover this average lead-time (2 nets), then trying progressively larger values of Q and R until a combination of Q and R are found found for which TAC is less than any preceding value and also less than the next succeeding value.

The basic formulae for the three cost elements are:

1. Annual Ordering Cost = (cost per order) x $\frac{\text{total estimated annual demand (AD)}}{\text{Number per order (Q)}}$

   or, in terms of Hectic, = \$20 x $\frac{365}{Q}$

2. Annual Inventory Holding Cost = $\begin{matrix}\text{holding}\\ \text{cost rate}\end{matrix}$ x $\begin{matrix}\text{cost}\\ \text{per unit}\end{matrix}$ x $(\frac{Q}{2} + R - DDLT)$

   As inspection will reveal, the last expression is the average quantity on hand,

   or, in terms of Hectic, $= \frac{Q}{2} + R - 2$ (since average lead-time is 2 days and average demand per day is 1 net)

3. Annual Stock-Out Cost = (cost per stock-out) x $E(DDLT > R)$ x $\frac{\text{annual demand}}{Q}$

   or, for Hectic, = \$40 x $E(DDLT\ R)$ x $\frac{365}{Q}$

How do the minimum values of (Q = 2, R = 2) work out for Hectic?

$\frac{\text{Cost of holding inventory}}{\text{year}}$ = .20(\$500) x (2/2 + 2 - 2) = .20 x \$500 x 1 = \$100

Annual ordering cost = \$20 x $\frac{365}{2}$ = \$3650

Annual Stock-Out Cost = \$40 x .3470 x $\frac{365}{2}$ = \$3430

Then TAC = \$100 + \$3650 + \$3430 = \$6180

For Hectic, it is obvious that the company could afford to carry a larger stock in order to reduce the frequency with which orders are placed, and cut down on inventory shortages. Increasing <u>Q</u> substantially, say to 8, would raise holding costs by only another $300 per year, even with (R = 2), but drop ordering cost to only $912.50 and stock-out costs to $857.50. Increasing <u>R</u> to 3 at the same time would increase holding cost by only $100, but cut <u>E(DDLT > R)</u> from .3470 to .1673 and thus further reduce stock-out costs by more than one-half of the $857.50. So, obviously, we must search further. A complete search will reveal that the minimum expected <u>TAC</u> will be $1534 with a <u>Q</u> of 13 nets and an <u>R</u> of 4 nets, if we can rely on our cost estimates.

But one item in our cost estimate is the roughest of approximations, if that much: our estimate of stock-out cost. In fact, stock-out cost is probably a volatile value, its level probably depending on the general tightness of supplies and our competitors' delivery policies. Whenever demand tends to outrun current supply, everybody may have trouble making delivery of nets on time, and our fisherman customers may be so aware of the problem that frequent stock-outs may mean the loss of little goodwill, if any. When supplies are plentiful and most competitors vying with each other for service, a single stock-out may cost us a major customer.

So we need to find out <u>how sensitive our policy calculation</u> is to the estimate of stock-out cost. In Table 5-9 are our sensitivity analysis calculations of the

TABLE 5-9. Comparison of Optimum Inventory Policy Costs at Varying Stock-out Costs, Between $10 and $80, and Annual Cost Based on an an Estimate of $40 for Stock-Out Cost

Actual Stock-Out Cost Per Unit	Optimum Inventory Policy <u>Q</u>	<u>R</u>	Minimum Annual Cost	<u>TAC</u> if Policy Based on Estimate of $40 Stock-Out	Added Inventory Cost of Ignorance of Actual Stock-Out Cost (in per cent)
$10	14	2	$1384	$1442	5.6%
20	14	3	1466	1473	0.5
30	13	4	1503	1503	--
40	13	4	1534	1534	--
50	13	5	1561	1564	0.2
60	13	5	1571	1595	1.5
70	13	5	1581	1625	2.8
80	13	5	1591	1657	4.2

differences between estimated TAC and actual TAC if the actual (and to some degree unknowable) stock-out costs were at various points in the wide range from \$10 to \$80. In the Hectic case, at least, a considerable error in the stock-out cost estimate can be tolerated without serious consequences.

Suppose, however, an abrupt easing in the market supply of nets makes quick delivery almost imperative if the patronage of Hectic's largest customers is to be retained. How many stock-outs are we risking with a (Q = 13, R = 4) policy? Referring back to the cumulative probability column in Table 5-8, we find that the probability of a stock-out of at least 1 net is .0738 with R = 4. In other words, out of about 28, lead-times per year $(\frac{365}{13})$, Hectic will experience stock-outs 7.4% of the time, or about twice a year. If we now run a sensitivity analysis on the values of Q, R combinations, we find that TAC is no more than 10% above the minimum for any of the values of Q between 11 and 16 ($11 < Q < 16$), and R between 3 and 6 ($3 < R < 6$). By reordering at R = 6, instead of when R = 4, the stock-out risk is reduced to 0.0071, or about once in five years. (P = 0.0071, 0.0071 x 28 = 0.199/year). By ordering only 12, instead of 13 nets when R = 6, Hectic's total inventory cost per year will rise only about 5% from \$1534 to \$1619, even without recalculating for a new value for stock-out cost. Hectic might consider this cheap insurance.

Inventory and The Inventory Model

Inventory models neither apply to all kinds of inventory situations, nor to inventory situations alone. They fit any situation, and all those situations in which both underestimates and overestimates result in cost proportional to the error. Such an "inventory model" might thus apply to the scheduling of a final "lifetime" production run of spare parts for a discontinued engine design if, in case of an underestimate, all additional orders would be filled individually by the model shop without the aid of special tooling, so that all additional parts costs were variable (and, of course, higher than before). And as already indicated, shortages can result in lump-sum losses in some conceivable inventory situations. For the latter, the inventory policy is best optimized by use of the lump-sum loss production scheduling model outlined below.

The Lump-Sum Loss Production Scheduling Model

The Basic Approach

When scheduling production runs of special designs or nonstandard dimensions, the percentage of defectives can only be estimated as a probability variable developed on the basis of analogous experience from operations thought to be similar. Over-runs normally result in some loss proportional to the over-run; at the extreme, the excess units must be treated as scrap, or at least unloaded at a substantial discount. Or the product may be unstable and deteriorate before sold or used, and losses suffered in this manner. Overage losses of this sort are the same sort of proportional costs as overages in inventory.

But quite often, if the percentage defective proves to be greater than allowed for, by even as little as one unit, a lump-sum cost be incurred regardless of the actual size of the shortage (as, for example, when it results in the need for a new machine setup). Such a lump-sum loss situation yields an optimum solution through a simple form of graphic analysis.

To visualize the lump-sum model approach, we need to think of each item scheduled as being one of a series, each with its own serial number, and the decision as being whether or not to schedule a particular numbered item, j, to be the last one run. The problem is worked out in terms of two pairs of quantities:

Q--the total number of pieces scheduled for production, of which j is the serial number of the last piece run

G--the total number of good pieces actually produced, of which n is the serial number of the last good piece needed to fill the order and n_{ac} is the actual serial number of the last good piece produced.

The aim is to schedule the quantity Q so that the last piece run, j, is equal to n, the last good piece needed, which is equal in turn to Q. With a known process and a repeat run of an item on which there has been accumulated a lot of experience, this means only that enough be scheduled to allow for a known number of defectives. But when we have no direct experience with the item, we must make some kind of probability estimate of the percentage of defectives to be expected, basing the estimate usually on the analogy between the item being scheduled and other items with production requirements we consider comparable, and whose defect percentages are likely to vary over some kind of range.

In such a situation, we can have 3 possible kinds of outcomes:

1. We may, by luck, schedule just enough production that $j = n = Q$, that is, such that the last piece produced just fills the order.

2. We may produce an over-run, so that $j > n$, in which case we sustain some unit loss k on each piece produced beyond those ordered.

3. We may schedule too few to produce n good pieces-- $j < n$ -- in which case, however few or many the shortage, we have the same lump-sum loss, K, because of the need for a new machine setup, for example.

In the case of an over-run, our actual total loss is equal to $k(Q - n)$. In the case of any shortfall, it is K. We do not know the value of <u>n</u> (the serial number of the last good piece needed), in advance, so that we must choose the best value of Q to schedule on the basis of our estimate of the expected value of two possible losses. Thus for every individual j, the last piece scheduled, there are two expected loss values:

1. the expected loss from an overage, due to scheduling: $j \times k\, P(n < j)$, that is, (the unit loss from one surplus piece) x (the probability that <u>j</u> will be greater than the serial number of the last piece needed)

2. the expected loss from a shortage if j is not scheduled: $K\, P(n - j)$.

<u>In order for it to be profitable</u> to schedule the jth piece, <u>the expected loss from scheduling it must be less than the expected loss of not scheduling it</u>, or

$kP(n < j) < KP(n = j)$.

A transposed form of this inequality is more revealing as to the condition the most profitable decision will meet:

$$\frac{P(n = j)}{P(n < j)} > \frac{k}{K}$$

The value of this form is that $\frac{k}{K}$ is a value known in advance: <u>the ratio of the unit loss incurred for each unwanted piece produced, to the lump-sum loss incurred in the event of any shortage of any size</u>.

We need, then, to make estimates of the two related probability distributions, $P(n = j)$ and $P(n < j)$, prepare some kind of summary of their ratios, and match $\frac{k}{K}$ with one of these ratios.

To take a simple example, assume we require a special production run of 10 good skyhooks, and that past experience with other designs leads us to conclude that the 10 good skyhooks can be any of the pieces from the 10th to the 14th, with individual probabilities as shown in the second column of Table 5-10, under $P(n = j)$.

TABLE 5-10. Individual and Cumulative Probabilities That $(n_{ac} = j)$ for Different Values of <u>j</u>, with 10 Good Skyhooks Required.

j	$P(n_{ac} = j)$	$P(n_{ac} < j)$ (cumulative)	P(=)/P(<)
10	.20	0	∞ (infinity)
11	.40	.20	2.0
12	.25	.60	.42
13	.10	.85	.12
14	.05	.95	.05
15	0.0	1.00	0

Note that $P(n_{ac} < j)$ is derived from $P(n_{ac} = j)$

Let us assume that k, the loss occasioned by producing one unwanted skyhook is \$10 and that a setup cost to make a second run is \$50. Then

$$\frac{k}{K} = \frac{\$10}{\$50} = .20$$

By inspection of our table, the profitable run to schedule is thus 13 skyhooks.

To deal with the long production runs of real life, with their large numbers, such a table would be too long, and data not available in such neat form. We use instead a graphic approximation technique that also gives us an answer by inspection and comparison of the probability ratio $\frac{P(n_{ac} = j)}{P(n_{ac} < j)}$ with $\frac{k}{K}$.

Graphic Technique for Estimation of Optimum Long Production Runs

Probability estimates for long production runs must usually start with information on the gross percentage defectives experienced on a handful of previous runs of other designs believed to have similar process requirements to the item being scheduled. Starting with this limited handful of observations, we usually proceed with a 6-step graphic estimating procedure as follows:

1. Treating each run experience, ranked by percentage defectives, as a proportional fractile of the total process probability, plot these points on a graph, then fit a smoothed curve to the plot as an estimate of the continuous probability distribution of the ratios of total produced to good (of Q/G, or n_{ac}/G)

2. Rescale this graph to represent the cumulative probability $P(n_{ac} < n)$ on the vertical and of n on the horizontal scale, for the size of run desired.

3. Read off from this graph a set of grouped probability values of $P(n_{ac} = n)$ and calculate from this the distribution of $P(n_{ac} = n)$.

4. Use these grouped data estimates to calculate grouped data estimates of the ratio $P(n_{ac} = n)/P(n_{ac} < n)$.

5. Plot this grouped data ratio on a log-scale graph and fit a smoothed curve as an estimate of the continuous probability distribution of the ratio $P(=)/P(<)$ with values of n as the horizontal scale.

6. Locate on this graph the value of the ratio $P(n_{ac} = n)/P(n_{ac} < n)$ corresponding to the value of k/K, and read off the corresponding value of n, the serial number of the last good piece needed to fill the order (that is, Q, the size of the run needed).

The Graphic Technique, in Terms of an Example

A realistic example of graphic technique might be the scheduling of 5000 acceptable NG1099 port valves for a special modification kit for the now obsolescent SN 365 aircraft engine, a lifetime supply with no expectation of additional sales after this one order. Each valve made after the 5000th good one will cost us \$5.00 in variable manufacturing cost and unsalvageable material loss. If we underestimate the number Q that should be run, a second setup cost of \$1000 will have to be incurred to make up the shortage. We can assume that after the first run, enough will be known about the probability of defective production that the second run can be scheduled rather accurately, but we have never produced the NG1099 before and so must rely on data from other valve production runs which required the same 25 operations, and our experience with which is judged by our engineers to be as comparable as it is possible to be. There were nine such runs, with the variable experience shown in Table 5-11. We wish to use this experience to estimate the value of Q for which $P(n_{ac} = n)/P(n_{ac} < n)$ will be less than \$5/\$1000, or ($< .005$).

TABLE 5-11. Production Experience for 9 Analogous Runs in The Past

Run Number	Total No. of Pieces	Number Good	Number Defective	Fraction Defective	Ratio of Total-To-Good
1	6100	4873	1227	.201	1.25
2	7300	5184	2116	.290	1.41
3	8200	6673	1537	.190	1.23
4	6700	5119	1581	.248	1.33
5	7900	6589	1314	.164	1.20
6	8100	5588	2512	.310	1.45
7	6600	5128	1472	.223	1.28
8	7600	5623	1977	.260	1.35
9	6400	5088	1312	.195	1.24

None of these runs produced exactly 5000 good valves, but we feel that the numbers are large enough that the difference has no significance. We really do not know, either, that the last valve in each run was a good one, but even if as many as 30 defective valves in succession were produced at the end of the run, our ratio of total-to-good would not be changed for any of the runs, within the 3 significant figure precision being used here.

FIGURE 5-6

ESTIMATING CHART FOR DETERMINATION OF $P(n_{ac} < n)$

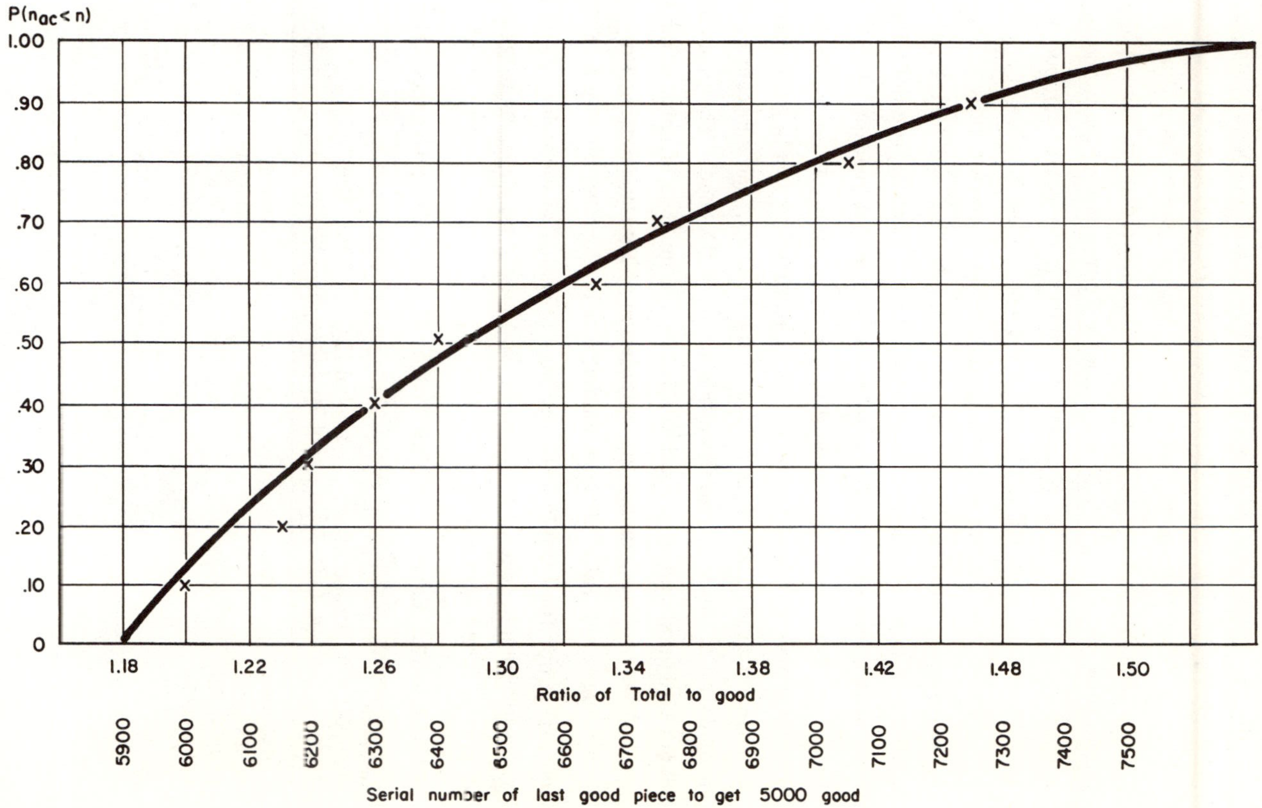

The next step is to rank these Q/G ratios in order of size. Then, since we have no reason to believe any of them is a more applicable experience than any of the others, treat them as fractile points on a continuous probability distribution, each accounting for 1/(9 + 1), or 1/10th of the total cumulative probability from 0 to 1.0. Thus the lowest value, 1.20, will be plotted as a $P(n_{ac} < n)$ of .10, the next lowest, 1.23, as .20, etc., as has been done in Figure 5-6. The points thus plotted, we draw the smoothed curve fitting them and then put a second scale label on the horizontal signifying the serial number n, of the last good piece needed to fill the order for 5000, for each value of n_{ac}/G.

From this we can now construct a table of conveniently grouped values of n, showing the total probabilities for each bracket, and derive the average probability of n per unit width within the bracket. For purposes of illustration, Table 5-12 utilized brackets of 100 (except for the initial bracket), but in practice, much narrower brackets would probably be used for slightly greater precision. The total probability of the bracket is estimated by reading the cumulative probabilities at the left and right edges of the bracket, and subtracting the cumulative probability at the left edge from that at the right edge. The probability per unit width is then simply this total divided by the number of units in the bracket, 100 in this case. Then, using this calculation of P(n) and getting $P(n_{ac} < n)$ by referring to the value at the midpoint of each bracket on Figure 5-6 we can construct our final Table 5-13, giving estimates of the value of our probability ratio for each bracket. From this, we plot the points on semilog paper as in Figure 5-7 and smooth the fitted line.

TABLE 5-12. Estimate of Unit Values of P(n), Using Grouped Data

n-value Bracket	Cumulative Probability at Left Edge	Total Probability of Bracket	Probability Per Unit Width
5890-5999	0	.120	.0011
6000-6999	.121	.094	.00094
6100-6199	.22	.081	.00081
6200-6299	.292	.072	.00072
etc.			

FIGURE 5-7

ESTIMATING CHART FOR DETERMINATION OF Q, GIVEN $\frac{P(n_{ac}=n)}{P(n_{ac}<n)}$

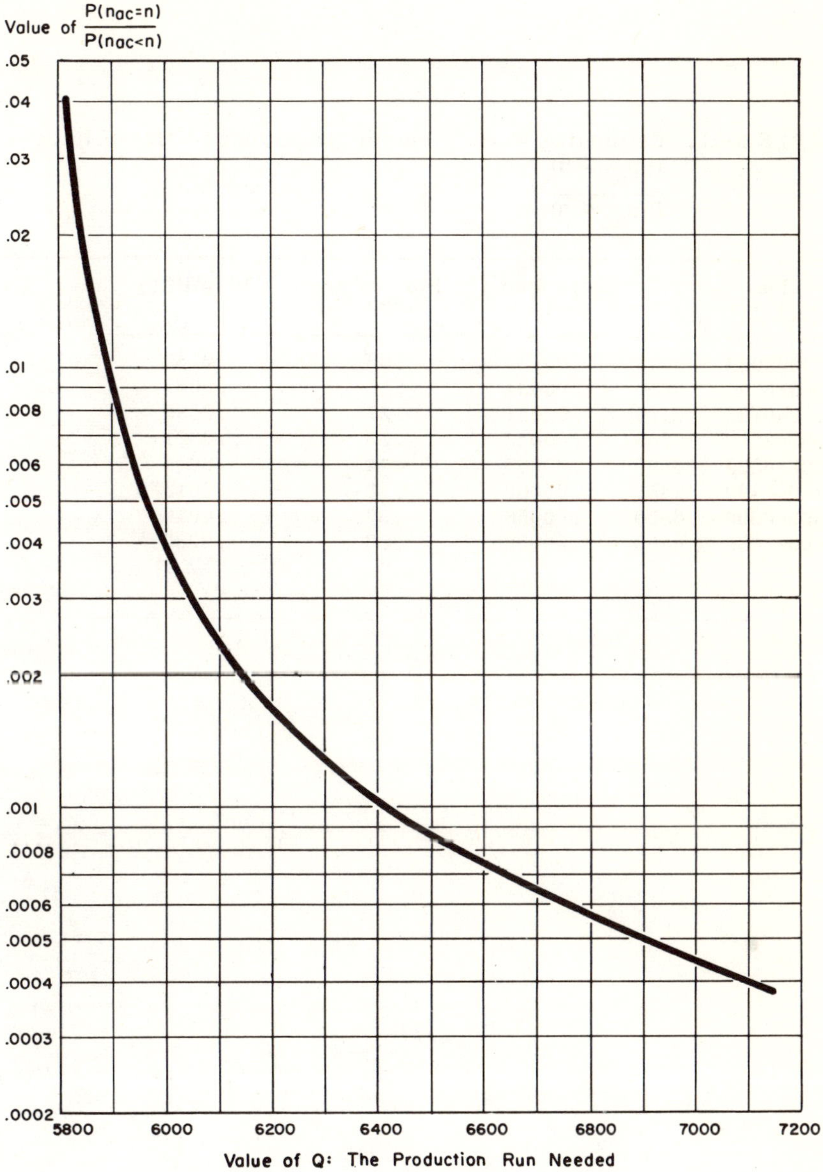

We can now read our optimum value of Q directly from this graph. Recall that for our valve schedule of 5000, the value of $\frac{k}{K}$ was .005. Reading for a value of $\frac{P(n_{ac} = n)}{P(n_{ac} < n)}$ of .005 on our graph we find it equivalent to 6092, the number to be scheduled.

TABLE 5-13. Estimating Work Table for Determining Value of Ratio $\frac{P(n_{ac} = n)}{P(n_{ac} < n)}$

n-value Bracket	n	Estimated P(n)	$P(n_{ac} < n)$	P(=)/P(<)
5890-5999	5945	.0011	.06	.018
6000-6099	6050	.00094	.18	.0052
6100-6199	6150	.00081	.27	,0030
6200-6299	6250	.00072	.35	.0021
6300-6399	6350	.00065	.44	.0015
6400-6499	6450	.00060	.50	.0012
6500-6599	6550	.00056	.56	.0010
6600-6699	6650	.000525	.63	.0083
etc.				

SUMMARY

1. Bayesian analysis furnished a method of dealing objectively with the quantitative side of subjective judgments and of spelling out the implications of what we deem to be the probabilities for profit expectations. Four very useful Bayesian decision tools are: sequential decision theory, competitive bidding strategy, the inventory model, and the production run and scrap loss model.

2. Sequential decision theory helps us reduce, to an objective statement of comparable present values, each of the decision paths in a situation in which some of the action alternatives lead to the need to make further choices in series of chains of unequal lengths and probability composition.

3. Competitive bidding strategy uses the kind of background experience normally considered in a subjective manner in any competitive bidding situation, to arrive at an objectively stated estimate of the probability of winning at any given bid level, and the consequent profit position value of any given bid.

4. The inventory model helps us minimize costs in any logistics situation in which , (a) there is a lag between ordering an input and having that input available, (b) the usage during this lead-time is not completely predictable, (c) there are fixed costs associated with each acquisition of an input, and (d) there are variable costs associated with any discrepancies between the amount available for use during the lead-time and the amount needed. The model is more widely useful than the label indicates, important as physical inventory problems can be.

5. The production run and scrap loss model is a helpful solution, using graphic methods, for any situation in which the cost of an overage is proportional to its size, but in which an underage of any amount results in a given substantial lump-sum loss.

GLOSSARY OF BAYESIAN MODEL TERMS

SEQUENTIAL DECISION: a decision which can result in the need for additional decisions rather than in a definite outcome for all of the acts.

Profit position of a decision sequence: the final profit which would be realized if every act in the chain of decisions has a favorable outcome, discounted by the cumulative probability of that favorable outcome.

Risk affordability: the ability, psychological and physical, of the decision maker to withstand the kinds of losses inherent in the risks to be taken.

Utility of a profit return: the marginal value which a decision maker might attach to the profit he would realize if successful.

COMPETITIVE BIDDING STRATEGY: an approach to estimating the worth, the profit position, to a potential bidder of each of the bids he might make on a specific contract, given his assessment of the past history of competitor bidding and of the current interest of the industry in this particular contract.

INVENTORY MODEL: an approach to estimating the least cost rule for input action in a system of repeated batch inputs with an appreciable time lag between the act of ordering the inputs and their availability for use, and with uncertainty concerning the output demand during this lead time. The model requires that there be substantial fixed costs associated with the input act, regardless of size of input, and that costs be variable for any shortages or overages resulting from the prescribed input. Applies to any situation meeting these conditions, not just inventory problems.

Cost of acquisition: all costs other than the cost of the items themselves, associated with the input act itself. In the case of an actual inventory problem, this would be such costs as the cost of preparing orders, receiving goods, putting them in stock, and the like.

Cost of carrying inventory: all of the costs associated with maintaining the availability of an input until it is needed as an output. In the case of a physical inventory, the financial cost of carrying the goods, cost of warehouse space, deterioration in value during storage, and the like.

Lead-time and demand during lead-time: lead-time is the time which elapses between the initiation of an act of acquisition of an input and the time such inputs become available as potential outputs. Demand during lead-time is the potential need for output during this lead-time, the potential usage for the items of input.

Order quantity (Q): the quantity to be ordered under the rule as calculated.

Reorder point (R): the stock level (level of available outputs) at which an input acquisition act is to be initiated (an order to be placed).

Stockout cost: the loss associated with the unavailability of an output item would be composed of any opportunity losses from missed sales, for example, plus other costs such as loss of customer goodwill.

PRODUCTION RUN AND SCRAP LOSS MODEL: An approach for the estimation of the least cost rule for scheduling acquisition in any situation in which exact useful output to be obtained is uncertain, there are substantial fixed costs associated with the initiation of the act of acquisition, variable costs associated with any resulting overages, but lump sum fixed costs associated with an underage of any size.

CHAPTER 6: FOUR MATRIX DECISION MODELS

A new form of algebraic notation, matrix algebra, is the main common element of four quite different mathematical decision models of differing degrees of utility. These four are game theory, linear programming, and two kinds of Markov chains--absorbing and nonabsorbing. While an appreciation of the values of these tools really does not require familiarity with matrix algebra, a brief note on the nature of this modern form of notation is worth some passing attention.

Matrix Algebra

Matrix algebra is not a different branch of mathematics but simply a different form of notation made useful by wide dependence on the digital computer for lengthy and sometimes complex calculations. In matrix notation, the coefficients in our mathematical expressions are listed in tabular form, separated from the variables they modify. Traditional notation couples the coefficient with the variable to which it applies--$10x + 3y$, for instance, placing the coefficient 10 adjacent to the variable x. In matrix notation, the coefficients alone are listed in rows, and the variables which they modify are indicated separately, to one side in a particular format. A matrix is merely one particular form of table similar to those we constantly use in summarizing numerical data, and in which we also separate the coefficients from the variables to which they apply.

Assume, for example, that we are showing the September sales records of the three salesmen in the Metropolis District of the Industrial Fastener Corp. Industrial has only three classes of products, bolts at \$1.50 per gross, nuts at \$1.00 per gross, and rivets at \$.75 per gross. We would usually summarize the monthly unit sales in some such form as:

TABLE 6-1. September Sales For District 9

Item (gross)	Jim	Joe	Jerry
Bolts	9,372	10,169	8,791
Nuts	7,867	11,243	13,319
Rivets	12,289	3,918	7,913

We would be somewhat astonished if our statistician gave us the table in the same form we have always used for our algebra:

TABLE 6-2. September Sales for District 9

Jim =		Joe =		Jerry =
9,372 gross bolts	+	10,169 gross bolts	+	8,791 gross bolts
7,867 gross nuts	+	11,243 gross nuts	+	13,391 gross nuts
12,289 gross rivets	+	3,918 gross rivets	+	7,913 gross rivets

We would consider the repetition of the item labels (bolts, nuts, and rivets) as superfluous, and mathematicians have come to feel that this does not make sense when those labels are the symbols of algebra. Matrix notation format differs slightly from Table 6-1, and it uses terms which could be unfamiliar. The term vector, for example, denotes any single collection of numbers or symbols written either in a row or in a column. The number or symbol is itself called a component. A combination of row vectors or column vectors in a specific tabular form is called a matrix. Examples of row vectors are:

$$(1,\ -3,\ 5) \qquad\qquad (x,\ y,\ z,\ -k)$$

If arranged vertically instead of horizontally, these same components would be in the form of column vectors:

$$\begin{pmatrix} 1 \\ -3 \\ 5 \end{pmatrix} \qquad\qquad \begin{pmatrix} x \\ y \\ z \\ -k \end{pmatrix}$$

A series of equations is represented as a matrix of their coefficients, with the variables listed as a row vector to the left to designate the label variables in the column. Thus if written in the form of matrix notation, Table 6-1 would look like:

$$(\text{bolts, nuts, rivets}) \qquad \begin{vmatrix} 9,372 & 10,169 & 8,791 \\ 7,867 & 11,243 & 13,319 \\ 12,289 & 3,918 & 7,913 \end{vmatrix}$$

If we were to put this in the form of instructions for getting the dollar value of the sales of each salesman, it would be shown as follows:

$$(1.50,\ 1.00,\ .75) \qquad \begin{vmatrix} 9,372 & 10,169 & 8,791 \\ 7,867 & 11,243 & 13,319 \\ 12,289 & 3,918 & 7,913 \end{vmatrix}$$

leading to the following result:

$$\begin{vmatrix} 14,058 & 15,253 & 13,186 \\ 7,867 & 11,243 & 13,319 \\ 9,173 & 2,939 & 5,935 \end{vmatrix}$$

If, in addition, the bonus commission rates differed, with Jim receiving

12%, Joe 10%, and Jerry 11%, instructions for computing the commission rates for each class of product sold would be shown as follows, with a column vector listing the amounts by which successive columns would be multiplied:

$$\begin{vmatrix} 14,058 & 15,253 & 13,186 \\ 7,867 & 11,243 & 13,319 \\ 9,173 & 2,939 & 5,935 \end{vmatrix} \begin{pmatrix} .12 \\ .10 \\ .11 \end{pmatrix}$$

This would be read as instructions to obtain the total commissions on bolts by solving the expression:

$$(14,058 \times .12) + (15,253 \times .10) + (13,186 \times .11)$$

and similarly for the other two rows, giving commission payouts on nuts and rivets. Note that the symbol + is always understood unless a minus sign is indicated.

Convenience of use in computer input is the main reason for matrix notation. The tedium of the necessary computation involved in each of the four tools to be discussed in this chapter usually requires access to a computer.

Game theory notation clearly illustrates the tabular nature of a matrix, and makes a good starting point. This tool has been touted so widely that we need to understand the limitations which have disappointed the hopes that were aroused.

The Theory of Games: Forestalling the Moves of a Competitor

Game theory has had such useful application to strategic military thinking that high hopes have been held for adapting it to competitive business decision. But military conflict is a much simpler type of confrontation than the differentiated competition of business enterprises. The hopes have not been fulfilled, and any expectation that game theory will ever play a major role in the business decision process seems to be wishful thinking. Thus two expert sources have concluded that the theory contains too much simplification for business use:

"It is not surprising that the 13 years that have elapsed since the publication of The Theory of Games have seen no important applications of game theory to concrete economic problems."*

(With reference to nonzero-sum games and proposed solutions:) "The fact that none (of these various solutions) fits every conceivable nonzero-sum game is perhaps an indication that such games do not reveal enough of the richness of real-world situations to provide universally satisfactory answers."**

*Robert Dorfman et al., Linear Programming and Economic Analysis, McGraw-Hill (New York, 1958) p. 445.

**Kemeny, et al., Finite Mathematics With Business Applications, Prentice-Hall (Englewood Cliffs, N.J., 1962) pp. 461-462.

At least one problem is the very necessary simplification which the use of numbers themselves entails. Although a real source of strength in the normal use of mathematical models, this very simplification becomes a fatal weakness in attempts to estimate the outcome of complex multidirectional competition characteristic of the marketplace.

Nevertheless, the game theory approach does yield qualitative insights into the incentives leading to such various business phenomena as cartels and other coalitions, price leadership, and the emphasis on so-called "nonprice competition" more properly designated as product and promotion competition (see the author's Economics of Managerial Decision, Appleton-Century-Crofts, 1965). Game models do indicate the kinds of rational decisions managers will arrive at in the absence of knowledge of a competitor's plans, and the pressures that may exist to soften competition.

Basically, there are three types of game structures:

1. zero-sum, strictly determined games
2. zero-sum, nonstrictly determined games
3. nonzero-sum games.

Definite solutions exist only for the first category--zero-sum, strictly determined games--and then only when limited to two players in direct conflict, or to a multiplayer game reduced in essence to a two-player game by coalitions. Workable probabilistic solutions exist for two-person zero-sum, nonstrictly determined games. For the nonzero-sum game, even when limited to two persons, no satisfactory general solutions have been developed. Regardless of game type, no really satisfactory solutions have been developed for games of more than two persons.

The Two-Person, Zero-Sum, Strictly-Determined Game

A two-person zero-sum game is one limited to two players, and one in which the gains of one just offset the losses of the other. Let us consider the simplest form of such a game in terms of two players. Max Row (R) and Min Column (C). Each has two cards: R has a red 7 and a black 7, C a black 7 and a red 5. The rules of their game call for both to expose one of their cards on an agreed upon signal. If the cards match in color, R wins by any amount by which his card is higher than that of C. If R does not match the color of C's card, then C wins by the amount of the difference in the card values. The game can be represented by the payoff table (matrix) for either one of the players. In this case we will use R's table and look at it on the assumption that Max Row is trying to maximize his gain, and Min Column's aim would therefore be, from this representation of R's table, to minimize his losses. A positive entry means a gain for R and a loss for C; a negative entry, a loss for R, and a gain for C. (If we were to look at it from the standpoint of C's payoff table, the values would be reversed.) Conventionally, R, the maximizing player's strategies are represented by the horizontal row strategies (thus R for Row), and the minimizing players (since this is not his table), by the vertical columns (thus C for Column). Thus if R chooses to expose his black 7 and C turns up his black 7, then R matches, but wins nothing, while if C turns up his red 5 instead, R loses 2, and

		Player C plays	
		Black 7	Red 5
Player R plays	Black 7	0	-2
	Red 7	0	2

thus our table shows a -2 for this event. Obviously, then R would not pick the strategy of turning up his black 7, but expose his red 7 instead. In the latter case, he might still not win anything if C chooses to turn up his black 7, but could win 2 if C exposes his red 5. C, on the other hand, hoping to keep his possible losses down, will choose to expose his black 7, since he will never lose if he does, whereas he can lose 2 if he turns up his red 5 and R chooses to expose his red 7. Thus in this game, there is one clear strategy for each player, one play he would always choose to come out best. R should always play his red 7, since he can thus make certain he never loses, and has a chance to gain the maximum amount. His <u>optimum strategy</u> is thus: play red 7. C will always play black 7, since this way, he achieves his aim of minimum losses: he can never lose (and never win either). His optimum strategy for minimizing losses is thus: play black 7. This particular game is also a <u>fair</u> game, so-called because neither player has either a net gain or a net loss if both play their optimum strategies. The <u>value of this game</u> (<u>v</u>), is zero, since this is the best either player can make sure of winning. If one of them could assure himself of any particular gain--say 2-- then the value of the game would be 2, and the player who could assure himself of that much should pay an entry fee of 2 to get in, if the play is to be fair.

This is a <u>strictly determined game</u> because there is one entry in the matrix, the value designated above as <u>v</u>, which is at one and the same time the <u>minimum</u>

for the row designating a strategy of the row, or maximizing, player, and the maximum of the strategy for a column, or minimizing, player.

The table by which we have represented this game is a conventionalized table of gain and loss values for the row (R) player, the one who is viewed as on the offensive (in military terms), or as trying to maximize his gains (in economic language). Each row in the table represents one of his possible strategies by listing the contingent values for each of the defensive strategies of the column (C) player. The latter is assumed to be trying to minimize his losses. The table above has been couched in terms of a specific card gamble, but is really a generalized representation for any situation in which the respective gains and losses for two opponents have the same relative values listed. The situation could be some other kind of gambling game, in which the figures stand for money gains and losses, a military skirmish in which gains might be casualties, or amount of territory gains, or some other strategic objectives. Or, if we could find such an uncomplicated business situation, the values could be business profits and losses, or market share gains and losses of two opponents with identical products seeking the identical market segment, one seeking to take over, the other to hold his position.

We need only the bare bones of the matrix itself to represent any two-person, zero-sum, straight-conflict situation, since each horizontal row is always understood to represent all possible value outcomes of one alternative strategy of the maximizing player (R) and each vertical column represents the results for R of each of the counter strategies of the opposing minimizing player (C, for column). Like all symbolic abstractions, this convention enables us to strip down and analyse the essentials of the gains and losses involved without concerning ourselves with the details of any given situation (such as the rules of the game) which result in the listed values, or to invent some simplified gambling situation to fit the results.

A conflict situation can be strictly determined without being fair, both in the casino and in textbooks. Any game in which one player can assure himself of a consistent profit is a zero-sum game if the losses of one are equal to the gains of his opponent. The following matrix represents such a game:

		C: Strategy C_1	C: Strategy C_2
R	Strategy R_1	9	6
	Strategy R_2	-8	-4

Given the knowledge that this is the situation, R will always play strategy R_1, since he will always win whatever C does: 9 if C plays strategy C_1 and 6 if C plays strategy C_2. C, on the other hand, since his objective is to minimize his losses, will always play strategy C_2, since he can lose only 6 this way, whereas with strategy C_1 he could lose 9. The value of this game is thus 6, and it can only be made fair by means of a compensating side payment of R to C to enter the game.

Nonstrictly Determined, Two-Person Zero-Sum Games

The strictly-determined game has little practical value except as a method of introducing the general principal of game analysis. No one knowingly enters conflict when the outcome is so foreordained. Conflict of any sort usually arises only when both opponents feel there is some uncertainty about the outcome of a given confrontation, and each believes that under some possible moves of his opponent, he can hope to win. When the proper choice of the move hinges on knowing the specific move of the opponent, the game is nonstrictly determined, even if it is also zero-sum. Consider the matrix:

		C: Strategy C_1	C: Strategy C_2
R	Strategy R_1	0	4
	Strategy R_2	6	0

If R plays his bottom row strategy, R_2, he can maximize his gains only if he can know that C will certainly play his left-hand column strategy, C_1. But C would do better, if he plays the right-hand column strategy, C_2, since the maximum possible loss is less in this column. If R foresees that C will play C_2, he would play R_1 to win 4. But if C were to know or guess this would be R's move, he would choose strategy C_1 and come out even. Thus any move either makes depends on his knowledge or estimate of the likely move of the other, and this move is uncertain on both sides.

Note that in the strictly determined games previously discussed, any move made by an opponent could be determined from the structure of the game, and the knowledge of his objectives (to maximize or to minimize). But in the nonstrictly determined game as above, any player needs advance knowledge of the opponent's immediate intentions to determine his best strategy. And knowledge of your own intended play by your opponent can enable him to defeat your hopes.

Thus your own play must not be consistent, or the opponent will know what that strategy is. So the optimum strategy would have to be some kind of inconsistent one which would leave the opponent guessing, and thus help you win part of the time, at least: a mixed strategy.

A nonstrictly determined game is characterized by the fact that all of the payoff values on one diagonal of the matrix are greater than any of the values on the opposite diagonal. Thus in the matrix just above, both the 6 and the 4 on the one diagonal are greater than the 0's on the other. Put in general terms, if we consider only a simple 2 x 2 matrix such as we have been using (there could be more strategies for each player, and thus a larger matrix), a game is nonstrictly determined if in the matrix.

a	b
c	d

either: $a > b$, $a > c$, $d > b$, and $d > c$

or: $a < b$, $a < c$, $d < b$, and $d < c$

As already indicated, there cannot be a single optimum strategy in such a game, since this permits the opponent to choose an offsetting strategy which can let him deprive you of the maximum gains or saddle you with more than minimum losses. Suppose in the matrix

0	4
6	0

, however, R chooses the top-row strategy four-tenths of the time, and the bottom-row strategy six-tenths of the time, and does so in a completely random manner, so that C never knows what his opponents next move will be, and that C chooses some independent set of mixed strategies, then R can assure himself of some expected value v at the least, depending on C's choice. For each there will be an optimum mixed strategy such that when both play at their optimum, R will get just the expected value, v, and C will also realize v as his minimum loss. If C chooses a strategy with a probability mix of less than the optimum, his losses will be greater than v, and R's gain greater. If C chooses the optimum probability mix, and R does not pick his, then C will lose less, and R gain less, over the long run. For a two-person, two-strategy game (a 2 x 2 matrix) the following five formulas tell what those strategies are, and the value of the game, v; in the matrix

a	b
c	d

with R playing rows 1 and 2 in the ratio $\frac{r_1}{r_2}$ and C playing columns 1 and 2 in ratio $\frac{c_1}{c_2}$:

$$r_1 = \frac{d - c}{a + d - b - c} \qquad r_2 = \frac{a - b}{a + d - b - c}$$

$$c_1 = \frac{d - b}{a + d - b - c} \qquad c_2 = \frac{a - c}{a + d - b - c}$$

$$v = \frac{ad - bc}{a + d - b - c}$$

For larger matrices, the solution is the same calculation as for linear programming, once the problem is expressed in positive numbers, as it can be. The right probability ratio and the inconsistency of individual play sequence are maintained by use of some randomizing device to choose the strategy for each play, such as a table of random numbers.

Nonzero-sum Games and More-Than-Two Person Games

Solutions of the two-person game type have been well-developed both because they yield definite generalized solutions, and because they are applicable to problems of military confrontations. Military showdowns normally tend to become two-sided pure-conflict situations in which what one side gains, the other loses. But business competition is almost never that simple. The number of "players" usually exceeds two, and it is seldom possible to really identify and define the total number of "players." When the number of players is more than two, then competition is not direct conflict, unless coalitions form that reduce the effective number to two. Even when there are only two sides, net losses and net gains are possible to both sides.

Consider a highly simplified situation such as we might have with two gasoline service stations on opposite corners, say the C Oil Co. and R Gas, with just two possible price strategies: a high price strategy, and a low price strategy. Assume also, that no other service stations are close by, and that the total sales possible in any one day are represented by the following matrix in which R's payoff is the first listed, and C's the second in each square. (Note that the payoff must be listed for both in a nonzero-sum game, because they differ in more than just the sign.) Assume that prices must stay at the level fixed when the station opens in the morning, and that fixed costs are the same for both--$20--so that either one loses money if his sales are less than this.

		C prices	
		High	Low
R prices	High	(26,26)	(16,42)
	Low	(42,16)	(17,17)

Note one difference between such a matrix and the payoff matrix for the zero-sum games. In the zero-sum game, all payoffs were of the form that the payoff for C was always the negative of that for R. In the nonzero-sum game, some of the payoffs are not complementary. (In the one used, none of them are.)

Note that we now actually have two different matrixes, R's and C's.

R's =	High	Low
High	26	16
Low	42	17

C's =	High	Low
High	26	16
Low	42	17

Each now has a maximin strategy, defined as any optimal strategy for him in his own payoff matrix. In the case above, R's optimum strategy in his matrix is obviously "quote low price." But C's matrix indicates his is also "quote low price." In this case, both will then end up with a payoff of 17, and be operating at a loss. Unfortunately, this "gas war situation" is also an equilibrium point, defined as a pair of strategies such that neither player can increase his payoff by any strategy change, assuming that his opponent does not change his strategy. Thus, if R were to change to a high price strategy while C stayed with his low quotation, R would reduce his payoff to 16. Similarly, if C switches to a high price strategy while R stays at low, he also reduces his payoff from 17 to 16.

Such is not always the outcome of every nonzero-sum game, as can be demonstrated later. But it is a realistic one in cases in which the product sold is, so far as the consumer is concerned, homogeneous as between competitors. Obviously, such a situation cannot go on indefinitely, for either R or C or both will be bankrupted eventually. If one has stronger financial resources than the other, he might be tempted to let this happen--except that in real life, there are antitrust laws which pose the threat of legal penalties to any large competitor which attempts such a solution. Or they both might continue the "war" until the stronger one feels that the other is tired of it, and raises his price first. If he is right in assuming "price leadership" at the opportune moment, the other follows, to the same high price policy, and both are better off.

But neither will be doing nearly as well as he might with a different strategy, with a low price against the other high price. In addition, the matrix indicates that both together would be somewhat better off--that is, combined sales would be higher--if one had a low price and the other a high price. War having failed, what might they do? They might form a cartel, with one agreeing to stick to the high price segment of the market for a side payment which would make up for the business he would lose, plus a share of the additional combined payoff total of 6 resulting when both follow the high price policy (26 + 26 = 52 as compared with 42 + 16 = 58). Or they might actually merge, and the new company sell under two labels at the two stations: one station with a low price label, the other with a high price label. Or, if one is very much stronger financially than the other, he might enforce a split giving himself the lion's share of the profits of a high-low policy under the threat of pursuing a low price policy until the other went bankrupt. A solution such as this does give us some insight into the forces which give rise to various non-competitive arrangements in business.

There is another type of strategy not reflected in the matrix which is the most common one followed in business--remove the core of the problem, the homogeneity of the product. One station owner may decide to let the other specialize in selling gasoline, at a low price to that part of the market to which price is important. He would go after more business per customer from each one he does reach by offering added services--mechanical work, lubricating services, road conditions information, or other services highly valued by a different market segment. Or he may up his profit margin by differentiating his product in the consumer's mind by intensive, well-planned advertising. Then we no longer have a direct conflict situation, but two stations selling somewhat different products to different market segments, and our game theory is no longer of much help, even in the case of a <u>hardship equilibrium point</u> such as we have hypothesized in the problem above.

Not all nonzero-sum situations lead to hardship equilibrium points. The fact that nearly all business competition is differentiated competition leads to situations in which what looks like competition can often be a direct benefit to both participants, and the maximum strategy leads to the maximum level for both parties. Thus shopping centers have learned that having two department stores in the center will not only increase business for the center, but that both stores will sell more than either would alone. Women's clothing stores nearly always do better if there are at least three in the same shopping district. In such a situation we might have a matrix like this:

		C Store Location 1	C Store Location 2
R Store	Location 1	(33, 31)	(14, 21)
	Location 2	(21, 14)	(20, 26)

In this case, obviously both R and C will chose location 1 by mutual agreement, and this is not the sort of agreement that needs to be hidden from legal view. At other times, both may have somewhat different talents for serving different market segments, and a matrix like the following may result:

		C Mfg. Co. Product Variation 1	C Mfg. Co. Product Variation 2
R Mfg. Co.	Product Var. 1	(26, 20)	(36, 31)
	Product Var. 2	(21, 14)	(20, 26)

In this case, each participant's matrix leads to a maximin strategy that is the same no matter what the other does: R will make the product variation 1 which one market segment desires, and C will make product variation 2, at which he is better, and which has a good demand in a different market segment. The result will be a payoff of 36 for R, and 31 for C.

Thus some nonzero-sum games have profitable equilibrium points, and others do not. Those that do not must have solutions outside the terms of the calculations. Or there may be more than one equilibrium point. Thus, game theory provides some qualitative insight into the general direction in which competitive forces may push business action. But the alternatives lie in so many directions (collusion, market leadership, product differentiation of several kinds, etc.) that general solutions are not likely to be formulated for the really critical situations, nor the calculations to give precise answers on the correct strategies.

Linear Programming: Striking The Right Proportions

In linear programming, the operating side of business has gained an invaluable tool for use in those situations in which the problem is to find the least costly mix of alternate components or the most profitably proportioned output mix from limited resources. All of the various kinds of problems that may be solved with linear programming have four elements in common:

1. We have a limited number of resources and of choices, and we wish to sustain the least input cost or obtain the most valuable output mix. (The goal of minimum cost or maximum profit is sometimes referred to as the objective function.)

2. There are certain restraints on the choices we can make--certain conditions of "not more than" or "not less than." A general one for all linear programming problems is that all inputs and outputs must be nonnegative (that is, they must either be positive in value, or zero).

3. Within limits we are free to vary the proportions of components in such a way as to satisfy the restraints and arrive at an optimum (maximum or minimum) solution or solutions. (There may be more than one solution.) The quantities we proportion are sometimes referred to as the choice variables.

4. Restraints are, or can, be expressed as linear (straight-line) equations and the objective function can be attained by direct (or linear) proportioning of the choice variables, or by some mathematical transformation of them into linear form. A linear equation has the general mathematical form $y = ax + b$, where a and b are constants.

Most operating relationships and requirements are linear in form.* Within plant or shift capacity limits, variable production costs tend to be linear, and so do many price-quantity relationships within the narrow range open to decision. Many decision requirements are in the form of linear restraints, the stipulation that they be "at least" or "no more than."

Even when the relationship itself is not linear, transformation into linear form is often easy. Relationships characterized by a constant percentage change--exponential relationships--become linear when expressed in logarithms. Total production cost, including both the fixed and variable components, is hyperbolic in form: $y = 1/x + c$ in its simplest form. By substituting $z = 1/x$, and maximiz-

* The discussion of method which follows is adapted from Chester R. Wasson, The Economics of Managerial Decision, Appleton-Century-Crofts, New York, 1965, pp. 211-213.

ing z, we can minimize x. Such usable tricks are familiar to anyone with even a moderate training in mathematics. For a broad range of middle management decisions, data from repetitive operations is usually available for linear programming of extremal points, by setting the relationships up as a series of simultaneous equations which can be solved by the simplex method. This latter is a version of the method we learned in high school, except that in linear programming we usually do not have enough equations to solve for every variable and must resort to a tedious cut-and-try approach on a computer. The basic principle can be illustrated with a highly simplified textbook example.*

The maker of both passenger cars and trucks has a factory divided into two shops: (1) Assembly Shop 1, which requires 5 man-days for a truck and 2 man-days for each passenger vehicle, and (2) Shop 2, which does the finishing at the rate of 3 man-days per vehicle, whether passenger car or truck. Shop 1 uses 180 man-days per week at capacity operation, Shop 2, 135 man-days per week. Profit on each truck completed is $300, on each passenger car $200. To maximize operating profit, what mix of trucks and passenger cars should be scheduled?

In mathematical notation, the problem is stated as follows:

Let x_1 = no. of trucks built, x_2 = no. of cars

Then the values of x_1 and x_2 must satisfy the following conditions:

$$5x_1 + 2x_2 \leq 180$$

$$\text{and } 3x_1 + 3x_2 \leq 135$$

Subject to the restrictions that $300x_1 + 200x_2$ has at least one real value and $x_1 \leq 0 \leq x_2$ (that is, that some cars and/or trucks will be built)

Every possible solution to the problem as thus defined lies in the shaded area of the graph in Figure 6-1, on which all of the conditions laid down appear as straight lines. Not all of the infinity of points within this area are at a maximum, of course, and in this case, only one is. The maximum can only be located by comparing all of the points which could be at the maximum profit. Fortunately, we need to consider only those points at the intersection of the lines, as indicated. Were there not some such limit on the number of solutions, even a computer would be useless--the number of possible solution points is truly infinite.

---

* Adapted from Kemeny, Schleifer, Snell, and Thompson, Finite Mathematics with Business Applications (Englewood Cliffs, N.J.: Prentice-Hall, Inc., 1962), pp. 379-380.

Figure 6-1. Graphic Representation of Truck-Car Production Problem

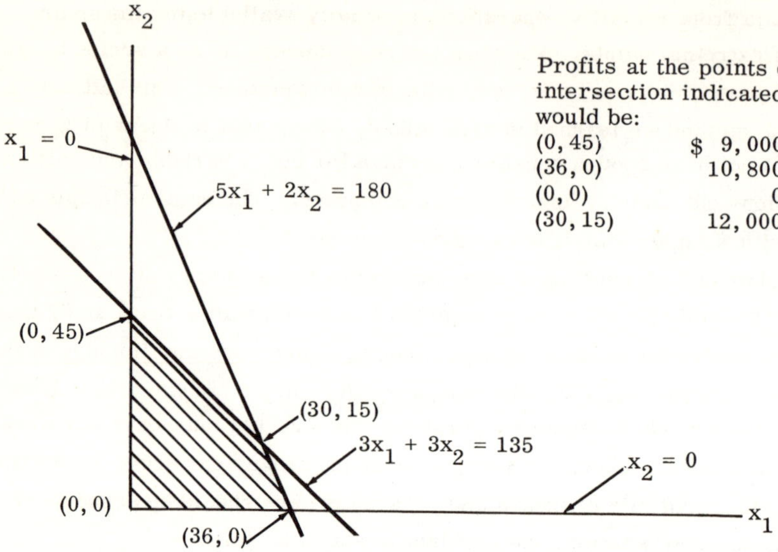

Profits at the points of intersection indicated would be:

(0, 45)	\$ 9,000
(36, 0)	10,800
(0, 0)	0
(30, 15)	12,000 = Max.

(All possible solutions lie within the shaded area and its boundaries.)

Not all such problems are soluble; sometimes the conditions are incompatible. Sometimes there are two or more solutions meeting all conditions equally, and management will make a choice between them on some other basis.

Linear programming applications are many and varied, because the allocation of scarce resources to get maximum profit is at the heart of all business operations decisions. Indeed, one form was developed before the computer was invented or the general linear programming algorithm discovered. This was the transportation model, originally so designated because its first uses were to find the best shipping plan from a series of points to different receiving points, with differing shipping costs from each shipping point. Certain universal simplicities in this type of problem permit calculation by hand. Though the name transportation model still persists, some of its more useful applications are not concerned with transportation or transportation costs. The model is applicable to any business or economic problem in which we seek a minimum or maximum of some resultant allocation of the inputs subject to restraints on both inputs and outputs. It is, for example, of value in determining the best disposition of a military force or in any other assignment of a limited number of skilled personnel of various abilities to varied responsibilities, provided we can arrive at some measure of individual output value. Or it can be used to determine the assignment of various kinds of competing machines or other capital equipment to an assortment of scheduled jobs, to minimize time, or costs, or some other relevant measure.

The typical transportation problem starts with limits on the inputs of each component, such as the capacity of the individual factories out of which shipments are being made. These limited inputs are usually completely used up to meet and just satisfy numerically limited outputs, such as shipments to designated localities. There are effective restraints on both the inputs and the outputs.

In general, however, linear programming requires only that there be restraints on one or the other, either on the inputs or on the outputs. In one typical linear programming model, the so-called diet, or feed-mix problem, the restraint is on input cost, not quantity. In the kind of problem from which this model takes its name, the aim is to produce a diet meeting certain minimum standards of nutritive composition (protein, fat, carbohydrate, vitamins, minerals, etc.) at least cost, given a set of ingredients containing various proportions of the elements. All "diet" problems are not feed cost problems. Any problem of allocating a freely available output to get a minimum cost can be a diet model problem, so long as the proportions can be combined linearly. The production of a mixed fertilizer fits the model.

In other cases, there may be no effective quantitative restraints on the output, only the objective of getting the most profitable mix within broad limits of proportionality. Oil refinery product mix has been one important application. Processing of the crude oil and other feedstock elements can be so regulated as to yield varying quantities of gasoline, kerosene, diesel fuel, heavy fuel oil, lubricating oils, etc. All of the products can be disposed of at some price, but the price and profit per unit of input will vary between products, and the yield will vary depending on the mix.

Although there is no published account of using linear programming to allocate shelf space in a store, the problem of maximizing profitability of the merchandise mix would seem to be identical, up to a point at least, with that of optimizing the output of an oil refinery. One recent interesting application of linear programming is the development of optimum operating plans for individual farms, given a known mix of land types and capital equipment.

Not all allocation problems can be solved by linear programming, however. After considerable experimentation, the Young and Rubicam advertising agency decided that the optimum decision rules for allocating an advertising campaign between media did not fit the requirements for linear programming and developed a different computer model which did seem to be of value.*

Markov Chain Analysis: Predicting the Outcome of a Dynamic Situation

Most mathematical models postulate a relatively stable set of relationships. Markov chains (or Markov processes), by contrast, are useful only when we can assume some underlying force for changes in the relationships between some sets of universes. A fictional example will illustrate the nature of the two kinds of Markov chains--absorbing and nonabsorbing, of which the nonabsorbing is the simpler.

Consider the mythical Republic of Rurbania (ROR), a country in which, for the moment, no one dies and no babies are born. The population of ROR, however, is not static--there is a constant two-way flow of migrants between city and the country, as can be seen from the following table:

Residence type at the beginning of the year	Percentage distribution of the same people at year's-end: City	Rural
City	90	10
Rural	30	70

This cross-migratory flow goes on year after year, continuously altering the rural-urban balance until some equilibrium point is reached--a point at which 10% of the city population just equals in number the 30% it gains from the rural-to-city flow, and the residential composition is in dynamic balance.

In Markov language, the table above would be labelled a matrix of transitional underlying probabilities. "Residence type at beginning of the year" denotes the previous state of nature (whether city residence or rural in this case). "Residence at year's-end" is the succeeding state of nature. The equilibrium point at which the process will come into dynamic balance (in this case, at the point of 75% city) is known as the fixed point.

All of the states of nature in the above example were nonabsorbing. That is, all were reversible. Those who moved to the country did not necessarily remain, nor did those moving to the city. We need merely bow to the reality of death,

*William T. Moran, "Practical Media Decisions and the Computer," Journal of Marketing, Vol. 27, No. 3 (July, 1963), pp. 26-30.

however, to convert our ROR example to an illustration of an absorbing chain--of a chain containing one or more states of nature, transition into which is not reversible. Death, of course, is not the only irreversible state in life. Graduation is an absorbing state in a study of school populations, completion of the transaction and bagging of groceries in a supermarket check-out line, etc. Because of this absorbing state, the fixed point of any absorbing chain is zero for all nonabsorbing states. Clearly, the potential values of the two types of Markovian analysis differ. The widest-spread use of the nonabsorbing chain has probably been in the analysis of brand-switching.

Where Are We Heading? The Nonabsorbing Markov Chain*

Consider our problem as members of the marketing team of Blue Sky Detergents who are evaluating the effects of our introduction of a new special duty detergent, Orion, formulated to capture parts of the market segments of two established brands, Castor and Pollux. We put Orion into test markets three months ago, with suitable promotional fanfare, and simultaneously commissioned the tabulations of a consumer purchase diary panel to be able to follow consumer buying of ours and competing products. We have met to discuss the significance of the tabulations drawn from the panel purchases in the second and third months and to see if we can divine how well we are doing. Our research analyst informs us we had 18.5 percent of the market in the third month, as compared with 43 percent for Castor and 39.5 percent for Pollux. He interprets the panel data to mean we are going to get an even larger share of the market. The tabulations, he points out, indicate that we hang onto more initial users than either Castor or Pollux do, and gain a larger share of their previous users than they get back from us.

TABLE 6-3. Brand-Switching Pattern During Third Month After Introduction of Orion Brand into the Subopolis Test Market. (The numbers denote the fraction of those who were purchasers of the brand listed to the left during the second month.)

Brand bought during the second month	Brand purchased during the third month: Castor	Pollux	Orion
Castor	.57	.15	.28
Pollux	.15	.52	.33
Orion	.17	.16	.67

* The illustration which follows has been borrowed from Chester R. Wasson, The Economics of Managerial Decision, Appleton-Century-Crofts, (New York, 1965) pp. 46-48.

It certainly seems to us that the analyst is right, and that we have indeed a detergent whose characteristics do meet, better than either of the competing brands, the desires of a substantial segment of the market they have been getting. But we would like a more specific fix on how big that segment is. It certainly looks like better than one-fifth, but how much better? Just looking at the table as is, it is pretty hard to tell.

But suppose we look at this table as a transitional probability matrix, as an estimate of what the brand-switching pattern in any one month may be, at least as long as there is no change in competitor's products or in their sales promotion elements. The first state of nature is then the brand purchased during the second month, the succeeding state of nature is the brand purchased during the third month, and the fixed point we calculate from this matrix tells us our ultimate market share for Orion. The calculation itself is not very intricate, but, for a 3 x 3 table such as this, could involve quite a few steps. However, we can simplify the problem by not concerning ourselves with how the segments we do not snare divide up between Castor and Pollux.

We therefore revamp our tabulation into a simpler 2 x 2 table as follows:

TABLE 6-4. Simplified Brand-Switching Pattern

Purchases in second month	Purchases in third month	
	Orion	Not-Orion
Orion	.67	.33
Not-Orion	.30	.70

Viewed as a transition matrix, each line is viewed as the coefficients of two variables, standing for Orion and Not-Orion, and we make use of the known properties of transition probability matrices that are nonabsorbing: As the process proceeds through successive time periods, it approaches (and usually rather quickly) a limiting value we call a fixed point. This can be demonstrated empirically by trying these switching percentages out over several periods, from any starting point of quantities. At this fixed point, the customers being gained by switching from other brands just compensate for the number of customers being lost to other brands.

The calculation of this simpler 2 x 2 table in terms of traditional algebraic notation is possible if we let:

$\underline{x}$ be the Orion market share

$\underline{y}$ be the Not-Orion market share

We then solve for two conditions which must hold at the point of equilibrium:

(1) The Orion and Not-Orion market shares together comprise the whole market, or

$$x + y = 1$$

(2) The number of Orion purchasers lost to Not-Orion just equals the number of Not-Orion purchasers switching to Orion, or

$$.33\underline{x} = .30\underline{y}$$

and thus

$$\frac{.33}{.30}\underline{x} = \underline{y} = \frac{11}{10}\underline{x}$$

Substituting this value of $\underline{y}$ in the first equation gives:

$$x = \frac{11}{10}\underline{x} = 1 = \frac{21}{10}\underline{x}$$

and thus

$$21\underline{x} = 10$$

$$\underline{x} = \frac{10}{21}$$

Since

$$\underline{x} + \underline{y} = 1$$

then

$$\underline{y} = 1 - \underline{x} - \frac{11}{21}$$

Hence our table of brand-switching during the third month implies that Orion will get about 10/21 of the market. Exactly 10/21? Probably not. For a number of reasons, our data for the third month is not a precise estimate of the actual transition probabilities. And we probably cannot assume that the makers of Castor and Pollux are going to stand still as Orion threatens to take over a large part of their market shares. But as of now, we have a product capable of sustaining a differential advantage for perhaps between 40 percent and 60 percent of the market, and can lay out future strategy on this basis.

Note that in none of this calculation were we concerned with what the current market share was. All we needed to know was the estimate of the percentages of brand loyalty and switching, i.e., the transitional probability matrix. The Markov chain might well be dubbed the rumor-mill model. The final result is solely dependent on the built-in bias toward change and is unaffected by state of origin.

The nonabsorbing Markov chain would be a useful but rather specialized model to know if brand-switching problems were its only use. But it would seem a useful technique to determine the possibility of changes that might be taking place in underlying probabilities of other sorts, e.g., changes in the trend in public taste and fashion, whether they concern clothing, automobile designs, or forms of investment. Any change in basic trend would show up as a significant change in the fixed point.

What Are The Implications of The Dynamics? The Absorbing Chain

In our brand-switching problem, no transition was irreversible. None of the detergents was so completely preferred that none of the users, once they tried it, might not go back to some other brand. The situation simply shifted until a point was reached at which the shifting and shifting back cancelled out.* But there are various kinds of changes over time in business and elsewhere in which some of the states are absorbing. Once the change reaches one of these states, there is no reversal. Consider, for instance, the following table, showing the experience of a hypothetical trailer rental agency operating in three cities: A, B, and C. While the majority of the rentals are for local use, trailers are rented on a one-way basis and thus may start in any one of the three cities and end up in any other of the three. But trailers may come to another kind of end, too: They may be stolen or wrecked. Such trailers never return; they reach an absorbing state, as shown in the following table giving a typical month's experience:

TABLE 6-5. Starting Point and Destination of Drivuron Trailers Rented During the Month

(In percentages of those from the designated origin)

Place of Origin	Terminal City or Condition A	B	C	Lost or Wrecked (L)
A	58	20	19	3
B	18	63	15	4
C	13	21	62	1
Lost, wrecked(L)	0	0	0	100

* The illustration which follows has been borrowed from Chester R. Wasson, The Economics of Managerial Decision, Appleton-Century-Crofts, New York, 1965, pp. 214-17.

Computational Format

	L	A	B	C
L	1	0	0	0
A	.03	.58	.20	.19
B	.04	.18	.63	.15
C	.01	.13	.21	.62

If we change the percentages to decimals, we have a table of transition probabilities, or a Markov matrix, with one absorbing state, lost or wrecked. If no new trailers are purchased, we need no computer to calculate the end result: all trailers will finally end up lost or wrecked. If we had more than one absorbing state--if, for example, trailers were sold on reaching a certain point of service or dilapidation--we would have to make a calculation to determine how many would end up in each of the absorbing states.

But our principal interest is likely to be in the answers to some different questions:

1. How long, on the average, will it be before the process is absorbed? In terms of our illustration, how long will a trailer be in service, on the average?

2. How many periods of time will the process be in each nonabsorbing state? That is, how many months is a trailer likely to be in each of the cities during its term of service?

3. How much input is needed to stabilize the process at some desired point of equilibrium? How many trailers must we buy each month to hold the stock at the current level?

4. At what points in the process should the input be injected to hold the process in some form of desired balance? In this case, where should we have new trailers shipped to start their service, A, B, or C, and in what proportion? If we look at the original table, we can see that A loses more to B and C than it gets back from either. Likewise, C ships more to B than it gets in return.

The answers to each of these questions comes from a different calculation, but one that follows a generalized standard and is a simple computer program. Even for a highly simplified illustration such as the one given, the tedium of calculation requires a computer, and even a short explanation of the process requires use of matrix notation. Those who are familiar with this form of mathematical symbolism, will find an explanation of nonabsorbing chains and some uses in Kemeny, et al., Finite Mathematics with Business Applications (Prentice-Hall, Inc., 1962), pages 282-298.

In other types of problems, other questions would be asked, and a calculable answer would be available. For example, one whole branch of Markov analysis deals with waiting-line, or queuing problems. The line at the supermarket can fluctuate erratically in length. The states of nature of interest to the store management would be the various possible lengths of line, and the units of time measurement would be the smallest interval of time in which at least one customer would arrive at the counter. Presumably, management's interest would lie in balancing out two antithetical costs: (1) the costs of checkout clerks, whose number determines the maximum length a line can attain, and (2) loss of good will and patronage from impatient customers. With some empirical observation on line lengths and customer time intervals and service intervals, he can find out how long the line will grow with any counter checkout force. His estimate of the cost of this force is likely to be very accurate, but he will have more difficulty determining the costs and probabilities of patronage loss due to waiting, i.e., just how long, on the average, and at the maximum, a line can get before significant numbers of customers shift at least part of their buying elsewhere, and how much loss this will entail. But there is such a cost, and if he can make a rough estimate, he will know how many counters he should operate and with what personnel.

While the details of the calculations are not particularly intricate, mastering the tedious procedure requires hours of drill and had best be done in a mathematics course. The computer programming needed is standard, and very simple. The important thing, as with all these mathematical implements, is to understand its uses and meaning. Outside of production processes, it is safe to say most of the uses of Markov chains have not even been explored. One interested mathematician has used it to analyze a department store's charge account system, determining what the distribution of delinquency can be expected to approach after a period of time, and in what length of time. (The absorbing states were two here: bad debts turned over for collection and paid-up customers.) He has also experimented with it to project the expected teaching load in a graduate program subject to student turnover due to transfers and other causes and thus to estimate the intake permissible with a given available teaching staff. By analogy, a firm with a large management training program could estimate the needed recruit intake to get the eventual supply of middle and top managers needed.

Although no case has come to public attention, Markov analysis of a mail-order customer file would seem a useful way of predicting how long a customer will remain active.

As with most mathematical calculations, the actual answers that come out of a Markov analysis look very precise. But their true accuracy is no greater than the accuracy of the somewhat limited empirical observations on which the initial probability tables are built. The approximations resulting are, of course, far better than we are likely to use in the absence of such analyses and are normally quite adequate to the needs of business decision.

SUMMARY

1. Four matrix tools have received wide publicity as models for business decision: game theory, linear programming, and two kinds of Markov chains (transitional probability matrixes). All four are usually formulated as algebraic matrixes, and game theory and linear programming use the same method of computation.

2. Game theory has shown some utility in military analysis, apparently, where the two person zero-sum game has proved a reasonable simplification of reality. But business situations are representable only by the more complex multiperson nonzero-sum game for which no satisfactory solutions have been or seem likely to be developed. Construction of such game matrixes have been of value principally in providing qualitative insight, but no quantitative answers, concerning the incentive effect of some aspects of competition.

3. Production functions in business have proven amenable to the allocation help rendered by linear programming. This tool will identify the optimum allocation of scarce resources when: (a) resources, or some of them, are limited, (b) some of our choices are restrained--can be expressed in terms of "not more than" or "not less than," (c) there is some freedom to vary the quantities of the "choice variables" within the restraints, and (d) restraints are, or can be, expressed as linear equations. It has proven useful in such matters as allocating shipments from several sources to several destinations (the transportation model), assignment of skilled personnel for most efficient use of their abilities in total, calculating the most economical mix of complex components (the diet problem) in such things as feedstuffs, fertilizers, etc., or in getting the most valuable product mix, as for an oil refinery.

4. Markov chains are of two types: (a) the nonabsorbing chain, which permits an estimate of where a dynamic change can be expected to stabilize (such as the market share of a recently introduced new product variation) and (b) the absorbing chain, used in "waiting line theory" to investigate the proper policies of handling any waiting line, backlog, or other situation in which inputs must be or are introduced continually to balance outputs which are not reversible.

GLOSSARY OF MATRIX DECISION MODEL TERMS

MATRIX ALGEBRA: a system of algebraic notation set up in the form of tables of coefficients, with the variables denoted separately.

GAME THEORY MODELS: Models designed to reveal optimal strategies in situations of pure conflict. Calculation methods are the same as for linear programming, but the uses are quite different. The model has proven of value for the analysis of military strategy situations, which can be reduced to conditions of pure conflict and tend to be limited to two sets of opposing forces, but has not yet proven to of any real value in giving quantitative answers to problems of business strategy, mainly because business situations are almost never matters of pure conflict, nor are the number of participants reducible to two, or any clearly defined number.

Games are of two types: zero-sum games, in which the losses of of one side are exactly the same as the gains of the other, and nonzero-sum games, in which the combined losses and gains of the two sides do not cancel out.

Strictly-determined games: Games in which there is a single clearly defined strategy for each side, which will maximize the gains of one side and minimize the losses of the other.

Nonstrictly determined games: situations in which there is not a single clear strategy for each participant.

Mixed strategy: a strategy in which a player varies his moves in some random manner, according to some previously decided-upon ratio.

LINEAR PROGRAMMING: a method for calculating the best allocation mix of scarce resources in any situation in which the important relationships, cost and otherwise, are either approximately linear in form, or can be transformed into linear expressions. This is a special case of the more general method known as mathematical programming for situations in which some of the relationships cannot be reduced to linear form. However, only the linear form of programming has proved to be of much utility.

Choice variable: any of the factors subject to allocation which we can, if we choose, vary.

Diet model: one form of linear programming in which the physical quantities which may be proportioned are not subject to any limitations, but in which the costs must be carefully proportioned.

Objective function: the goal we hope to achieve with our allocation: minimization of cost, maximization of profit, and the like.

Restraint: any limitation on what can be done, on the supply of a particular resource, on the relationship of resources used, and the like.

Transportation model: the earliest form of linear program developed, so-called because it was initially used to work out the best shipment pattern out of a number of factories or warehouses of limited capacity to a number of different shipping points. It is applicable to any problem in which there are limits on both the inputs and on the outputs, with both being just exactly satisfied. Can often be calculated without the aid of a computer.

MARKOV CHAIN PROCESS MODELS: models for deciding where a dynamic process is heading and how, if desired, the course of events might be modified. In Markov processes, some "system" such as a body of customers (or a group of vehicles on the road, for another example) moves from one state of nature, such as the purchase of one brand of soap, to a different state of nature (purchase of different brands) in the next time period, in some probabilistic manner. This transition from one state to another depends only on the state of nature in the previous time period. A table representing the probabilities of change from each state to each possible succeeding state during one transition period is known as a transitional probabilities table.

Markov absorbing chains: Markov processes in which the transition to certain states is irreversible. If the process is not continuously interfered with by the introduction of new inputs into the nonabsorbing states, the system ends up divided between the absorbing states after some calculable number of time periods (it becomes absorbed).

Markov nonabsorbing chains: Markov chain processes in which all transitions are reversible--in which, for example, the switch from the purchase of one brand to another brand is not permanent. Nonabsorbing processes end up at a calculable fixed point, a stable distribution of the system over all of the states. Each brand of soap, to carry out the original example, would then have a stable market share, gaining as many customers during each time period as it loses to other brands.

Queuing theory or waiting line theory: a variant of the absorbing chain approach aimed at balancing out the costs associated with the buildup of a waiting line (as, for example, the number of cars delayed by a slow moving truck on a two-lane highway, or the number of customers waiting to be checked out at the supermarket) with the costs of reducing the length of the waiting line (putting in an extra passing lane, or adding more checkout counters in the market).

CHAPTER 7: NETWORK ANALYSIS: MAKING THE BEST USE OF AVAILABLE TIME

The time needed to get a job done is often the scarcest of the resources we have for carrying it out. Minimizing the time between the start and finish of a job nearly always yields direct cash benefits, and in new product introductions can mean the difference between major success and mediocre success or even failure. Network analysis is the general term given to a set of valuable tools for searching out the best timing pattern: CPM (critical path method) and PERT (program evaluation and review technique). The basic scheme is the same for all of the variations of both. The difference lies in the kind of data available for planning. CPM requires reasonably close estimates of the time requirements for individual component tasks, tasks with a past history that can be used to get at least Bayesian approximations. PERT was developed to handle the planning of complex jobs in which a really close estimate of the time requirements was not possible and a probability statement of the time requirement had to be used; it is the most useful of the two for planning research and development projects. Both methods aim at the same objective: the pinpointing of those tasks for which any delay means a delay in completion of the entire project, the bottleneck tasks. Typically, these are only a minority of the component tasks in any project. Once these few tasks are identified, executive attention and funds, if necessary, can be concentrated on the expeditious handling of these few jobs, and not squandered on the speeding up of other tasks that do not need concentrated attention and crash handling.

The efficiency of the execution of a wide variety of jobs has been greatly improved through scheduling based on network analysis; from the development of the Polaris submarine, for which PERT was perfected, through all sorts of new construction projects, to plant maintenance shutdowns and development of new product marketing operations.

Analysis and control is a nine-step process:

1. Describe the entire job in terms of the simplest component tasks.
2. Estimate the time required to carry out each component task.
3. List the tasks in their technological sequence. This means determining which tasks must be finished before others dependent on their completion can be started. The result is usually the identification of a number of semi-independent sequences.

4. If the job is simple enough to permit it, prepare a project graph with arrows connecting boxes or circles representing each task, ordered in the proper technological sequence and indicating completion time for each task.

5. For each task, as originally sequenced and planned, compute the earliest starting time by counting forward from the project start. Similarly, obtain the latest starting time by counting backward from the "end date" or "due date". Enter both times on the project graph. (On very complex projects, a computer can handle this part by use of a program published by F. K. Levy, G. L. Thompson, and J. D. Wiest as Chapter 22 in Industrial Scheduling, edited by J. F. Muth and G. L. Thompson--Englewood Cliffs, N. J., Prentice-Hall, Inc., 1963.)

6. Sum the times required for each path on the project and identify the path requiring the longest time. For this sequence, the earliest and latest possible starting times will be identical for every component task, and this path is thus the critical one--the path on which any delay in any task will delay the entire job. Any other kind of sequence will contain some slack time, some permissible delays which can occur, as shown by a difference between the earliest and latest possible starting times indicated.

7. Reexamine the original critical path to determine if more tasks can be carried out concurrently, even at some extra cost, and in what way and at what extra cost the time span of individual tasks can be shortened.

8. After these adjustments have been made in the plan, draw up a new project graph or revise the old one and reinspect the whole to determine whether or not another path may now be the bottleneck. If so, decide on new adjustments needed until a satisfactory schedule is arrived at and the final critical path tasks defined.

9. Set up a formal control system to keep a continuous check on the progress being made in the accomplishment of the bottleneck tasks.

To put the mechanics of this process into more concrete terms, let us look at a simplified example. A company which currently sells a product on a limited scale through small specialty stores would like to broaden the market by introducing a variant into supermarkets. Let us see how a critical path analysis of their plan could be used to improve its execution and then consider a more typical and therefore more complex product introduction effort.

A Simple Example: Planning a New Package and New Channel of Distribution

Let us say we have decided to broaden the market for a successful pet supply specialty by introducing it into supermarkets, limiting initial expansion plans to three major metropolitan areas. To protect our present sales through pet stores, we shall develop a new label and a new package specifically designed for supermarket display and sale. Sales will be pushed through newly appointed food brokers, and the initial contacts with chain warehouse buyers will be done by the sales manager together with the broker in each area. Production itself will be no problem. We will continue to have the product processed and packaged by a contract supplier. But we will in addition, have to get a new source of supply for a potentially greater market, and we will have to work with this source in setting up his processing and packaging operations--a relatively simple matter requiring only a little new equipment.

After careful consideration of past experience, we have analyzed the whole project as composed of the following basic steps, with time requirements as indicated:

Item	Time Required (weeks)	Prerequisite Step
a. Arrange for new manufacturing source	4	--
b. Produce preliminary package copy and label designs	1	--
c. Consumer test preliminary designs	1	b
d. Develop final package design	1	c
e. Consult with package sources and get quotations	3	d
f. Send package copy and get plates made and proofed	2	e
g. Prepare portfolio of sales presentation material	1	d
h. Interview and select brokers	2	g
i. Sales calls on chains	2	h
j. Consideration and acceptance by chain buying committees	3	i
k. Manufacturing and delivering packages to source	5	a, f
l. Manufacturing product and delivering to stores, getting display	2	i, f, k
TOTAL TIME	27 weeks	

FIGURE 7-1. Project Graph For Introduction Of A New Package Into A New Channel

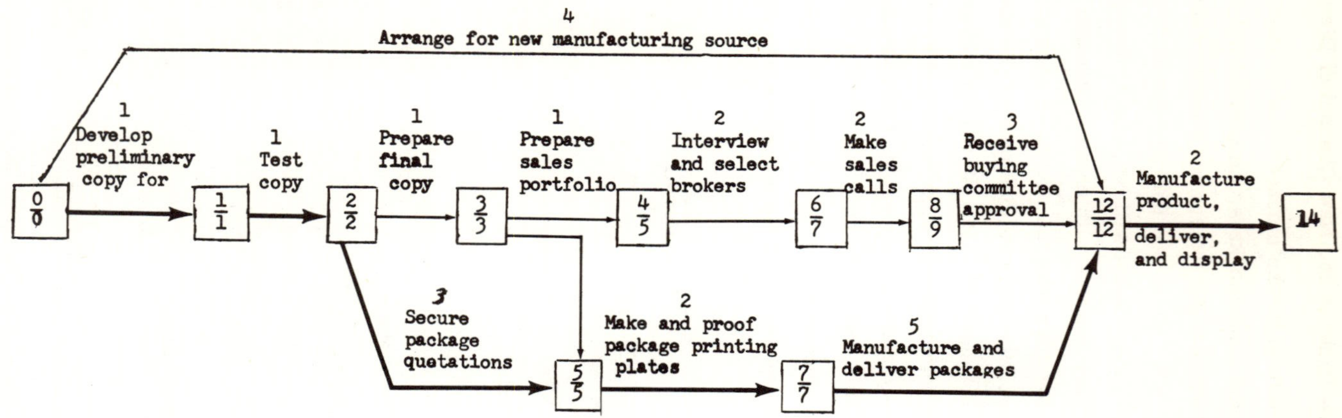

1	Numeral alone:	Duration of activity in weeks
2/3 (box)	Numerals in box:	Upper numeral--earliest finish in weeks after start, of preceding activity, earliest start in weeks after project start, of activity which follows Lower numeral--latest finish for preceding activity, latest start for activity which follows
Heavy arrow	Heavy arrows:	Critical path
Light arrow	Light arrows:	non-critical paths.

Clearly, if we take these steps one at a time, it will be six months before the new label gets on the market. But we know we ought to be on the store shelves by mid-September, when there is a seasonal pick up in sales and we are making the decision to go-ahead at the end of the first week in June. We need to do the job in 14 weeks, not 27. And we see we can do it in this time without any crash program, by carrying on some aspects of the project concurrently with others. Looking at the list and at the prerequisite tasks, there seems no good reason why we cannot start designing the package at the same time we start arranging for a new source. Nor, once the package copy is frozen, is there any reason not to arrange for the stock of packages at the same time we are setting up our sales organization and getting the orders. Graphing the project in this fashion, we find we can come out at just 14 weeks, with the critical path indicated by the heavy arrows in Figure 7-1.

Normally, of course, in as uncomplicated a project as this, the paralleling of tasks is so obvious that no formal analysis need be made, and the plan is worked out with minimum resort to paper and pencil. But product introductions as well as construction projects can involve so many sequences and subsequences that it becomes impossible to carry all the details in our head, and foolish to try to work out all the needed adjustments without the help of formal graphics and even the computer. Consider the situation which might realistically occur when a radically new office reproducer-copier is introduced by a business machines firm. The machine is sufficiently complex that it requires a new missionary sales force to get industry acceptance rolling.

Using Network Analysis to Improve Scheduling: An Example

Suppose that, as the members of the New Product Committee of the Weuns Office Equipment Company, we are met to make a final decision giving the go-ahead to a complete pilot testing and market introduction program for the Ocoprep, an exciting new office copier and fast multicopy reproducing machine which our laboratory has developed and proved out in internal operation with a hand-built model. In previous meetings and in individual study of reports on the potential market and on performance tests in our own operations, we have pretty much convinced ourselves that this machine holds promise of a major breakthrough, and have tentatively agreed that a pilot test program in outside companies should be conducted to get the bugs out of the design. Following this, preparations for a full-scale market introduction program should be

FIGURE 7-2. Initial Project Outline For Ocoprep Introduction, Following Normal Procedure

A. OVERALL NETWORK

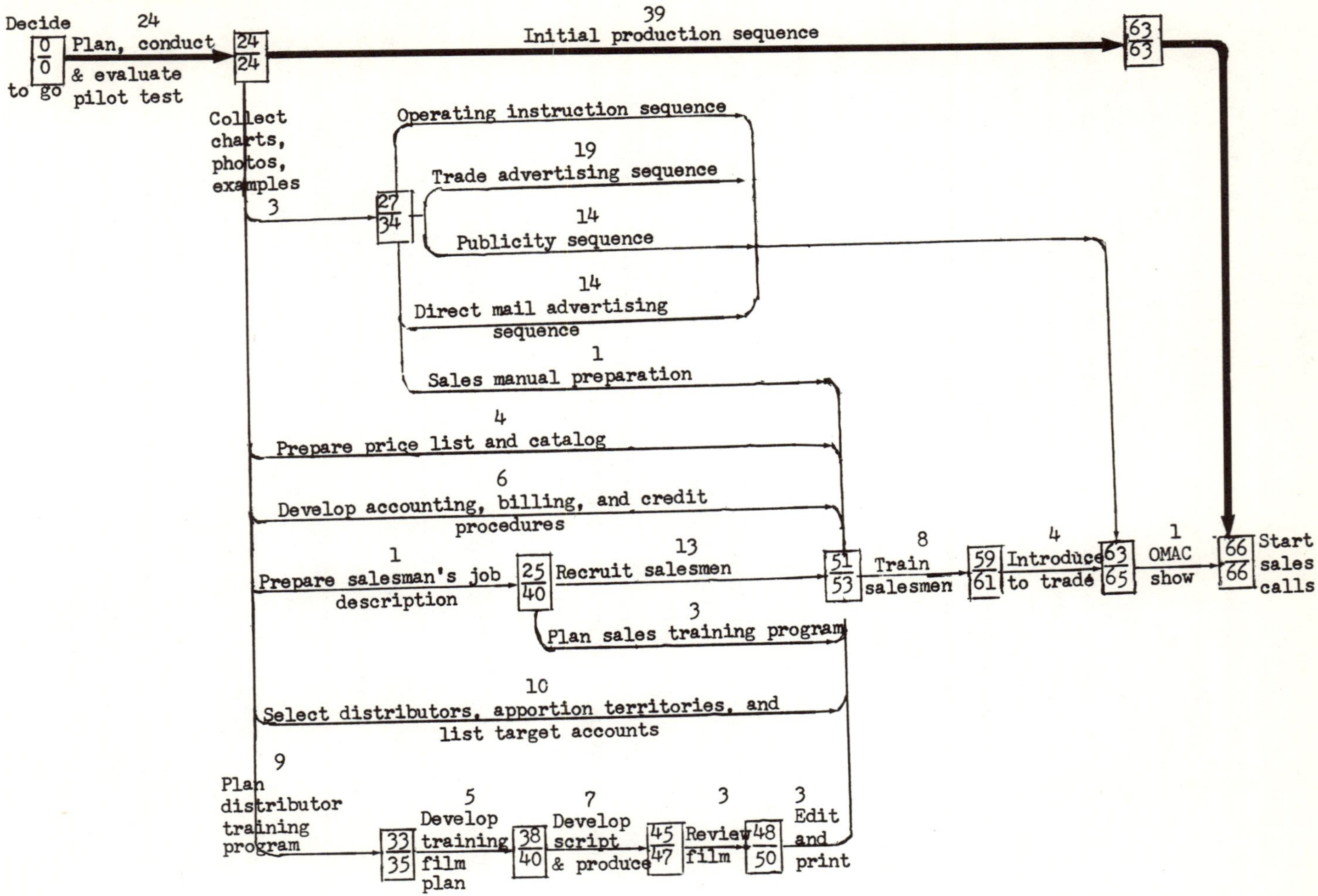

B. NORMAL PILOT TEST SEQUENCE (Estimated Total: 24 weeks)

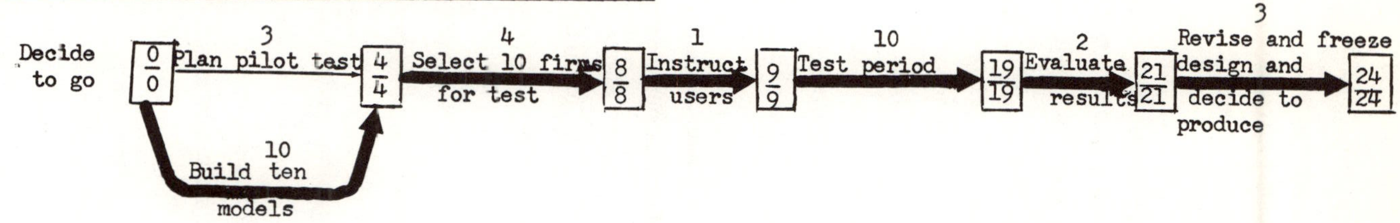

C. NORMAL INITIAL PRODUCTION PROCEDURE DETAIL (Estimated Total: 39 weeks)

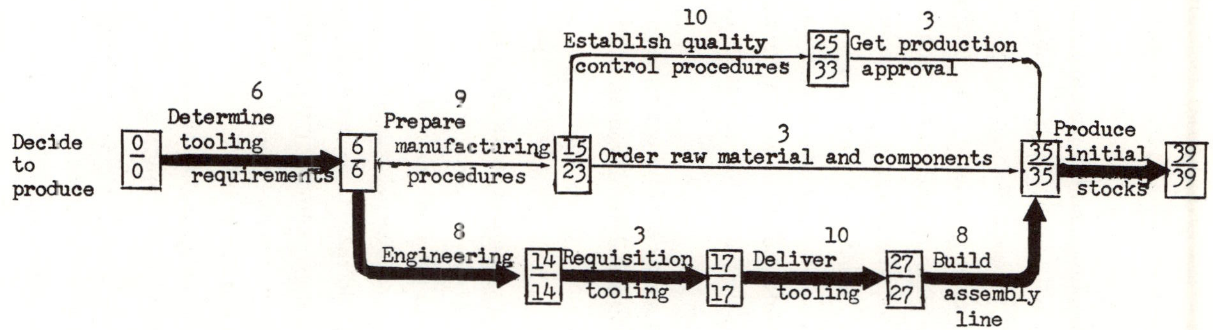

1 Numeral alone: Duration of activity in weeks

2/3 Numerals in box: Upper numeral--earliest finish in weeks after start, of preceding activity, earliest start in weeks after project start, of preceding activity, Lower numeral--latest finish for preceding activity, latest start for activity which follows

Heavy arrows: Critical path — Light arrows: non-critical paths.

pushed as rapidly as possible. We are all aware that the ideal time to unveil the Ocoprep to potential customers is the coming OMAC show, to be held in the week following February 29 next, a bare nine months away. We have asked first that an initial project graph be prepared according to our usual introductory procedure of an initial pilot test followed by the development of the program for marketing.

However, both the planning and the preparation for marketing will be unusually elaborate. This will require a different kind of selling from our other machines and the training of a special missionary sales force. The test itself must proceed for a minimum of 10 weeks if the companies in the test are to become accustomed to the machine and learn, both for themselves and us, what its capabilities and problems are in normal office use. We anticipate some minor design changes as a result of the test, as well as important leads both for the instruction manual and for promotion themes. Ten outside firms to be asked will have to be carefully selected to cover a wide variety of office conditions and copier and reproduction needs, and their cooperation will have to be secured for the placements.

To our dismay when our best time estimates are put into our usual new product production procedure and displayed as in Figure 7-2, the time between now and the OMAC show is impossibly short. The normal test sequence alone would eat up 24 of the available 39 weeks, leaving only 15 weeks for the critical initial production and delivery sequence which is estimated at 42 weeks. In addition, even if we were to shorten the initial production sequence by some kind of crash program, we would need 39 weeks to get the distributor training program worked out and train and introduce the salesmen. Even operating instructions, as normally scheduled, would take 31 weeks after completion of the pilot test.

Of course, not all activities form critical paths or near-critical paths. We have adequate time to develop accounting, billing and credit procedures, for sales manual preparation and for at least two of the advertising and publicity sequences. Others can be managed if some adjustments are made in the length of the test cycle. For this reason, only the total estimates for these sequences are indicated on the chart in Figure 7-2. The detailed time estimates are (the first figure indicates time required for that phase, the figure in parentheses indicates the total elapsed time since beginning of the task):

TRADE ADVERTISING SEQUENCE	(weeks)	
Choose media	1	(1)
Rough out advtg. copy & layout	4	(5)
Review	2	(7)
Prepare final copy	4	(11)
Approval	2	(13)
Place with media	6	(19)

PUBLICITY SEQUENCE	(weeks)	
Prepare rough copy	3	(3)
Review	1	(4)
Revise copy	2	(6)
Print	2	(8)
Release for publication	6	(14)

DIRECT MAIL ADVTG. SEQUENCE	(weeks)	
Develop direct mail piece	4	(4)
Review	1	(5)
Prepare final copy	4	(9)
Approval	1	(10)
Print & mail	4	(14)

Since the Committee has already been informed that the OMAC show introduction date is a must, justifying abnormal expenditures, we start to look for ways to speed up the process. The obvious first choices are the test sequence and the initial production and delivery sequence.

In looking over the details of the normal test procedure sequence, we see no way to safely reduce the actual 10-week test duration, or to cut down the 4 weeks allotted to hand-build the 10 test models. But someone points out there is no need to wait until we have those models before lining up firms to cooperate in the test, and that if we start immediately on this, we can save the whole 4 weeks. Another member asks why we have to wait until the end of the test to make our evaluations and to gather materials for the instructions and advertising. Why, he wants to know, can't those responsible take time to monitor the tests at least weekly as they proceed, making decisions on any last minute design changes as we go. We decide if we handle things this way, we should be able to make all final evaluations within a week after the end of the test, and revise and freeze the final design within 19 weeks from the go-ahead, instead of 24 weeks.

The 20 weeks remaining would still be far too short for 3 post-test sequences:

1. the manufacturing and initial delivery sequence estimated at 42 weeks
2. the distributor and sales training programs which take 39 weeks as set up

3. preparation of the operating instructions, programmed to take 31 weeks.

Moreover, no further internal concurrence of tasks seems feasible in any of the three tasks. We note no reason, however, why the review process in the development of the distributor program should really require 3 weeks. Everyone agrees to give top priority attention to any reviews, reducing them to a maximum of 1 week each. Planning the distributor training program could also be started concurrently with the pilot test, and if this is done, we should even gain a couple of weeks slack in this sequence.

We find no further ways of shrinking the time requirements without time or cost penalties of some sort, such as diverting executive attention from other important matters, making substantial use of overtime for key personnel, and risking wasted effort by proceeding with some engineering before the design is finally frozen.

If we are willing to accept the costs, we find four manufacturing sequence activities which can be shortened by throwing in more manpower, using overtime, and diverting skilled manpower from less critical projects:

1. determination of tooling requirements can be cut from 6 weeks to 4
2. engineering can be cut from 8 weeks to 4
3. requisitioning the tooling can be reduced from 3 weeks to 2
4. the assembly line can be built in 4 weeks, at a considerably higher cost, rather than 8.

Air shipment would reduce delivery of initial stock to more distant distributors. If we took all of these steps, we could shrink the manufacturing sequence steps to 29 weeks, it seems. But a second look tells us it would still take 31 weeks because the quality control subsequence has now become a bottleneck. So we find ways to shrink this by 2 weeks and are satisfied that 29 weeks is the least we must have from start of the sequence to final delivery of initial distributor stocks. This is still more time than is available before the OMAC show unless we can see a way to telescope the testing and manufacturing operations together in some manner.

Clearly, any attempt to start the manufacturing sequence before firming up the design will cost something in duplication of effort and design change confusion. But it should be equally obvious that the changes in design would be minor at this point and that most of the tooling for the machine could be started even before the testing begins, if necessary. If we wait until the test is half over, changes should not be too disruptive provided we have carefully monitored the test as it proceeds, and evaluated what we observed as we went along. If we start planning the tooling at the midpoint of the test and accept some wasted effort, we can have the Ocoprep machines in stock by the end of the OMAC show without crashing as many of the steps as we could if necessary.

Finally, we could very easily pick up the photographs, charts, and work examples we need for the various promotion programs and the operating instruction in the first 6 weeks of the test. We should have nearly all of the information we need for preparation of good operating instructions and a trouble shooting guide, if we continuously monitor progress of the test. So we can get this path within needed time dimensions with only a more intense and compressed review period.

As a result, we draw up the revised project graph of Figure 7-3. To avoid crash operation of too many activities, we settle for three critical paths, all of which will have to be carefully watched and controlled. In the process, however, we have created even more slack in the noncritical activities. The biggest price we have had to pay is in creating more work in the planning of the tooling and the manufacturing procedures, by starting them before the design can be frozen--a necessity in any case if we are to keep within the desired deadline. We have even managed to avoid crashing the development of the assembly line. We now have a tool to help us control execution of our plan--a definite statement of the timing needed for every activity in the plan, and a knowledge of which activities must get constant surveillance to assure success.

Controlling the Network

Network analysis, like every effective planning tool, includes a built-in management control mechanism. The initial plan makes certain that deadlines will be met if diligently followed. The completed plan should save top management resources by spotlighting the small minority of tasks whose planned progress is critical to meeting these deadlines. The control value lies in minimizing the number of tasks and sequences requiring close observation. However, the number of these must be kept small, and this hinges on the delineation of component task elements themselves and on adequate delegation of details.

By definition, a component task represents an action sequence which, <u>for the purpose of analysis and control,</u> is indivisible, and would be carried out

Figure 7-3. Final Revised Project Graph for Ocoprep Introduction Program

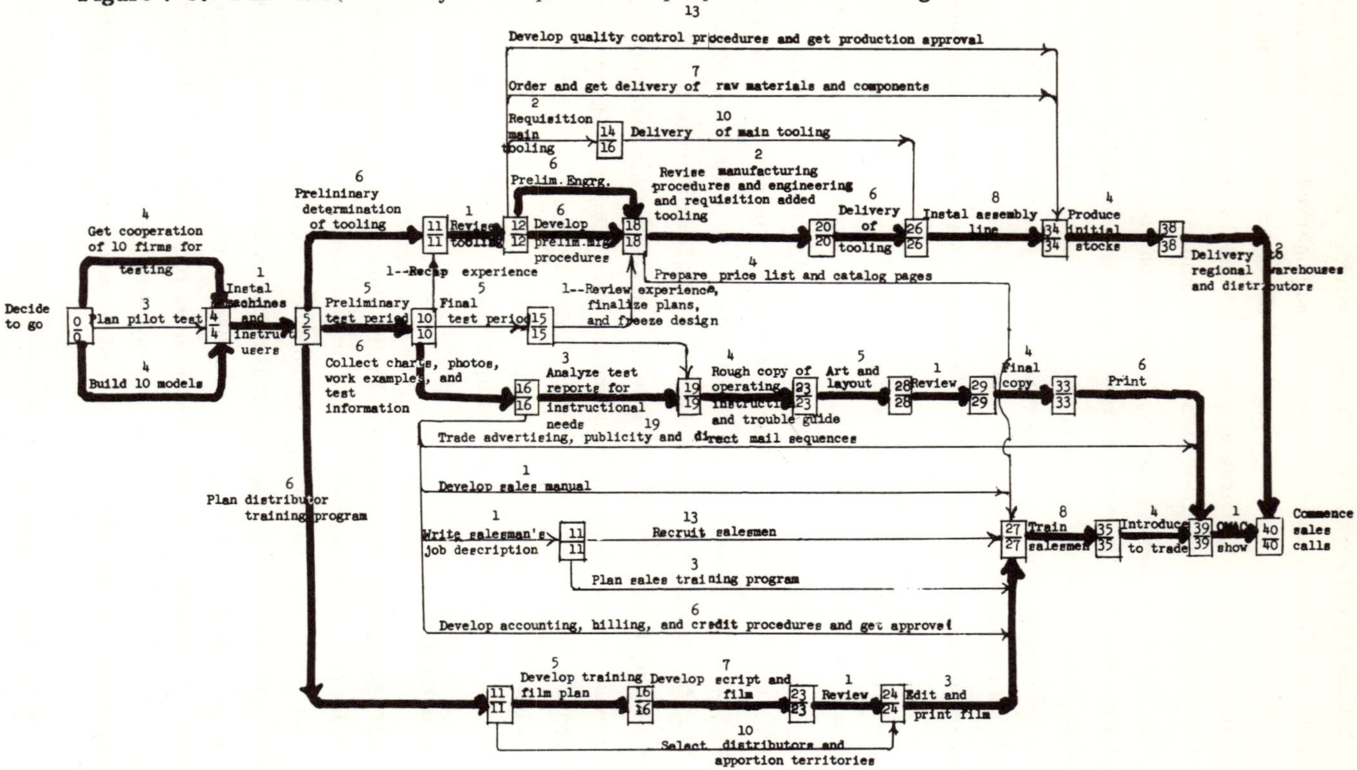

without interruption and close oversight. The indivisibility and freedom from close supervision are thus dependent, like all quantitative methods, on human judgment and on the needs and objectives in the situation.

Each of the steps in our first simple example of a new package introduction (page 175) clearly involved whole sequences of individual actions, each of which had some degree of elasticity of time requirement. "Arranging for a new manufacturing source" calls for numerous telephone calls, letters, personal visits, and contract preparations. Similarly, production of a series of preliminary package and label designs is not something done with a few strokes of a pen. These actions can be considered indivisible components for planning purposes only if we can be assured that those responsible for the sequences can be relied upon to complete the task in the alloted time without prodding and oversight. We must, however, be sure that those to whom we delegate such responsibilities both understand what their deadlines are, and can be trusted to meet them.

The alternative to such delegation is continual checks on a myriad of details of task performance. At the extreme, this alternative could mean an attempt to foresee each necessary phone call and each tentative sketch of a label design, to count them and insist on reports and checks on them. To even state the problem in this manner is to sketch the problem at its most absurd extreme, of course, and we need not undertake it to realize that the administrative burden would defeat the very purpose of planning. But it is easy to attempt too detailed a breakdown unless the necessity of delegating responsibility and minimizing supervision is kept as clearly in view as the need to meet the deadline.

Maintaining that correct balance in practice means that management will delegate whole sequence deadlines to lower levels, and that such lower levels will themselves set up such production control procedures as they find necessary--preferably informal procedures, but conscious ones. If this is done, network planning will achieve its real aim--limiting top management concern to just those details which are really crucial, and making certain management concentrates on performance in these areas.

SUMMARY

1. Network analysis is the general term for graphic and computer methods of breaking down the time requirement of parts of a project in such a way as to reveal the bottleneck component tasks and thus finding least costly ways to minimize the time between project start and completion.

2. CPM methods require reasonably firm estimates of the time requirements of component tasks, PERT systems were developed to analyze tasks with major components whose time requirements were less predictable. The general procedure is the same in both methods.

3. Analysis starts with a careful breakdown and listing of stages of the project into simple component tasks, an estimate of the time requirements for each such component, and a listing of related tasks in their technological sequence. The whole is then charted as the tasks would normally proceed, or so programmed on a computer, the cumulative time requirements calculated, and the result analyzed for task sequences which are critical in the sense that any delay in their performance will cause similar delay in the completion of the project.

4. Attention is then focused on such critical paths only, to determine whether and how some of the included tasks might be made concurrent (paralleled) or their time requirements reduced, and at what cost.

5. The entire new project plan is then reanalyzed to determine if other task sequences have not now become critical paths, and further adjustments made until a plan with a satisfactory job schedule and completion date is achieved.

6. The critical paths in this final plan will then be earmarked for special attention to make sure that they are carried out on schedule. The analysis thus also serves as a way of minimizing the executive attention needed to follow meaningful progress, focusing attention on only those details essential to successful performance.

7. The principal problem is to maintain the proper balance between detailed specification of tasks and timing and delegation of responsibility for the less critical detail. Too much fineness of detailing can defeat the very purpose of network analysis.

NETWORK ANALYSIS: GLOSSARY OF TERMS

Component task: a stage of the project which can be considered indivisible for the purpose of analysis and control and would be carried out without interruption and need for close supervision.

CPM (Critical Path Method): The form of network analysis used when the time requirements of all important tasks are subject to relatively firm estimate.

Crashing a task: Putting more than the normal optimum effort and expense into a task to gain substantial time in its completion.

Critical path: Any sequence of tasks between the start and completion of a project, all of whose earliest possible finish times coincide with the latest finish time necessary if the project as a whole is to be completed on schedule; sequences in which there is no slack for any component task. Any delay in even one of the component tasks in such a sequence thus means a corresponding delay in the completion of the total project unless specific provision is made to shorten the time of some subsequent task.

Earliest finish time: The earliest point in the project time schedule at which, under the scheduled sequence charted, a task can be completed, taking into account the minimum time estimated for this task and all preceding tasks in its sequence.

Early starting time: The earliest point in the project schedule at which a task can be initiated, based on the minimum estimated time required for all preceding tasks in the same task sequence.

Late finish time: The latest time at which a task can be completed without delaying completion of the project.

Late start time: The latest point of time at which a task can be started and still leave enough time available to meet its estimated requirement without delaying the project.

Paralleling: Scheduling independent tasks or independent task sequences so that they will be carried out concurrently.

PERT (Program Evaluation and Review Technique): a group of variations of network analysis designed for projects having components whose completion time requirements cannot be firmly predicted, and thus must be estimated on a probability basis.

Slack: Any difference between the early finish time estimated for a task and its late finish time. All tasks on a critical path have zero slack.

Technological sequence: The specific sequence in which tasks must be carried out because of their physical interrelationship. For example, if we are putting in a concrete foundation for a building, we would have the following five component tasks in the technological sequence as follows:

1. Excavate for foundation
2. Build forms for the concrete
3. Pour concrete
4. Allow concrete to set
5. Strip off forms

We could not put the forms in place until the excavation is complete, pour the concrete until the forms are in place, etc.

CHAPTER 8: THE BASIC AIDS TO MANAGEMENT CONTROL: CHARTS AND AVERAGES

In the excitement generated by complex computer aids to decision, we may overlook the more widely useful and powerful role which the simple charts, averages, and cross-tabulations of traditional statistics can play in operational and management control. No glamor attaches to these simple graphs, tables, averages, and measures of dispersion. They look so elementary that we are not inclined to endow them with the awesome mesmerism we often associate with the expression of other mathematical tools. Yet as often as not, a simple average, with or without some measure of dispersion, is all we really need to make a desired comparison or to learn how well our plans are working out. Whenever we seek to discover the basic facts behind our variable measurements or the dominant forces giving the principal shape to events, our best divining rod is the analysis of the carefully ordered frequency of the measurements in the form of a table or, most dramatically, in the form of a graph which shows the figures of the table in a sharply focussed whole whose meaning can be absorbed at a single glance. Or we may compress everything into a single figure--an average--supplemented by some measure of the degree of the variation of values around this central location.

The simpler-seeming statistical techniques of objective probability, whose computation has a comfortable familiarity for most of us, uses the analysis of directly comparable repetitive experience to answer one or more of these fundamental questions:

1. Does some one single important fact, measurement, or dominant force underlie the surface variations of our necessarily inexact measurements?

2. Are we getting deviations from what we expected?

3. What has been happening when, where, and under what conditions, and where have we been heading?

All these ends can often be accomplished by familiar statistical devices needing little real mathematical expertise (although quite a little non-mathematical judgment) in their application. Five of the most useful are:

1. The averages: primarily the arithmetic mean, the median, and the mode.

2. Measures of variation of individual items from the average: the standard deviation from the mean, and the percentile or fractile distribution.

3. Ordinary relative frequency distribution tables and charts: a simple listing of the number of items in each category, or a chart presenting this information.

4. Measures of interrelationship: most often, simple cross-tabulation tables (distribution of the numbers in each category by some independent category, such as the number of women wearing size 36 dresses who bought slacks, sweaters, and toreador pants), comparison charts (the superposition of a chart showing one kind of frequency distribution for a group on one showing the distribution for a different category). Or we may use a scatter diagram or calculate a correlation coefficient.

5. Time trend charts.

The purpose of such statistical devices is to reduce the actual complexities of original data to some simplified summary form such as a condensed table, a carefully ordered chart, or even a single figure, which can make it easier to grasp those aspects of the complex reality which are relevant and important to a decision. Thus even this most objective form of statistics does what all other mathematical methods do: it simplifies reality, discarding some aspects of disorder in order that we may understand those aspects we judge to be most important. Thus a considerable, though usually unrecognized, element of subjective judgment enters into the use of all objective statistical tools. The summary simplicity of end expressions from well-conducted analysis may obscure the degree of skill and judgment that entered into their preparation. Let us review these devices briefly.

Complete Suppression of Detail: Averages

The averages come close to that ideal of all statistical simplification: a single figure or measure which merges all individual variation to focus on some one aspect of the clustering of those values. Most of us are aware of the names and meanings given to the three most widely used ones:

1. the median: the middle item, the 50% point when items are ranked by size.
2. the mode: the most common or most frequently occurring item usually meant when we speak of "the average Iowa farm."
3. the arithmetic mean: The balance point or center of gravity of the group. It is a rate: that value which, when multiplied by the total number of items,

gives us the total value of the whole group, as when we talk of "the average value" of the 100,000 orders received being $10: indicating total receipts of $1,000,000.

Of these three, the mean is unquestionably the most widely used. One sound reason for such wide use is that our interest is often in the comparison of totals for groups of different size. We are concerned with the comparison of the relative size of the units in two or more groups independent of the size of the groups rather than the characteristics of some sort of center. It is important to keep in mind that the mean and median may differ substantially in value and that only the median is always representative of the value at the center of the distribution. Since extreme values influence the location of the mean, it often does not fall at the 50% point, nor does it necessarily designate that item which occurs most frequently. If the distribution of the data is symmetrical, the mean, median and mode tend to cluster. However, symmetry is not the characteristic form of the distribution of most social and economic data. Commonly, these exhibit a characteristically lopsided ("skewed") distribution like that in Figure 8-1. Characteristically, something like two-thirds or three-fourths of the values will be accounted for by one-third to one-fourth of the total items when we deal with matters affected by human action. For any one business firm, four-fifths of the sales volume may originate with one-fifth of the customers. Whatever the size of the individual customers, one-fifth or one-third of the orders will probably account for between four-fifths and two-thirds of the dollar volume. When dealing with production personnel, analysis will generally reveal that a large portion of the grievances or of the absenteeism are traceable to a small portion of the employees. The phenomenon is so prevalent that business writers sometimes elevate it to a principle—the "70-30 principle" or the "80-20 principle". It is one reason for the effectiveness of management by exception.

The Mean As A Device for Projecting or Comparing Totals

Of course when data are so skewed, the location of the mean is far from the center of the distribution and it does not represent the more frequent or common values. If, however, we can assume that the distribution will remain relatively stable (as it quite usually does for any individual phenomenon), the mean can help us project from a group of one size to one of a different magnitude. Since the mean is related to (divided by) the total count, it is a device for comparison

FIGURE 8-1. Typical Normal Social Curves: Percentages of Farms by Value of Product and Percentage of Total Value of Farm Product by Value of Product per Farm, 1959

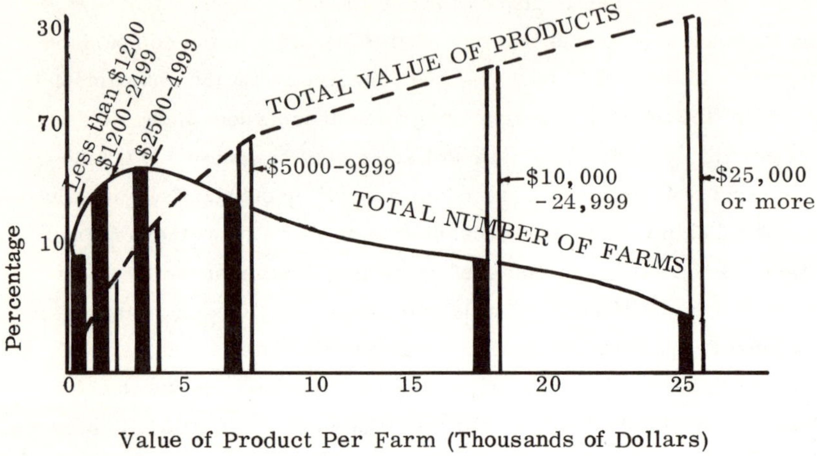

of the size tendency for individual items in groups of unlike total number. For the mean is truly a rate: a way of comparing totals.

Consider, for instance, the estimates which the executives of Rural Mail Order House must make as it completes its catalog circulation plans for the next season. Rural's sales will depend on the number of catalogs it mails, and its profits depend on mailing only to customer lists which will average out at some profitable level of sales per catalog in the case of each particular list. Rural mailed 3 million catalogs last season and did $120 million worth of business. Meanwhile, the customer list has grown to 3.5 million customers of the type qualified to get a catalog, and the committee has concluded booming business conditions will lead to 10% more business per customer. If Rural adopts the same catalog circulation standard as last season, what volume of business should it plan for? That is easy you say: the average sale per catalog last season was $40, and the 10% increase would bring that up to $44. If we multiply $44 by 3.5 million, Rural's total estimate should be $154, if their economic projections are right. Of course, because of the lopsided distribution of order size (a mere 5% of the orders accounts for a fourth of the dollar sales), far less than half of the customers bought as much as $40 worth last season, but those sending in the large orders counterbalanced this, to get the average value of $40. There is no reason to doubt that the distribution will be just as skewed next season, so there is nothing wrong with this $44 projection.

The executive committee's interest in the sales average of $40 was not in the average itself, but in the average as a convenient way of translating last season's total sales experience into an estimate of what next season's could be expected to be. Their real focus is on total sales, not the average, and the latter is simply a useful device in projecting a new total. At other times and for other purposes, they might be interested in the average as a device for management control. Thus if the average price paid by customers per dress in the dress department were to show a decline, they would view this variation in the average as a signal that something might be wrong with the selection of higher price merchandise in the department. Or if Rural's average rate of net profit on sales were to be substantially lower than that of its much bigger competitor, Sears Montgomery, they might begin to investigate circulation policy, or merchandising as a whole, or some other list of suspected factors. In every case, of course, they would be interested in the average as an indicator of some trouble in the total.

Sometimes, however, we forget that our true interest is in some total value and seek a rate for its empty self. We forget that a rate is only a multiplier, an "adjective," deriving whatever meaning it has from the total to which it is applied. We may forget that the reason we drove 60 miles per hour on the freeway was to make the 120-mile trip in 2 hours. At a rate of 40 miles per hour it would have required 3 hours. The 120-mile total is forgotten, however, when we speed at 60 miles per hour on a 1-mile trip through side streets where the time saving is infinitesimal and the increased risk quite substantial.

Or we may, as merchants occasionally do, look at the wrong rate and give valuable display space to a slow moving item because it gives us a high gross margin rate, perhaps a rate of 35%. We may neglect to look at the rate of turnover, which reflects a total sales of $50 per year. Another item in the same department might have a margin of only 10% but its sales of $2,000 per year yields nearly 12 times the total margin and 6 times the return per dollar invested in inventory.

Last, it is obvious that some of us may be inclined to ignore the fact that all rates have a denominator, that they are so much per something, particularly interest rates. Although expressed in numbers, a rate is not a quantity, but an expression of a relationship of two other quantities. Rates such as averages and percentages cannot be added, subtracted, or otherwise dealt with as quantities. If, for example, the unemployment rate is 10% in Ohio, 12% in Illinois, and 11% in Indiana, we cannot assume that the average rate for the area equals $\frac{10 + 12 + 11}{3}$, or $\frac{33}{3} = 11\%$. The total numbers of the labor force varies in the three states, and to get the average, we must go back to the original quantities, add the total unemployed, divide by the total of the three labor forces. Thus there is no such thing as an interest rate of 1-1/2%, but only 1-1/2% per month, or per year, and the two are definitely far from the same thing. Furthermore, in these days of amortized loans, which we pay off a little each month as the loan matures, we need to distinguish carefully between the rate on the total originally borrowed, and the rate on the balance still due.

How many bright-eyed young couples who would be scandalized at an interest rate stated as 18% per annum blithely sign up for a charge account at this same rate stated as 1-1/2% per month? And what about your cousin who thinks he is getting money at a very low rate on the time payments on his $3,000 car because he is being charged "only" $4.50 per $100 per year in addition to the principal of $100 per month over the next three years? Has he forgotten that he has the use of the full $3,000 only one month, and that in the last month of the loan he is in effect paying 4-1/2% per year on $3,000 for the use of a mere $100: in effect nearly 9% real interest, because the average value he owes during the three years is just over $1,500 (since he pays off to zero in the time the loan runs).

Even academia is not always immune to the misuse of rates. Early in the Great Depression, one of the professional schools boasted that "only 10% of our graduates were placed immediately last year, but business has picked up. This year, 25% obtained jobs." The publicity neglected to mention that the 1931 class had numbered 300 graduates, the succeeding class only 40. Jobs landed had actually dropped from 30 to a mere 10! The total figure to which an average refers is important.

Charting to Highlight Variation and Stability

The focus of traditional statistics on repetitive phenomena helps us implement management by exception by measuring the likelihood of exceptions. And in nearly every case, the quickest and most certain way to spot the exceptions and observe the constant aspects in a situation is to look, literally, at a picture of the whole--to draw a simple chart.

It is unfortunate that many who must regularly make choices based on quantitative data (and who can avoid such choices?) do not automatically draw simple charts of the data. No other method of presentation of our figures can reveal so clearly the basic regularities hidden in the fog of individual variations. No other device can so dramatize and make obvious the unexpected comparisons and exceptions. No tool is simpler to use, for the best charts are the simplest: line charts and bar charts requiring no artistic skill. Furthermore, their interpretation, when properly planned, is nearly automatic, needing little more than a conception of what might be expected. Statistical charts, like all pictures, use the detailed information only to represent the whole and shift attention from the confusing details to reveal the pattern of relationships underlying them. The oft-quoted story of the five blind men and the elephant is very much to the point, for it was their inability to use their eyes which led to their concentration on the one detail they could grasp, and thus to disagreement.

Charts can draw attention to four kinds of relationships:

1. How values cluster, and how they vary, what the principal values are which are obscured by the variations, and how dominant these principal values are.

2. How quantities or sets of measurements compare. It takes a little mental gymnastics to see that 72 is 3 times 24, but when translated into bars on a chart, the relationship is obvious. Again, our interest in Miss America's dimensions are better satisfied with a simple snapshot than by the numbers 36-26-40.

3. How values vary and are related in space--revealed by graphic maps.

4. How relationships vary over time and what the trends and regularities are.

One of the most useful habits we can acquire is always to draw a rough chart or picture of our quantitative information. Simple sketched charts can furnish important leads to basic forces otherwise overlooked in the underbrush of specific detail. The simplest is, of course, the frequency distribution chart, a line or bar representing the total count arranged by some classification, for example, the number of buyers of our product, by age-group.

Investigating the Shape of Things: Frequency Distribution Analysis

Even the most intimate familiarity with a set of figures may not reveal

FIGURE 8-2. A Simple Frequency Bar Chart: Number of Ladies Slacks Sold, by Size

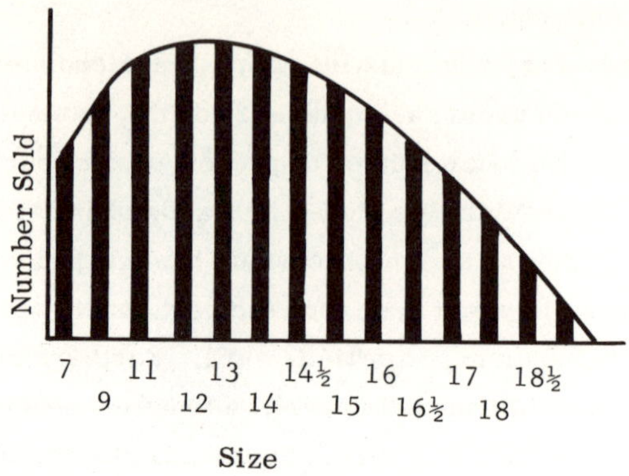

the basic relationships. Indeed, too much familiarity with the individual numbers, and concentration on them, can blind us to the underlying factors shaping them. A buyer for women's sportswear, for example, was aware that he did not carry as complete a size selection in his casual items as did the buyers of better dresses in his mail order firm. His only answer as to "Why?" was to point to past practice. An analyst with whom the problem was discussed drew a graph, Figure 8-2, based on sales figures taken from the buyer's own working copy of the catalog. Clearly, larger sizes of his items did not sell--sales volume dropped off rapidly as sizes increased. In his concentration on the trees and bushes of the numbers he consulted every day in planning his orders, the buyer missed the shape of the forest revealed when the graph subordinated this detail to show the picture as a whole.

Likewise, firms using standard costing and cost variances are prone to look at the individual variances and find explanations for each one, but are very likely to overlook the clues to quite different cost problems which only the graphs of the distribution of variances are likely to reveal. For the shape and the character of the whole is determined by more fundamental and usually quite different forces from those shaping the individual variations from the standard. Both the forecasts of costs and their improvement depend more on locating and understanding these underlying forces, whose presence a simple frequency chart can reveal, than on the less significant factors which cause the smaller temporary variations.

Cost variances, like all other measurement variations, are sure to fluctuate around some central point--the average. The important facts are the location of this average, the extent of the scatter around it, and the change in this location, if any, over time. If we wish to evaluate and control costs, we have a simple model with which to compare the frequency distribution of our cost variances, and alerting us to any possible need for further digging: the bell-shaped normal curve. (For the trend over time, we must use some other model, discussed below.)

What can comparison of any frequency distribution with the normal curve tell us? First, we have learned from the long history of measurement that if the set of measurements all come from the same "universe"--if they all measure the same thing with no significant disturbing or conflicting factors--the fluctuations should assume the shape of the well-behaved normal curve, the pleasantly bell-shaped distribution with a clearly marked mode and limited, but not too limited, dispersion, as in Figure 8-3A, below. If this is the way our data plot, then our cost variances, or product quality, or whatever, are under control. But if the distribution, while still bell-shaped, has acquired a middle-aged spread like that of Figure 8-3B, we have begun to lose control of costs or product quality, or whatever we are measuring, and we better start looking for the "how"

FIGURE 8-3. Some Variations of the Normal Distribution

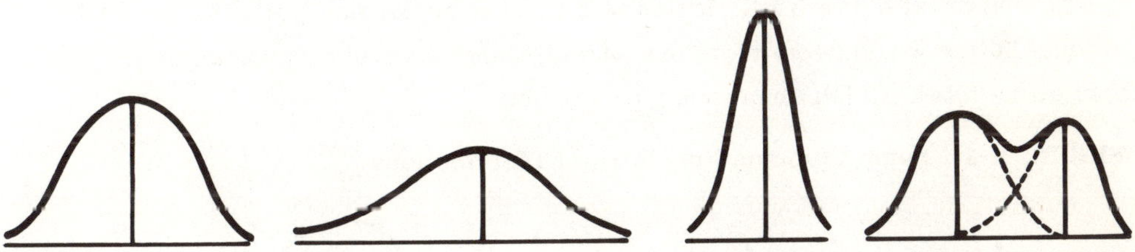

A. Normal-normal

B. The Flat Normal

C. Tall Normal

D. The Bi-Modal-Two Normals Combined

and "why." On the other hand if our bell assumes that pinched-in corsetted look seen in Figure 8-3C, control has become artifically tight--too tight. If this were output per worker in a piece-rate operation, for example, we might suspect a tacit agreement on some norm which nearly every worker can meet. Any such tight bell needs investigation to see if some artificial constriction is not exacting some cost of its own.

Not all frequency distributions look like bells, with their single peaks, or modes. Some are two humped, like the Bactrian camel, which can result from adding two sets of measurements, each from a different universe and gives us overlapping bells; (Figure 8-3D). Two machines in the production line may be set up so as to produce to slightly different mean dimensions. A frequency distribution of their combined output would be bimodal. Again if we are interested in selling trips to Europe, we might find that the ages of the adults in the families who take such trips follows a bimodal distribution: they tend to go before children come along, or after they are fairly well grown. (There may be still a third hump, of course, representing families who wait till after the young are established on their own).

Many distributions will have no recognizable kinship to the normal bell. Some have the lumpy shapelessness of the person who likes his food too well--the rectangular distribution that results from complete lack of control, as in Figure 8-4A. When costs or product quality exhibit this kind of distribution, production procedures, control measures, or whatever is reflected obviously need a fundamental and drastic overhaul. If this is a market preference pattern, the smart product policy would seem to be that of well-selected custom production for some part of the total, rather than mass production.

FIGURE 8-4. Some Common Non-Normal Distributions

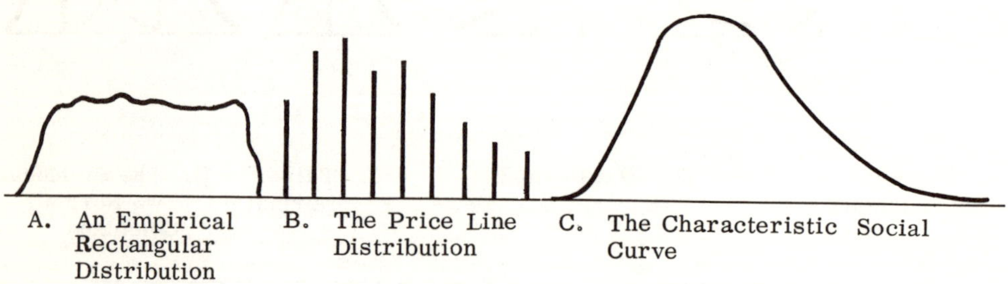

Or we may find we have nothing like a continuous frequency distribution, but a series of tightly-defined, clearly separated values like those shown in Figure 8-4B, typical of prices of major garments of any sort--the price line phenomenon. (In some other context, this might be the distribution of acceptable quality grades.) In such a situation, production must be "engineered" to meet the accepted price line points, and quite exactly. In cases like this, buyers and merchants both have built up expectations and habits around such price line points, and woe to the seller who tries to buck the pattern. A clothier of the author's acquaintance pointed to a suit in his store which did not fit the current price line structure. It was made to sell at a price in between two price lines. "It really is one of the best values we have in the store," he said, "but we can't sell very many. Its price is higher than one class of our buyers normally pays, and lower than the other group thinks they must pay."

The highly skewed characteristic social curve of Figure 8-4C has already been discussed. The profits lie in the interpretation and use of this curve--in the concentrated sales and dollar volume attributable to the handful of heavy buyers at the right end of this distribution.

Simple frequency charts can take on many other forms, of course. A not uncommon form is the U-shaped distribution which may result from the mixture of measurements from two completely different universes--such as taste preferences we might find in relation to grits-and-gravy for breakfast, in an Army outfit made up of equal parts of men from Albany, New York, and Albany, Georgia.

FIGURE 8-5. A Hypothetical U-Shaped Distribution of the Taste Reactions of a Mixed Army Outfit to Grits-and-Gravy

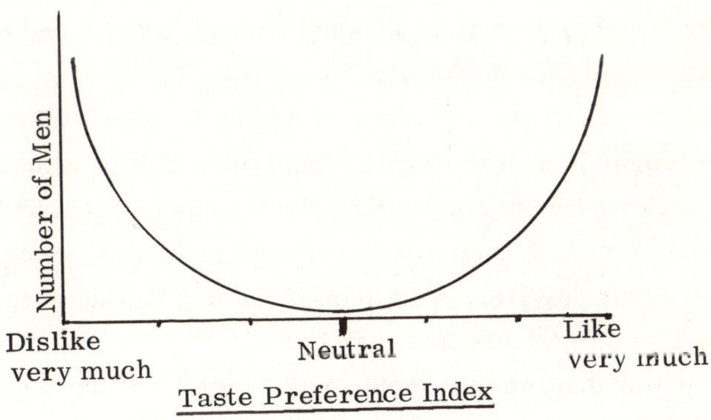

Whatever the shape of the distribution we find, charting it can furnish valuable leads to the factors which are likely to exert a major influence on any action we contemplate. Charting can brush from our mental eyes the cobwebs of abundant and confusing detail to reveal the clear outlines of the true shape of the matter under construction. It is then up to us to reason out what these forces may be. This neither our charts nor any other mathematical tools can do by themselves.

Even in charting, we should go beyond the straight frequency distribution, to plots which show the relationship to other distributions to space, or to time.

Comparison Charts to Reveal Relationships

The sportswear buyer already mentioned had called in the analyst to find out why attempts to expand his rather modest volume by expanding offerings had failed. The answer came rather quickly when the size distribution of sportswear items sold were plotted against the corresponding distribution of dresses by size. The resulting chart looked something like Figure 8-6, revealing that only a minority of the firm's clothing customers had the slim builds of the women who buy slacks and similar items. Other types of comparisons then corroborated the conclusion indicated by this comparison: the firm's clientele did not offer a potential target for the volume sales of many kinds of sportswear.

The clustering that a plot reveals is a better guide to the underlying truth than any individual item, as any range rifleman knows. When the marksman wants to know whether his gunsights are set correctly, he aims a few shots very carefully from the steady prone position, then checks how they "group." That is, he looks at where the center of the group of shots (the average, again) is located in reference to the bull's-eye. If he finds the center high and to the right, he will aim lower and to the left by an equal amount, even if one of his "zeroing" shots actually was in the bull's-eye.

Similarly, if a firm has been underbid by its competitors on too many occasions it might do well to chart a comparison of its estimate history with actual cost experience on jobs landed. Such a comparison, indeed would be a sound routine procedure even when no trouble is visible. Such a charted comparison (see Figure 8-7) revealed to one firm why it was being consistently underbid by an average of approximately 5%.

The scatter diagram can yield a quick picture of the degree of relationship between two factors without lengthy calculations and without any of the

FIGURE 8-6. A Charted Comparison of the Sales of Ladies Sportswear with the Sales of Ladies Better Dresses

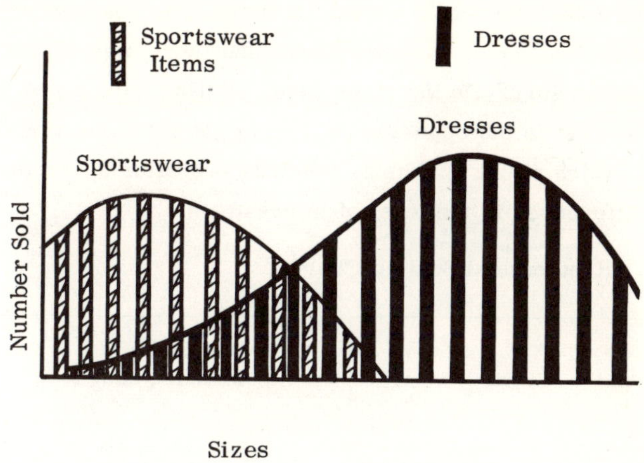

FIGURE 8-7. A Charted Comparison of the Relative Distribution of Cost Estimates and Actual Realized Costs Which Revealed To Company X Why It Was Being Underbid

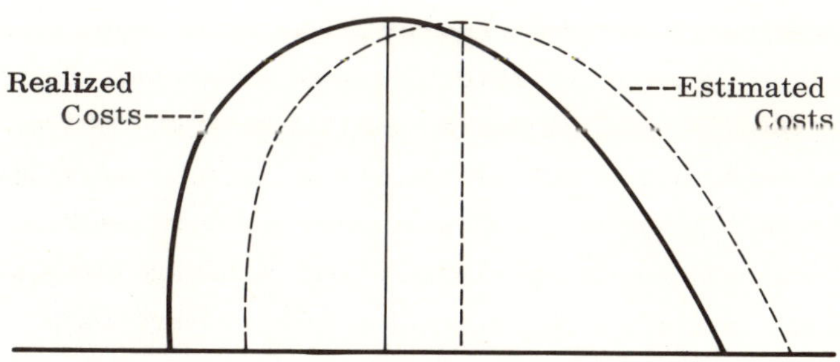

necessary assumptions about the nature of the relationship between the factors and the nature of the regression curve which underlie correlation calculations. We need only plot our pairs of observations on graph paper and observe the degree of tightness with which plotted points cling to the path of some kind of curve. If we get a close coincidence of paired values of, say, the age of women and their interest in diet foods, we can suspect that there may be a possible cause and effect of some sort. On the other hand, plotting the ages of men and solid evidence of interest in the opposite sex, we might get a correlation chart like Figure 8-8B, which might lead us to conclude that after a certain age, there are widespread differences in the level of interest.

FIGURE 8-8. Hypothetical Scatter Charts

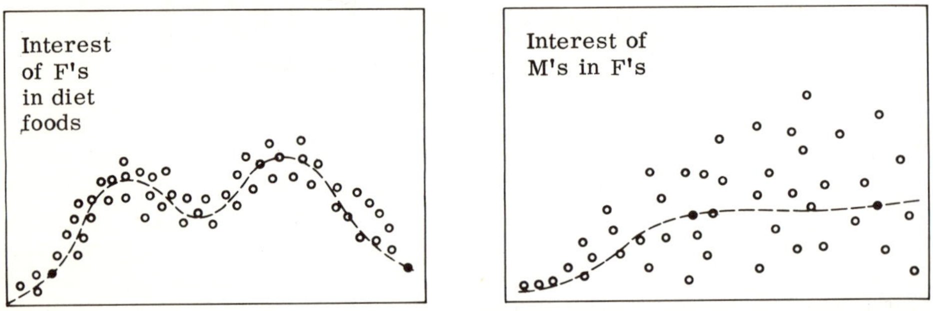

A. Close correlation

B. No significant correlation over most of the observations

Such a chart reveals close coincidence of any sort without regard to the shape of the regression line, whether straight or curving. It does not yield a number, of course, and if you need a number to convince someone else (nothing is more impressive), you will still have to do some calculating. By drawing a scatter diagram first, you will learn what to expect, what kind of line it is appropriate to assume, if any, and much other relevant information about your data. It would reveal the one or a few "wild shots" which, if present, could have a decisive influence on any calculations. Data which are grouped quite closely about a regression line, but which also include several "wild" ones far from the line, can yield the same numerical value for a correlation coefficient as data much more loosely grouped but including no exceptional values. The phenomena which produced such divergent series are quite different, but the numerical calculation alone will conceal the fine differences a plot will reveal.

Moreover, in the case of the tightly grouped data with a few wild deviants, critical examination of the exceptional values may yield the greatest illumination on the forces at work, and they should be carefully examined, not ignored. It is, then, a good general rule to plot all regression and correlation data whether or not calculations are conducted.

Spatial Charts to Reveal the Importance of Where

Knowing the where, geographically, of our profit opportunities, costs, sales, product problems of other matters of interest can be valuable in itself. Information revealed by relative concentrations on a geographic plot usually must be combined with other knowledge to tell us the "why." For geography is more than landscape: it is people and culture patterns; it is occupation, diet and all sorts of tastes; and it is climatic conditions. When a mail order seller became interested in the substantial profits from the sale of his garden tractor line, a simple plot of recent orders on a map pinpointed more than just the shipment destinations: it revealed to him that sales were predominantly in areas with heavy concentrations of part-time farming. This information, in turn indicated something about design needs.

A geographic plot of complaints about electrical equipment breakdown might point to humid areas as the problem, leading to an inference that some materials needed changing to give greater humidity tolerance.

Even tabulations made by geographic breakdowns are often more revealing if the numbers themselves are actually entered on an outline map, permitting direct two-dimensional comparisons.

Taking a Look at What Has Happened When--Trend Charts

If your individual cost variances have been staying within a reasonably narrow range for a considerable period, can you sit back and worry about some thing else? Maybe, but, again, maybe not. It would be wise to see first what they look like when plotted in chronological sequence. If Glamor Industries stock, which was selling for 75-1/2 last week dips to 66-1/4, is it a good buy if you find no reason to believe the company's financial position has not changed? Maybe, and again, maybe not. Better look at the trend, both absolutely, and in relation to other stock prices. In either of these situations, the ability of a chart to cut through detail to show underlying forces can reveal opportunities or warn of dangers.

Although your cost variances may all have been within what looks like reasonable limits, there may have been larger plusses than minuses on net recently. This may mean some new factor has entered which has tended to push up your costs. or, happily, the minuses may be overbalancing the plus fluctuations. Even such good news is worth an investigation to see the why of the trend, and what advantage can be taken of it.

And with respect to Glamor Industries (GI on the Board), any trader in the market knows that a dip of 9 points in one week is not unusual for this volatile issue. The sophisticated trader will consult his chart to see if this is a new low point in a period in which successive high points have each been lower, and successive lows progressively lower. If so, he may decide he better sell GI, no matter how good the financial news about the company. His chart suggests to him that the wild gyrations of this issue have hit a downslide in public favor, a fact that the naive investor who looks only at individual quotations (see Table 8-1) may easily have missed, but shows up clearly in the chart (see Figure 8-9).

TABLE 8-1. Price Fluctuations in Glamor Industries Stock

-2.37	-.37	-1.63	+.88
-.50	-.63	+.63	-1.88
+1.00	-1.00	-1.88	-.37
+.25	-.50	+1.50	-2.37
-.88	+1.25	+.88	+1.88
+.62	-1.37	+.25	-.37
-.62	-2.00	-1.12	+.37
-.37	+1.88	+1.00	-.50
+1.50	-1.50	-1.50	+2.12
-1.25	-1.63	-3.00	-1.63
+1.12	+3.50	-1.00	-.88
+1.00	+1.00	+1.50	+.37
-1.88	+.37	+.88	+1.12
-.50	+1.25	-.88	+.25

The Learning Curve: A Process Improvement Model

We now have reason to believe that in any industrial process, a continuing downtrend in cost and a continued uptrend in efficiency should take place over its entire lifetime: a relatively constant percentage decrease in cost and man-hours requirements in time. The size of the percentage seems to be closely related to the complexity of the process and the amount of human element involved, and the phenomenon has been labelled the learning curve. Plotted on ordinary rectangular graph paper, the trend is revealed as a downward sloping

FIGURE 8-9. Chart of Price Fluctuations in Glamor Industries Common

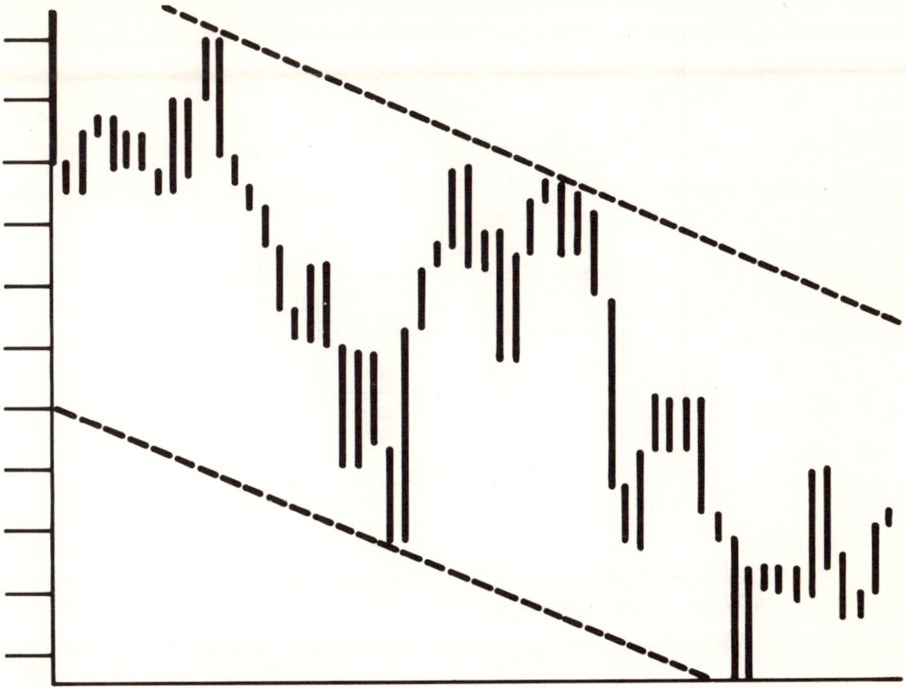

line of constantly decreasing slope as time passes, similar to Figure 8-10, that is, the actual physical quantity of improvement per month or year is constantly decreasing amount. Plotted on semi log paper, the results should approximate a straight line. (Figure 8-11)

Thus, management should expect any process to show such an improvement curve, and should view any absence or cessation of it as a control signal for investigation of possible artificial blocks to such improvement.

Outlining The Differences and Interrelationships: Tabulations and Cross-Tabulations

Charts enable us to deemphasize detail without ignoring it. They thus can be used either to get a picture of the general tendency or to see how much the details vary from the average. The purpose of ordinary simple tabulations is to reveal the outlines of the variations. We can then identify the sources of those variations and gain insight into possible action related to them by use of well-chosen cross-tabulation--tabulation of the relationship of the variations in one

FIGURE 8-10. Number of Man-Hours to Build a Widgimatic: Rectangular Coordinate Plot

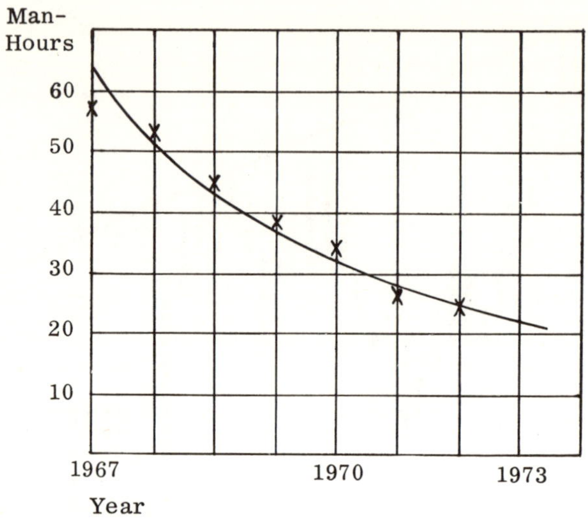

FIGURE 8-11. Number of Man-Hours to Build a Widgimatic: Semilog Plot

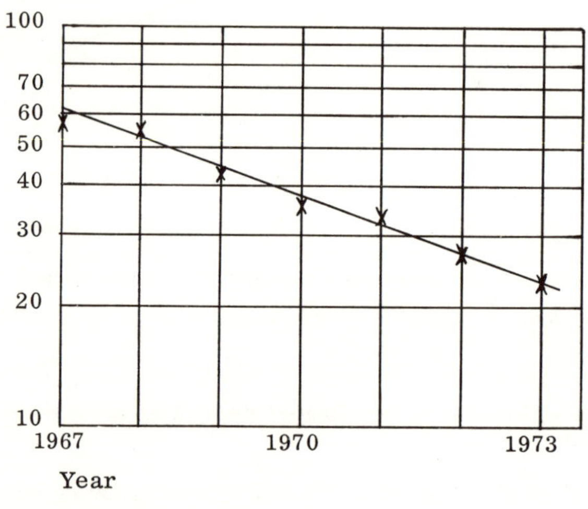

subclass of the universe studied to the variations in another. Cross-tabulation is such an obvious and easy to use device that it is a mystery why so many studies stop short with the simple tabulation of data without investigating the cross relationships. Omitting this highly informative step often leads to inferences the opposite of the truth. Simple tabulation of the sales to department store credit customers, for instance, might show that two-thirds of them were well-established families whose head was over 30 years of age. However, if the merchandising and the advertising were actually directed at this group, it would undoubtedly be a mistake. A cross-tabulation would almost certainly show that about two-thirds of the purchases of furniture and other large volume items came from the newer families whose head was under 30.

Indiscriminate cross-classification may not be much better than none at all, however, The cross-classifications should be based on some clear model as to which kinds of relationships can be expected to be meaningful, and they should be relevant to the decision to be made. Any form of classification suppresses detail. The detail suppressed should be that which is not significant in relation to the decision. The categories used should be those which are relatively homogeneous with respect to the evaluation to be made. This principle is violated by one of the most widely used classifications in marketing and economic planning--the use of income classes to denote differences in buying patterns. All studies of expenditure patterns clearly show that the social classes have markedly different expenditure patterns. And in recent decades, all of the income studies show that income is not closely correlated with social class. It is true that the average income of the various social classes does correlate directly with social status, but the dispersion within classes and the overlap between classes is so great as to rob income classification of any useful meaning as a measure of class and expenditure patterns. The best single indicator of class is occupation, and all other measures are highly correlated with occupational status. As the cross-tabulations of income and occupation in Table 8-2 show, substantial numbers of individual families in the lower-lower unskilled labor clas have incomes as high or higher than most members of the upper-middle professional and technical class. Table 8-3, carrying this cross-tabulation one step further, gives some indication of the major differences in consumption patterns which confusion of income class with social class can conceal. The lower we go in the social scale, the more of the same income will be spent for food. (The composition of the food bill itself will be different, too, as we know from other sources.) The higher we go in the social scale, the more of the same level of income which would be allotted for education and reading. There is a clear split between the white collar classes and the blue collar in the proportion of income they are willing to spend on shelter.

TABLE 8-2. Distribution of Income Levels for Each Major Occupational Grouping, 1960-61

Occupational Group	Percentage with a Family Income of ($000)								
	Under 3	3-4	4-5	5-6	6-7.5	7.5-10	10-14	15 or more	All income classes
White-Collar, Upper and Middle Classes									
Self-employed	14	10	11	12	12	15	13	12	100
Salaried professionals and officials	3	4	8	11	21	28	19	7	100
Clerical and sales	10	12	17	17	20	16	16	7	100
Manual Workers									
Skilled	4	8	14	17	27	21	7	0.5	100
Semiskilled	12	13	19	19	19	13	5	0.2	100
Unskilled	32	17	18	12	11	7	2	1	100

The information we can gain from such cross-tabulation is valuable in another important respect--it is more stable and trustworthy than the averages revealed by the whole of the sample measurement. The categories of any useful sub-classification are inevitably more homogeneous than is the whole of the universe, and thus less subject to sample variation and bias. In turn, if such categories also represent fundamental groupings in that whole, it is possible to make projections which reveal more than the grouped data alone tells us. In political polling, for example, knowledge of the overall percentage favorable to a given candidate or issue tells us much less than cross-classification of the responses of various groups. In one statewide poll in a closely contested election, for example, the survey organization was able to make a correct prediction over two months ahead of time, when almost a fourth of the electorate was undecided, by cross-classifying voter response of both the decided and the undecided according to voter background information. *

Indeed, the really important aspects of our measurements often lie in the exceptions to the usual turned up in the cross-tabulations. National economic

* Chester R. Wasson, The Strategy of Marketing Research, Appleton-Century-Crofts, New York, 1964, p. 220.

TABLE 8-3. Family Expenditures for Consumption by Families of Two or More in Each Major Occupational Grouping, for Four Principal Income Classes, 1960-61 (In percentage of total expenditure for personal consumption)

	Families with Income of ($000)			
	4-5	5-6	6-7.5	7.5-10
A. Food, Beverages, and Tobacco Expenditures by:				
Salaried professionals and officials	21	23	23	23
Clerical and sales	24	24	24	24
Skilled	25	26	24	25
Semiskilled	27	26	26	25
Unskilled	28	27	25	24
B. Shelter Expenditures by:				
Salaried professionals and officials	16	17	16	14
Clerical and sales	16	15	14	13
Skilled	14	13	12	11
Semiskilled	14	13	12	11
Unskilled	14	13	13	11
C. Home Furnishings and Equipment Expenditures by:				
Salaried professionals and officials	4.5	6.2	5.2	5.6
Clerical and sales	4.6	4.6	4.5	5.1
Skilled	4.9	5.4	5.5	5.2
Semiskilled	5.0	5.7	5.5	5.6
Unskilled	4.4	5.2	6.0	6.3
D. Education and Reading Expenditures by:				
Salaried professionals and officials	2.5	2.2	2.1	2.2
Clerical and sales	2.7	2.7	1.8	2.0
Skilled	1.3	1.4	1.5	2.0
Semiskilled	1.1	1.4	1.7	1.5
Unskilled	1.2	1.5	1.9	1.7

and employment policy in the United States might well have been different in the late 1950's had more attention been paid to the high unemployment in disadvantaged groups than to the low unemployment on the average. Detroit auto manufacturers might well have moved earlier and more wisely into varying their offerings had they paid less attention to the clear liking of the great majority of drivers for overpowered and oversized cars than to the growing number who did not like them.

Cross-tabulations are to statistical analysis what the hammer, saw and plane are to the carpenter--the tools which do most of the most important work. Although more complex mathematical methods have been developed to put numbers on relationships for purposes of comparison, their utility has not been great for most uses, although occasionally very valuable for specialized tasks.

Numerical Measures of Relationship: Regression, Correlation, Multiple Regression, and Multivariate Analysis

A scatter diagram, or correlation chart, gives a relatively accurate impression of the degree of relationship between the values of two variables but yields no numerical measure by which we can compare this relationship with that between two other variables. Furthermore, it can be used to visualize only the relationship between two variables. Quite often, many of us would like some simple figure which would enable us to compare two different sets of relationships. Sometimes we would also like to measure the relative effect of a number of variables acting together. Mathematicians have devised a number of related measures aimed at these ends which have proved valuable in solving some specialized problems when the assumptions on which they are based hold true. The assumptions, however, are relatively stringent. The tools are those of regression, correlation, multiple regression, and a variant of the latter sometimes labelled multivariate analysis or factor analysis. All tools derive from the basic one of regression analysis--the mathematical fitting of a smoothed trend line (or trend surface, if more than two variables) to the relationship between variables. The techniques of calculation can be found in any modern statistical text, and the calculation is a standard set of computer programs. As with most statistical tools, however, the textbook discussions spend little space discussing the limitations well known to the authors. These limitations involve the rather arbitrary nature of the curve-fitting process and the high quality of the data required for valid application.

A regression line is simply the calculated best fit of some chosen type of trend line to the relationship between two sets of measurements, such as the relationship between the height and the weight of a group of individuals, or the heights of a set of parents compared with that of their children. The computation does not itself choose the shape of the trend line. Generally, it is assumed that a straight line trend is a close enough approximation, although any smooth algebraic function may be designated, chosen arbitrarily on the basis of some assumed type of relationship, drawn from other knowledge, or inferred from an inspection of a preliminary scatter diagram. "Best fit" is defined as that version of the type of regression curve picked which follows the general trend of the measurements with the smallest average value of the square of the deviations of actual measurements from the theoretical values indicated by the line. When the calculation assumes, as is customary, that the regression is linear, it is assuming that the changes in the values of one variable always bear a constant proportion to changes in the other. The equation $x = 2y$ might be such a regression relationship, for example, indicating that for any change in the value of y, x will change twice as much.

The correlation coefficient--always less than 1, since the latter indicates perfection--is derived from the calculation for the regression and measures how well this line predicts the observed values. Mathematically, the simple correlation coefficient is the square root of the average of the squared deviations of the observed values from the regression trend. The coefficient does not itself really indicate the degree of predictability, but the square root of that value. Thus, a correlation coefficient of .70 seems and is quite high, but really means that a knowledge of the one variable's value only accounts for about half (.70 x .70 = .49) of the variation in the other variable.

Even when applicable, the two-dimensional qualities of simple correlation and simple regression are not adequate for most prediction. Most of the phenomena in which we are interested are the result of the action of more than a single factor, and we would usually like to measure how much of the value of an independent variable we can identify from the knowledge of several factors working together. We might wish, for example, to see how closely the sales of our principal product can be predicted from some kind of measurement of the quality and amount of our advertising, the amount of personal sales effort put behind it, the number and quality of our distributors, similar efforts of competitors, and the income prospects of potential buyers. Multiple regression would permit us to measure this if data of the kind and quality assumed were available, for results in the past. (With dynamic relationships such as we have in business competition, it is doubtful, however, whether the calculation would be worth much, and the relationships discovered cannot be taken to mean cause and effect, only coincident variation.)

Multivariate analysis, based on multiple regression calculations, has proved of value in attempts to determine whether test items developed for use in standard psychological and educational usage measured the same factors as other items, or different ones. Such analysis has also been used on occasion to determine the number of factors necessary to predict the readership score an advertisement will receive. However, multivariate and factor analysis do not tell us whether the test actually does test what we wish to find out about an individual nor whether the readership of the advertisement indicated its sales impact. These are personal judgments quite apart from the factor measurement score, even when the calculation itself is valid in terms of meeting the basic assumptions about the data.

Any sets of figures can be fed into a correlation, multiple regression, or factor analysis program on a computer, and a numerical answer will result. That answer has no valid meaning however unless five conditions are met by the data used:

1. That a linear regression or whatever other relationship is assumed correctly portrays the relationship between the variables

2. That the data is of interval (parametric) quality within the limits of approximation used

3. That measurement variation follow a normal distribution

4. That the variations are random

5. That the independent variables are not mutually correlated to some other variable.

Manifestly, if the true relationship is different from that assumed for the regression, any projections made as a result of the calculation will be in substantial error. If the data is not of interval quality, there can be no way of measuring the shape of that relationship, and thus no way of determining the degree of deviation. If measurement variation is not random and normal in distribution but skewed, then the implied assumption that deviations in one direction are as likely as those in the other is not valid. Unfortunately, almost no economic or social data fits these assumptions, accounting for the disapointment which has followed every period of enthusiastic endeavor to apply to business and social prediction a tool which has done some useful work in the natural sciences.

Like so many other kinds of attempts to get precise measurements, regression and related methods generally meet the twin frustrations of inadequate quality data and unstable and discontinuous relationships. This is one reason for the growing use of computer simulation, which pretends to no such high degree of precision.

SUMMARY

1. The great bulk of the quantitative data on which decision depends are still analyzed most effectively by the simpler tools of traditional statistics: such summary measures as the averages and measures of dispersion, and the visual dramatizations of charts and summary tables. They all enable us to cut through the complexities and confusing variations of individual figures to perceive the character of the underlying basic forces with which we are confronted.

2. Traditional statistics seeks to find clues in directly comparable repetitive experience as to the existence of a dominant force or forces underlying measurement variation, and the place, the time of, and the conditions surrounding major events, their trends, and the degree of precision we have achieved or can achieve with a limited amount of sample information.

3. The three most used averages--the arithmetic mean, the median and the mode--coincide and are all the most frequent and most central values only when measurement variations are symmetrical, most commonly in the form of the bell-shaped normal curve--a curve not characteristic of the kind of data involved in most business policy decisions. Otherwise the mode is the only average which is the most common value (or values, since there may be more than one). The median is defined as and is thus the central value always, which the others may not be. For economic and social data, the arithmetic mean is rarely the central or dominant value around which variations cluster. But it is the most widely used because it is always a rate: a means of comparing two distributions of different size or covering differing lengths of time, and thus also a means of projecting what can be expected under different conditions of quantity and time.

4. We must be especially careful, when using the arithmetic mean as a rate, that the time and quantity bases used for comparison are the same, and that the rate itself is the facet of interest, and not the gross quantity.

5. Simple graphic charts dramatize visually the underlying uniformities and the easily blurred-over presence of dominant values, without need for any kind of mental translation of the relationships involved.

6. The frequency chart shows at a glance both the presence of any dominant central values and the degree of strength of this dominance.

7. The trend chart can reveal forces for change unsuspected by one simply looking at the uncharted figures.

8. Charts showing the typical unbalanced or skew distribution of most business data can dramatize the need for concentrating effort for most efficient results.

9. Comparisons of different frequency distributions which can be supposed to be related helps uncover unsuspected elements in that relationship.

10. Well-planned tabulation enables us to see some of the important variations in the universe, and cross-tabulation should be used more widely to investigate the relationships which underlie the variations. When the categories on which the cross-tabulations are based are fundamental, the greater stability of the measurement of subclasses enables us to make more accurate predictions.

11. Mathematicians have developed a set of tools for giving a numerical value to the interrelationship of various factors in a situation when the data are of the right kind and quality. The basic device is the regression line--a line or surface fitted mathematically to the observed data. Correlation, multiple regression, multivariate analysis and factor analysis are all based on the regression calculation. All depend on the validity of the judgmental choice of type of regression relationship, and all require data which is parametric in quality and normal in its distribution. Otherwise the calculations are misleading and meaningless. Unfortunately, very little economic and social data fits the assumptions.

CHAPTER 9: WHEN ALL ELSE FAILS: COMPUTER SIMULATION MODELS AND SOLUTIONS

Previous chapters have sketched a number of formal models for finding the best decision choices in various types of situations. The term model has come into fashion in recent years to connote any general concept we may have of the mechanism by which some sets of action inputs get transformed into a specific set of outputs or results. The general idea is one we unconsciously use all of the time, since any model is simply some variant of the general proposition that "If ------------ is done (or happens, or is observed), then ----- will happen (or be the result." While some people use the term model to refer specifically to quantitatively formulated propositions, the term covers every such generalization, whether validated or not. (We have all heard the fallacious marketing model, "If you build a better mousetrap, the world will beat a path to your door.")

The advantage of the mathematical models lies in their objectively calculable nature. If we can fill in some relevant quantitative material, we can obtain a quantitative answer which can be verified against experience. Such a model also tells us something we always need to know--how much input is needed to get how much output.

Unfortunately, mathematical models are available only when we have thoroughly verified knowledge of the true input-output relationships and usually only when these relationships can be expressed in the form of continuous mathematical functions. We frequently have no sound knowledge of the pertinent relationships and even when we do, the relationships are not subject to translation into the smooth functions mathematicians prefer.

Thus linear programming is conceptually an ideal model for solution of warehousing and inventory problems. In practice, however, the constraints on which the solution depends are frequently not even approximately continuous functions. Transportation rates, an important variable in location problems, are a complex mixture of discontinuous functions. The rates change abruptly at the margin of arbitrary quantity boundaries (such as carload and less-than-carload). Moreover, there is a maze of special commodity rates and other special considerations.

Whenever we have no applicable model and whenever what should be an applicable model cannot be used, we can, thanks to the computer, fall back on trials of a number of suggested rule-of-thumb solutions--we can simulate.

Although some kind of simulation has always been used (the architect's blueprint is really a form of simulation), the computer's speed has vastly broadened the possibility of comparing many cheap trials of possible solutions.

The Computer and Simulation

Because the computer permits the ultimate in mathematical abstraction, it can be used to approximate all kinds of possible experience without the pain and cost in time and money of actually trying things out. The only input, output, and storage actually involved are simply electrical impulses and charges, which, because they are devoid of any kind of meaning, can be made to represent and actually read or produce and compare numbers, real words, sentences (in English, Swahili, or any other language), or geometric patterns or maps--all at the option of the programmer and operator, with suitable auxiliary machinery and equipment. Moreover, whatever the computer is instructed to do, in the infinitely detailed painstaking language we call a program, it carries out in millionths of a second, giving rise to a new term in business, real time, to indicate practically instantaneous availability of stored or processed information output in more than adequate time to use it for decision or action.

The functions of a computer are simply stated. First, it carries out the same basic operation that every mechanical computation device has ever performed: it adds quantities. This means it can also be used to subtract (negative addition), multiply (repetitive addition), and divide (repetitive negative addition). The computer can also store data, instructions, and results and can retrieve the stored information for internal calculations or for output. Because of its storage capability, it can make predetermined comparisons. Because it can make predetermined comparisons, it can make predetermined choices. Most important, each operation is performed in millionths of a second because the whole internal process is carried out by electrical currents and charges.

Programming is a tedious operation requiring tremendous patience in the preparation of minutely detailed instructions. But once we prepare a generalized program, we can use it over and over with new parameters and data. Time-consuming as the programming process frequently is, computational time savings in even a single use can be enormous. Assuming no errors in the programming itself, the utility of the answers depends only on two factors which the data user himself must evaluate.

1. the applicability of the general procedure programmed to the kind of decision to be made

2. the quality and meaning of the input data for the purposes of the decision.

Since both are matters of personal judgment, not mathematics, it is always well to consider how well the answer corresponds with experience.

The computer performs two major types of service for the decision maker:

1. the purely computation service of assuming the tedium of multitudinous and prolonged calculations, such as those required by more complex linear programming solutions, Markov chain analyses, network solutions, and statistical decision computations, when alternatives are many and complex

2. simulation: that is, a cut-and-try process for determining what the resulting patterns or quantities would be if a given procedural rule, policy, or course of action were adopted.

In one sense, the solutions of linear program or network algorithms are forms of simulation: the carrying out of successive trial solutions in an iterative operation which gets progressively closer to an optimum solution. But this is properly considered a simple calculation process. Simulation is more often applied to somewhat less structured trial-and-error procedures of four types:

1. Experimental application of accepted rules and relationships to discover their pertinence and meaning in specific circumstances and to compare the results with known experience, in the hope of arriving at better analytical formulas, or to develop designs. Thus a computer has been used to simulate wind tunnel fluid dynamics, revealing important details difficult to obtain in physical experiments. Pictures were produced on a cathode ray tube giving a "remarkably faithful impression of the behavior of smoke or dye filaments" in a wind tunnel experiment. The purpose of the experimental simulation was to try "to discover workable approximations that will simplify the mathematics needed to solve complicated problems," in a situation in which needed mathematical techniques for complete solutions have not yet been developed.* Such uses are not likely to have direct business decision application in the near future, but have great possibilities in physical sciences and in engineering.

---

* Francis H. Harlow and Jacob E. Fromm, "Computer Experiments in Fluid Dynamics." Scientific American, Vol. 212, No. 3 (March, 1965), pp. 104-110.

2. Monte Carlo simulation of a probability distribution, to construct a prolonged synthetic experience, based on limited observation data.

3. Heuristic programming or simulation, a pure cut-and-try procedure according to some arbitrary or intuitive rules, comparing the results obtained from the use of such rules when applied to situations with a known structure.

4. Simulation of population distributions in miniature and testing the effect of proposed actions in terms of its effects on these simulated populations.

Monte Carlo simulation is a very useful auxiliary device for developing a more prolonged series of experiences than would be economical through direct observation, when the variability of quantities is thought to be of a random character, within specified limits and under a given probability distribution.

Heuristic programming offers promising possibilities as a really cheap substitute for extensive practical trial-and-error in many business decision situations for which we have no very satisfactory mathematical models capable of yielding optimum solutions.

Population simulation has already proved its worth as a device for projecting the interacting results of planned political campaign efforts and commercial advertising media programs, and would seem to have more extensive possibilities for forecasting the results of other kinds of planned action when we have data on the impact of individual actions on various parts of the population.

Monte Carlo Simulation

Some kind of probability distribution is a basic assumption in the solution of many types of mathematical decision models--in inventory problems, in waiting line problems, and in some kinds of network analyses, for example. It is, of course, possible to fall back on an extended series of actual observations as an approximation to such a probability distribution, if such an extensive series is available. But often only limited observation is available, enough to indicate the extent of variation, and something as to its shape, but not quite enough by itself. The alternative is to generate an approximation by random selection, or the so-called Monte Carlo method.

In its essentials, Monte Carlo simulation consists of nothing more than production of a series of random numbers, according to some previously determined probability distributions, in order to develop the kind of unpredictable individual variations which might be expected in practice, with the distribution governed by previous probability experience. If the number needed is small, this is exactly what is done by hand.

Consider a previous example: the Hectic Fisheries Supply inventory control problem. To start with, Hectic had the frequency distributions of nets demanded per day and of the number of days lead-time per order. They might have simply programmed a computer with this daily experience, as it occurred, and compared various combination of Q (order quantity) and R (reorder level) with this one year's experience. But all possible combinations of 0-to-3 nets per day demand, and 1-to-3 days lead-time would not occur within 1 year, in the proportions to be expected. (Remember that one possible policy tested would result in a shortage only twice in 5 years, according to our calculations.) So we chose instead to calculate the probability of every possible combination of demand per day and lead-time and to compute the costs and risks of each possible policy of Q, R combinations until our computations indicated we had found the optimum one.

Even this simplified problem involved a rather burdensome series of hand calculations. Had the maximum demand-per-day been not a mere three items, but hundreds or thousands with comparable variability, counting and calculating would have been more work than most would feel is justified. Without a computer, we would certainly have tried a Monte Carlo approach to sample the possible combinations instead of trying to enumerate all of them. Even this would have been no spare-time task if carried out by hand. A computer would have short-cut the tedium of Monte Carlo methods or allowed us to evaluate more samples. If we had a long enough back series of experiential information, it would even have permitted us to consider enumerating all of the actual combinations of lead-time and demand-per-day and calculate the values directly.

If we chose the Monte Carlo approach, let us see how this would work in Hectic's case, starting with the tabulated frequency of demand-per-day and of lead-time per order, which were as follows:

Nets Demanded During Day	Percentage of Days
None	40
1	30
2	20
3	10

Lead-time per Order (Days)	Percentage of Orders
1	25
2	50
3	25

For each period, we would draw two sets of numbers from our random number table:

1. a number to represent the reorder lead-time for that period, to tell us whether the lead-time is 1, 2, or 3 days

2. a number for each of the lead-time days, to tell us whether demand on that day is 0, 1, 2, or 3 kippered herring nets.

For the lead-time number, using some arbitrary sequence for successive drawings, we will read off a 2-digit number from our table and interpret it as follows:

1 day's lead-time if number is between 1 and 25

2 days' lead-time if number is between 26 and 75

3 days' lead-time if number is between 76 and 00

Then for each of these lead-time days, we will read off a 1-digit number in the same way, interpreting it thusly:

0, 1, 2, or 3 means <u>0</u> demand

4, 5, or 6 means <u>1</u> net demand

7 or 8 means <u>2</u> nets demanded

9 means <u>3</u> nets demanded

If a computer is available, we can instruct it (program it) to do the same thing, no matter how large the series is likely to be (within reasonable limits), and then tabulate the results in a combined probability table as we did for the Hectic case. If we have the computer run the simulation for a large number of order periods, the results are the same as though the probabilities were calculated directly.

Pure Cut-And-Try: Heuristic Programming

Suppose you were the head of a large food processing firm--say H. J. Heinz, and you realized the time had come to modernize and streamline your complex processing, shipping, warehousing and selling system.* You have production plants scattered all over the country, each with a different product-mix capability, a complex of warehouses and shipping points handling scores of different products to serve literally thousands of customers of many sizes and differing demand patterns and ordering habits, you have the choice of shipping by rail or by truck, in full carloads or truckloads, or less than carload or

* The example which follows is based on the report of a study which H. J. Heinz made, as printed in Harvey N. Shycon and Richard B. Maffei, "Simulation--Tool for Distribution," <u>Harvard Business Review</u>, Vol. 38, No. 6 (Nov.-Dec., 1960) pp. 65-84.

truckload, under a complex rate structure whose costs are not linear nor representable by any simple equations. The nature of the relationships rules out any simple linear programming solutions. Two factors need optimizing: service time and overall cost. In studying any suggested distribution configuration, customers would have to be defined in terms of at least four variables (geographical location, order size and frequency, volume of purchases, variety requirements) and producing factories in terms of three variables (geographical location, production capability by product line, and product mix, both actual and potential). The distribution system would have to be represented by a model expressed in the following terms:

1. How frequently each customer orders, how much, which products and sizes, where located, and how they prefer to take delivery.
2. The kinds of goods which can be shipped from each specific factory point, in what quantities, and the location.
3. For truck and rail, the relationship between shipping rates and points of origin and destination, for different types and sizes of orders.
4. The relationship between total volume handled at warehouse and mixing points and total costs.
5. Knowledge of where these relationships differ, so that adjustments could be made in cost and volume estimates. (For example, at some given volume, direct shipping would be better than warehousing.)

Hand calculation would require 75 million computations for only one suggested configuration with this model; or about the output of 100 clerks working for a year, just to estimate the overall cost and service time results for a single set of assumptions as to the product mix at each factory, the warehousing points and mixing points to be used, and the transportation arrangements. And quite a number of such configurations would have to be tested. But once a computer is properly programmed, it could handle the calculations for any one configuration in one hour. To test the results of some variation in the detail of a configuration, such as the change of the product mix at any one plant, even less computer time is needed. This makes possible a form of dry-run experimentation which can add knowledge about the importance and effect of individual factors through systematic variation, one at a time. Some of the plans tested could thus be suggested by interim computer results. At the end you should know more than merely which of the plausible plans tested gives the best estimated combination of cost and service, but also why, and how sensitive the choice of a given configuration would be.

Carefully thought out computer simulation can be used to evaluate many kinds of business operating plans and procedures. Various studies have shown, for example, that a large part of any salesman's time is spent in travelling from one customer to another, and that an easy way to lower sales cost is to reduce this time by proper routing. The problem is made more complex by customer classification systems which vary the number of calls scheduled over time, between classifications, in order to optimize the sales per call. No known mathematical model is guaranteed to give an optimum answer to the routing problem, but various plausible routings can be tried and compared with each other. One such plausible rule might be to direct the salesman to the next nearest point in a clockwise direction, avoiding any backtracking, another to divide the territory into a number of subterritories, each with a focal point out of which all calls in the subterritory would be routed according to some specific rule of direction and sequence. The computer output might be available not only in numbers, but as a map on a graphic display terminal, which could be reproduced for study and use. Some rough mental model is needed to gain insight into alternatives of course. Pure blind simulation is unlikely to produce a usable result.

Even when no definitive model is available which yields an optimum answer, we can find the best of any suggested alternatives through computer simulation if we can express the factors influencing outcomes in some kind of quantitative terms (such as cost, distance, direction, time, and the like). In most such cases of heuristic simulation, the program against which we test our arbitrary rules are relatively simple static relationships: the geographical relationships of stops in a salesman's territory, the freight cost schedules and location of producing areas in customers for Heinz, the equations expressing the physical laws of aerodynamics when we want to try out alternate wing section designs for an airplane. Little or no actual statistical experience data is needed because the meaningful influences on the outcome are the statically simple relationships of the physical world.

But some kinds of usable simulation are concerned mainly with the dynamic and complex socioeconomic relationships of human behavior. The computer program we need for such simulations is not only many times more complex, but so dependent on meaningful statistical experience in the input and so in need of constant updating as to be a really different sort of simulation.

Population Behavior Simulation

When we wish to simulate the design of an airplane, we can program the computer with a few mathematical equations, representing such things as the behavior of structural materials under stress and of a wing surface under air flow. When we wish to simulate the response of the electorate to a potential campaign appeal, or test the possible impact of a given selection of advertising media on the national market, we have no equations, but only piles of more or less meaningful statistical tabulation from various surveys, in constant need of updating, classified by various socioeconomic groupings and geographical segments. The detail involved in the analysis of this mountain of tabulations, however incomplete at times, was far too much for computation before the computer became available, and would tax the capacity of the largest computers available if we tried to cover the full population. Fortunately, both in politics and in advertising, (in both of which population behavior simulation has proved useful), we are interested in significant segments of the population, rather than in individuals as such.

Computer capacity is adequate to permit us to develop a replica of the total population, representing what we can know about its composition socially and economically, by major market areas, and about major market reactions and exposure to advertising communications of various types. In politics, the method proved useful in the 1960 campaign as a means of testing how various subgroups would react to different candidates and statements of issues. The technique has begun to find use in the advertising area, particularly in the testing of possible advertising media choices. Each developer of such a program has put his own trademarked label on it, but the title at the head of this section appears to be as good a designation of the type of simulation as any the author can think of. In writing of their trademarked Data Breeder Model, the Young and Rubicam advertising agency has indicated:

"This model is an 18,000-sample simulation of consumer behavior. It takes as its data input what information is available about a brand's customers or media audience, and then produces estimates of the information that is missing. In the bank of information from which the model may draw are considerable data from the United States Census, from survey sources, and from syndicated services. The computer draws on these data as they are needed, to produce the best estimates of missing information.

"The Data Breeder Model also has the capability of analyzing reach and frequency patterns of existing and proposed media schedules among the entire population, or among a wide variety of different prospect groups."*

Obviously, such population behavioral simulations are of little value if they are static. They would soon be made obsolete by the changes constantly taking place in various aspects of population composition and in public tastes and attitudes. But one of the virtues of the computer is that stored data can be automatically updated by programming trends into the model, and by input corrections, both of which can be carried out with very little effort.

SUMMARY

1. The computer is simply a fantastically fast, automatically instructed electronic device which can store information and process it as instructed. Its flexibility and capacity are making it a major aid in the use of mathematical decision tools because the electrical impulses it generates can be designated and come out as numbers, other symbols, words, sentences, or diagrams.

2. The computer is often needed to carry out the lengthy calculation needed for solution of most of the quantitative tools discussed in previous chapters, but it has also given us a virtually new way of finding out how suggested plans might work: computer simulation.

3. The most common forms of computer simulation are:

(a) Experimental application of accepted rules and relationships to learn more about the results of their application and to develop more accurate knowledge. Largely limited to investigation in the physical sciences so far.

(b) Monte Carlo simulation for the construction of an extended synthetic experience series where the variations are thought to be random and actual experience data limited. Primarily an auxiliary tool in the solution of such problems as inventory and waiting line.

(c) Heuristic programming, or the calculation of the results of arbitrary rules and procedures and the comparison of these results with those obtained from variations in these rules and from alternative sets of rules. Very promising in the solution of business decision problems where no known form of quantitative analysis yields an optimum answer.

---

* William T. Moran, "Practical Media Decisions and the Computer," <u>Journal of Marketing</u>, Vol. 27, No. 3 (July, 1963) pp. 26-30.

(d) Population behavioral simulation: the creation of sample populations and their known behavior patterns relative to those characteristics in a given problem situation, against which we can try various planned actions to get an estimate of the net effect of complex interactions which may result. Has already proved its value in estimating the effect of political campaign actions, and in the handling of media mix problems in advertising.

GLOSSARY OF SIMULATION TERMS

ALGORITHM: a rule for carrying out a series of iterative (repeated) trial solutions for a problem, in which each attempt gets progressively closer to an optimum solution until it is reached, and includes a means of identifying that optimum solution.

COMPUTER PROGRAM: data and instructions stored in a computer for the purpose of producing a solution to a series of problems, or occasionally for a single problem.

CUT-AND-TRY: not an orthodox technical computer term, but the common sense elliptical form of saying "cut and try to see if it works," familiar to anyone whoever carried out a non-routine mechanical task. Used here because it is an apt description of many of the values of a computer--its ability to go through the tedium of numerous successive trial-and-error calculations speedily and cheaply, whether the calculation is an iterative algorithm such as in linear programming, or the calculation of arbitrary heuristic solution rules, as in pure simulation.

HEURISTIC PROGRAM: more understandably, and just as accurately, labelled "rule of thumb" programming. Use of the same kind of arbitrary rules for decision used by human problem solvers when standard analytical methods are not available, and calculating the effect of different variations of the quantities in the situation against these rules.

ITERATIVE SOLUTION: One in which the same mathematical procedure is repeated over and over again in reaching a solution.

MONTE CARLO SIMULATION: generation of a synthetic experience series by some variation of a random numbers system, to represent probable actual experience over a long period of time, in a situation in which such experience is thought to be subject to chance variation, within known limits.

POPULATION BEHAVIOR SIMULATION: the author's own label for a class of trademarked programs which provide a computer with large quantities of available statistical information about a given human population and its behavior in matters relevant to various advertising, marketing, political or other types of decision. The population is usually a scaled down simulated simplification of the actual population, and the factors programmed are usually subject to continual change and must be kept currently updated, a characteristic not generally true of most kinds of heuristic programming.

A SELECTIVE BIBLIOGRAPHY (In addition to such general works as those listed, publishers are beginning to bring out slim paperbacks with excellent treatments of individual subjects such as Vectors and Matrices, Operations Research Techniques, Models for Business Analysis, etc.. Most such are written for ease of understanding and are well worth investigation.)

Archibald, Russell D., and Villoria, Richard L., Network-Based Management Systems. New York: John Wiley and Sons, 1967. A relatively comprehensive review of the variant forms of network analysis and some of their applications.

Dorfman, Robert, Samuelson, Paul A., and Solow, Robert M., Linear Programming and Economic Analysis. New York: McGraw-Hill Book Co., Inc., 1958. A thorough and largely non-mathematical discussion of the related techniques of linear programming and game theory, the possible applications of linear algebra to economic analysis, and the limitations of game theory in relation to business decision. A brief exposition of matrix algebra is included in the appendix.

Kemeny, John G., Schleifer, Arthur Jr., Snell, J. Laurie, and Thompson, Gerald L., Finite Mathematics with Business Applications. Englewood Cliffs, N. J.: Prentice-Hall, Inc., 1962. A mathematics text giving complete elementary coverage to mathematical logic, statistical desision theory, matrix algebra, linear programming, queueing theory and game theory. Assumes an elementary knowledge of ordinary algebra.

McMillan, Claude, and Gonzalez, Richard F., Systems Analysis: a Computer Approach to Decision Models. Homewood, Ill.: Richard D. Irwin, Inc., 1965. Contains fairly full discussions of the inventory model, queueing, network analysis and computer simulation, together with specific outlines of Fortran computer programs for them.

Richman, Samuel B., Operations Research for Management Decision. New York: The Ronald Press, 1968. A thoroughly readable yet soundly basic textual treatment of all the tools discussed in this treatise, plus some more. The author is obviously quite at home with and interested in the Bayesian approach, and in the kinds of problems for which it is best suited.

Rummel, J. Francis, and Ballaine, Wesley C., Research Methodology in Business. New York: Harper & Row, Publishers, 1963. Appendix A is an extremely lucid 58-page "Review of Basic Statistical Concepts and Calculations."

Schlaifer, Robert, Probability and Statistics for Business Decisions. New York: McGraw-Hill Book Co., 1959. The first and still the most complete text on the Bayesian approach to business decision.

Spur, William A., and Bonini, Charles P., Statistical Analysis for Business Decision. Homewood, Ill.: Richard D. Irwin, Inc., 1967. A relatively comprehensive exposition of statistical tools, including Bayesian approaches, with some brief comments on their limitations.

GREEK ALPHABET

Alpha	A, α	Nu	N, ν
Beta	B, β	Xi	Ξ, ξ
Gamma	Γ, γ	Omicron	O, o
Delta	Δ, δ	Pi	Π, π
Epsilon	E, ϵ	Rho	P, ρ
Zeta	Z, ζ	Sigma	Σ, σ, s
Eta	H, η	Tau	T, τ
Theta	Θ, θ	Upsilon	Υ, υ
Iota	I, ι	Phi	Φ, ϕ
Kappa	K, κ	Chi	X, χ
Lambda	Λ, λ	Psi	Ψ, ψ
Mu	M, μ	Omega	Ω, ω

APPENDIX. SOME OF THE COMMON ABBREVIATIONS AND CONVENTIONS OF MATHEMATICAL LANGUAGE

ABSTRACT SYMBOLIC LABELS DENOTING QUANTITIES

GENERALIZED VARIABLES: x, y, z, x_1, x_2, x_3, etc.--denote a set of quantities which can, even in the context of a specific situation, be any one of an extremely large number of values depending on the circumstances. The choice of any particular letter is quite arbitrary, and it must be defined.

GENERALIZED COEFFICIENTS AND OTHER CONSTANTS: a, b, c, d, k, a_1, a_2, a_3, etc. Are called constants when standing alone (as in x = a), coefficients when they modify a variable (as in x = ay). They indicate quantities which have a single value in the context of a particular situation and a given mathematical relationship.

GENERALIZED SUBSCRIPTS: such as 1, 2, 3, k in a_1, x_1, x_2, a_3, x_k (read as "a-sub-1", etc.)--simply differentiating labels which distinguish x_1 as denoting a quite different quantity than does x_2, for example. They have no separate quantitative significance of their own, are simply a device for economizing in the use of separate symbols.

k, when used as a subscript refers to some specific but undesignated finite value of the variable or constant. (Similarly, when used as an exponent, it denotes a specific but undesignated finite power, and when used in such expressions as "the kth term" refers to some finite end, usually, of a series of similar terms.)

i, when used as a subscript, denotes "an individual value" of whatever it modifies. When used in a formula or in a table heading (x_i, for example), it indicates that the appropriate individual numerical value is to be substituted. Σx_i would be read as "the sum of the individual values of x."

GENERALIZED EXPONENTS: 2, 3, 4, a, b, x, y, k in x^2, y^3, a^x, etc. indicate power. That is, they indicate that the designated quantity is to be multiplied by itself as many times as designated by the exponent.

SPECIFIC STANDARD ABBREVIATIONS

UNIVERSAL:

(pi)--a single specific irrational number (approximately 3.1416 to the 5th significant figure) which is always the ratio of the circumference of any circle to its own diameter

e--another irrational number which is the base for natural logarithms

STATISTICAL CONVENTIONS:

$\bar{x}$, $\bar{y}$, etc. (usually read as "x-bar, y-bar") --the mean of all values of the designated variable

μ (mu)--often used to indicate the midpoint of a normal distribution, or sometimes used instead of $\bar{x}$, simply indicating the arithmetic mean.

p--the probability of whatever it modifies. Thus, p(x - y), meaning "the probability of (x - y).

q--the reverse probability. That is, the probability of <u>not-occurring</u>. By definition, (p + q) is always equal to 1.

n--the number of observations

(sigma)--the actual standard deviation of a distribution (the square root of the average of the squares of the deviations of individual items from the mean)

s--the standard error, that is, the estimate of σ calculated from a set of sample observations

SYMBOLIC OPERATING INSTRUCTIONS

+ (plus)--add the two quantities thus joined. That is, increase the first by the amount of the second

- (minus)--subtract the two quantities thus joined. That is, decrease the first of the two quantities by the amount of the second.

x or $\cdot$, as in x x y or x $\cdot$ a, or mere juxtaposition when using letter symbols as in ab and in (a + x)(b - y)--multiply one term by the other. That is, add the second term to itself as many times as indicated by the first term (or the other way around--it comes out the same).

$\div$, /, or ____, as in a $\div$ b, a/b and $\frac{a}{b}$, --"divide by"--that is, subtract the the second term from the first as many times as possible before it reaches zero.

Σ (Sigma), as in $\Sigma (x_i - \bar{X})$--the sum of all the individual values indicated by the symbol or expression which follows.

$\sum_{X=a}^{X=b} (\quad)$--the sum of all those values for the expression within the parenthesis which are between the value indicated at the bottom of the sign and the value indicated at the top.

SYMBOLS OF RELATIONSHIP

= ("equals"), as in $x = a$ --indicates that the quantities on either side of the sign can be considered as completely substitutable for each other for the specific purpose under consideration

$\cong$ ("approximately equal to"), as in $\pi \cong 3.1416$--indicates that the two quantities may not be quite equal, but the difference between them is not significant for the purpose under consideration

$\sqrt{\ }$ ("radical")--take the square root of whatever is under the sign. That is, find that number which, when multiplied by itself, will give the number under the radical. When the radical carries a number, as in $\sqrt[k]{\ }$, the kth root to be taken--that is, that number found which when multiplied by itself k times will give the number under the radical

$>$ ("greater than"), as in $a>b$ ("a is greater than b")--indicates a significant inequality in the stated direction. Can also be represented in the opposite direction, as in $b<a$, meaning "b is less than a." Thus $1 > p > 0$ is shorthand for "p is some value between 0 and 1, but is not equal to either"

$\geq$ ("equal to or greater than," and thus also means "at least, and may be more than")

$\leq$ ("equal to or less than," and thus "no more than, and it may be less")

$\cup$, as in $A \cup B$ ("the intersection of set A with set B," often read as "A cup B")--signifies all of those items which are part of both the set of phenomena designated by A and that set designated by B

$\cap$, as in $A \cap B$ ("the union of set A with set B," read as "A cap B")--signifies all items which are part of either set A or set B, or both.

f( ), as in f(x) ("some function of x")--signifies that whatever is defined as equal to it has a single definable value for each separate value of the variables enclosed in the parenthesis

$\int f(x)$ ("the integral of the function of x")--an analog of $\Sigma f(x)$, but applies whenever f(x) is a continuous relationship and the number of values of f(x) thus is infinite even for a small portion of it. $\int f(x)$ is a relationship whose solution defines the total area bounded by f(x).

$\int_{x=a}^{x=b} f(x)$--the area bounded by f(x) between the point where x = a and the point where x = b.

Δx--signifies an incremental change in the value of x

dx ("differential of x")--the infinitesimal change in the value of x as it passes through a single point in the function

$\frac{dx}{dy}$ ("the differential of x with respect to y")--signifies the expression which tells how to calculate the slope of the curve plotted by an equation, and thus is the equation for the rate of change in the curve from which it is derived

Logarithmic functions: log x (the logarithm of x to the base e) and $\log_{10}x$ (the logarithm of x to the base 10). Each of these indicates a number which, when it is the exponent of the base indicated, will give the value of x. Tables of these values, and slide rules scaled from them, have long served to ease the carrying out of multiplication, division, calculation of powers, and computation of roots. These functions have another valuable property, however. A great many relationships are exponential functions (such as $y = a^x$) or approximately so over sections of their curves. Substituting the logarithmic form ($\log y = x \log a$) changes the characteristically J-shaped exponential relationship to a straight line relationship which is easier to use in such computations as linear programming.

sin x, cos x ("Sine x, Cosine x")--the labels given to standard trigonometric functions which can be represented graphically by the familiar wavelike plots we call cycles.

REVIEW EXERCISES TO REINFORCE YOUR UNDERSTANDING

(For answers, see pages 248-260)

THE MEANING OF FIGURES

On the basis of the accompanying table listing the official 1960 population for the 25 largest cities in the United States, their land area, and the populations of the 25 largest standard metropolitan statistical areas (SMSA),*

a) What is the largest city in the U.S.A.?

b) What is the second largest?

c) Which is larger: Boston or Houston?

d) Which is the most important city?

---

*A standard metropolitan statistical area (SMSA) is an agreed upon compromise definition of the recognized metropolitan area of a central city with a population of 50,000 or more. It generally includes the total population of all of the counties containing the city and its suburbs. However, in some cases political considerations and local business pride enter in to split off parts of the generally recognized area as a separate metropolitan area. Thus the generally recognized metropolitan area of New York City clearly covers the northern New Jersey area but the Census Bureau has been forced to define this area as parts of two added SMSA's: Newark, N.J. and Paterson-Clifton-Passaic, N.J., and Jersey City, N.J. (pop. 611 thousand), all within sight of downtown Manhattan. Orange County, California would look to the outsider as inseparable from the Los Angeles area, yet has been redefined in recent years as the separate Anaheim-Santa Ana Garden Grove SMSA with a 1960 population of 704 thousand. The San Jose airport is officially recognized as part of the San Francisco area's air facilities, but a separate San Jose SMSA (pop. 643 thousand) is listed by the Census Bureau.

POPULATION, 1960, OF THE 25 LARGEST CITIES AND THE 25 LARGEST STANDARD METROPOLITAN STATISTICAL AREAS, U.S.A.

Rank Order City Pop.		Population, 1960 (Thousands) City Proper	SMSA	Land Area (sq. mi.)	Rank Order SMSA Pop.	SMSA Population Increase, 1960-1966 (Per cent)
1	New York, N.Y.	7,782	10,695	300	1	6.7
2	Chicago, Ill.	3,550	6,221	222	2	8.2
3	Los Angeles, Calif.	2,479	6,039	455	3	12.4
4	Philadelphia, Pa.	2,003	4,343	129	4	8.0
5	Detroit, Mich.	1,670	3,762	138	5	7.9
6	Baltimore, Md.	939	1,727	78	12	9.8
7	Houston, Tex.	938	1,243	321	17	22.7
8	Cleveland, Ohio	876	1,909	76	11	5.0
9	Washington, D.C.	764	2,002	61	10	26.7
10	St. Louis, Mo.	750	2,105	61	9	8.5
11	Milwaukee, Wis.	741	1,233	90	18	4.1
12	San Francisco, Calif.	740	2,649	45	6	11.7
13	Boston, Mass.	697	2,895	46	7	3.0
14	Dallas, Tex.	680	1,084	254	22	20.8
15	New Orleans, La.	627	907[a]	205	28	15.0
16	Pittsburgh, Pa.	604	2,405	55	8	-1.2
17	San Antonio, Tex.	588	716	148	37	16.1
18	San Diego, Calif.	573	1,033	195	23	13.0
19	Seattle, Wash.	557	1,107	82	20	9.7
20	Buffalo, N.Y.	533	1,307	41	15	1.2
21	Cincinnati, Ohio	503	1,268	77	16	6.7
22	Memphis, Tenn.	498	675	129	39	11.5
23	Denver, Colo.	494	929	68	26	16.5
24	Atlanta, Ga.	487	1,017	136	24	23.7
25	Minneapolis, Minn.	483)	1,482	(53	(14	9.9
(40)	St. Paul, Minn.	313)		(52	(	
27	Kansas City, Mo.	476	1,093	130	21	10.7
44	Miami, Fla.	292	935	34	25	15.6
30	Newark, N.J.	405	1,689	24	13	10.2
85	Paterson-Clifton-Passaic, N.J.	144	1,187	8	19	

2. Below are some Weather Bureau data for Minneapolis (as reported at the airport:

Item	Month								
	Jan.	Feb.	Mar.	Apr.	May	June	July	Aug.	Sept.
Temperature of record:									
Highest	58	59	78	92	95	100	104	102	98
Lowest	-41	-36	-28	-5	16	30	37	36	22

If this were all the information you had available, and you were asked what the temperature probably is as of an April date, what could you say? Express it in mathematical symbolism.

3. The map indicates that it is 841 miles from New York to Chicago, but the scale gives no information as to the distance from Chicago, Ill. to Elgin, just shows that it is west of Chicago, but not very far west. Express the distance from New York to Elgin, Ill., according to this information, in mathematical language.

4. You do not know how old Mary is, but you know she is one of John's younger sisters, and John was with you, grade for grade, all through school. You are 35. Give your statement as to her probable age, in mathematical language.

5. When you make out your income tax return, your total income for tax purposes is, according to Internal Revenue instructions, the total of your wages, salaries and tips, plus your "other income", less adjustments to income. Your "other income", however, is calculated by summing up:

a) Taxable dividends, defined as: Gross dividends and other distributions on stock, less exclusions not to exceed $100 each for husband and wife, less capital gain distributions, less nontaxable distributions (defined as return of capital).

b) Interest received.

c) Pensions and annuities, net rents (after expenses and depreciation) and royalties, partnerships, estates, or trusts.

d) Net business income or loss.

e) Net gains from sale and exchange of property. For tax purposes, these are defined as all of net short time gain (property held less than 6 months) plus one-half of long-term gain. However, if this total is negative (a loss), it can be subtracted from total income only up to $1,000 or to an amount equal to total income minus deductions.

Translate the above into mathematical language.

MEASUREMENT:

6. A building constructed to house a clerical operation cost $875,000 on land worth $100,000. Its specifications are such that the floor loads will not permit use as a warehouse, and no other organization would desire an office in that location. What is the value of the building as an asset?

7. A very practical form of classification is that of quality grading. From time to time, various groups propose that official government grades be applied to virtually all consumer goods. They point to market efficiencies achieved through application of official grades to such items as fresh eggs, meat, and butter sold at retail, and to a wide variety of commodities sold as raw material to industry (cotton and all grains, for example). How would you measure the grade of a given new passenger automobile, a house, or a ball gown?

8. One frequently meaningful way of classifying people is by age groupings. There are obvious similarities in the needs of those of primary school age, for example, and a different set of needs for those who are over 65. During the late 1960's, some people scanning the Census population projections were startled to discover that one possible projection indicated that people under 25 would be about half the total U.S. population by 1975. They began to insist that marketers and politicians focus their future plans on serving this group. In fact, a play was written around a take-over of the country by those under 25.

Comment on this "under 25" classification, used in this context.

9. How many significant figures are in:

a) 937.6 b) 001263 c) 3745 thousand

10. My tape measure is marked in eighths of an inch, and I am a little short of 6 feet tall. My height in the evening is about 1/2 inch less than in the morning. To how many significant figures am I justified in expressing my height?

11. The correlation coefficient in a validation test of entrance examination scores against the success of graduates was based on a study of 149 students. Even as history, to how many significant figures are we justified in carrying out the calculation?

12. Economists measure the growth and the fluctuations of the economy in terms of the Gross National Product (GNP), the best estimate they can make of "the total value of all goods and services produced" in a year's time, in a nation. In practice, GNP is defined solely in market terms, because of the difficulties of measuring services which do not go onto some market. For example, the unpaid homemaking services contributed by a housewife are not part of the GNP. But if she goes to work and hires a cleaning lady to take over some of her duties, the wages of the latter are part of GNP. The value of some items, such as total automobile production, are counted quite precisely and easily measured. Other items such as the total value of babysitting, are the roughest of approximate guesses. Many are hard to measure--such items as the total net creation of capital goods. The new construction of the latter are not too hard to get, but from them (and from all building construction) we must subtract the physical wear and tear and declines in market value due to obsolescence. Such items as the value of educational output produced, or value of governmental services, are measured in terms of cost. Many measurements are necessarily based on sample information, from biased samples.

To how many significant figures would you trust the expression of GNP?

13. Approximately 1,500 securities are listed on the New York Stock Exchange. Some trade every day in large volume, others skip days without a trade. The trading volume in any stock will vary greatly over time, independent of total

volume on the market, and the latter has wide swings.

The market as a whole has obvious up and downswings, but rarely or never do all stocks go in the same direction on a given day. While it is true that a buyer or seller deals in a few individual issues, never in the market as such, the general "climate" of the market is an important decision variable for traders and market watchers. Consequently, a number of indexes have been constructed to measure these swings. The most widely watched is the Dow-Jones Industrial Index, an "average" of the prices of a single share each of 30 well-known "blue chips", divided by an arbitrary divisor.. Since the advent of computers, the N. Y. Stock Exchange itself publishes an index composed of the average change in the prices of all common stock issued, obtained by adding the price of one share each of the listed issues, and dividing by the number of shares.

Which is the better index? Why are both called indexes, not measures? If you wished an accurate <u>measure</u> of the changes on the exchange, one which would enable you to plot trends accurately over time, how would you construct the measure?

14. Anyone who does much reading is bound to come across some quotations of by-gone prices, usually of the 1920's and 1930's: 5¢ transit fares, steak for 25¢ lb., milk for 10¢ a quart, steak dinners for 50¢, automobiles for $325, etc. To someone accustomed to the prices of more recent years, these look awfully attractive. Are they really? If not, why not, and how would you measure these prices to show that the glitter is false?

15. Temperatures can vary within relatively small areas. Thus, on one early spring morning, the readings at 6 different stations in the same city were reported as 19 degrees, 23 degrees, 27 degrees, 28 degrees, 30 degrees, and 32 degrees. The 30 degree reading was at the "official" station for the area--the one covered by the official forecast. Furthermore, the differences are sometimes much less than this, and not always in the same direction. As anyone who follows weather forecasts knows, the forecast itself is subject to some error, expressible in degrees. Suppose you owned a peach orchard in full bloom, within what range of precision would you wish the forecast of a minimum temperature of (a) 35, (b) of 52 degrees?

SAMPLING AND PROBABILITY DISTRIBUTIONS

16. We are trying to gauge public support for a bond proposal for a new school, and do not want to submit the proposal unless there is a high probability of passage. Information from past elections in this community indicates that the favorable vote has ranged on both sides of 50%, with an estimated standard error of 5%. Funds for the poll are limited, and interviews will cost at least $5 each. Spending $500 for an initial sample of 100 reveals 51 favorable.

a) Assuming no bias, what does this sample result reveal as to the probability of passage?

b) What would it cost to increase the sample to a size which, with the same percentage result, would give very strong assurance that an actual majority will vote favorably (a sample, in other words, in which three times the standard error of the favorable percentage is less than 1%).

17. All mail sampling involves the use of some kind of lists of names, and much other sampling is based on the use of lists for reasons of economy. All lists unfortunately, have a time bias. By the time they are available, they represent the population as it existed months, frequently a year or more before. Some have other biases in addition--one of telephone subscribers, for example, omits those parts of the population which have no telephone, or which resort to unlisted numbers. Of all biases, the effect of time bias is easiest to see.

(a) In a study of consumer preferences, what kind of bias is involved in the use of a city directory which presumably lists every household of approximately one year before?

(b) For what kinds of purchases would the bias be greater: the purchase of baby foods, or the purchase of soft drinks, and why?

BAYESIAN STATISTICS

18. One way to understand the difference between objective and personalistic probabilities is to look at the two sides of an insurance purchase--the seller's and the buyer's sides. An insurance firm bases its rates on "actuarial" experience--in life insurance, for example, on a very large series of specific death rates of people by age, sex, and occupation. The resulting mortality

experience tables are thus a series of objective probability calculations. The individual who is trying to decide whether the policy is a good buy for him would certainly look at these figures, but he would also note that some people die at every age interval, and some live much longer than the average on which rates are based.

What kinds of added information might be needed by such an individual making a personal evaluation of the value of a policy to him?

19. Bill and Mike, two young engineers earning $12,000 a year, have a chance to buy a franchise in a new shopping center amusement device for children. The total franchise cost is $40,000, of which $10,000 must be put up in cash, the rest as a note to be paid out of earnings. The device is new, and the only data they can get is based on a single installation in use for 6 months by the idea's developer. It looks to them that the satisfaction obtained is largely of a novelty character for most of the children, especially for the older ones, and its attraction for any individual would wear off in a few months of frequent use. If this were all it offers, then it would have the typical fad pattern, and might die off after 3 or 4 months, and before the first year is out, they would be bankrupt. However, one aspect of its use suggests it might have some special appeal for one market segment. They noted that some mothers with smaller children would leave the kids at the device with a handful of tickets while they were shopping. If this "baby-sitting" attribute is of much substantial value to many mothers, the appeal might last long enough for each new generation of 5-8 year olds to build a continuing demand. If it did, they estimated they could build up the business to a point where they could either quit their profession entirely, or resell the franchise at the end of the year for $100,000, after drawing salaries and profits of $20,000 each for the year. Running it, meantime, would require both to take a year's leave of absence from their jobs, as well as risk $10,000. The only immediately visible alternative use for their capital would be in securities yielding 6%. If they did not invest, they would have a combined income of $24,600--$24,000 in salary plus $600 in returns on securities. If they did invest, and the appeal proved to be a fad, they would lose their $24,000 in salary, the $10,000 invested, and the $600 opportunity loss on investment return, for a total loss of $34,600. If the demand proved stable, however, they would receive an estimated return

of $100,000 resale price plus $40,000 in income, for a net return of $130,000 ($140,000 less $10,000). They estimated the odds it was a fad at 90%.

(a) Construct the pay-off table, assuming the fad prior probability at 90%.

(b) Bill knows of a market research firm specializing in product acceptance investigations. How much would a study be worth which would distinguish with certainty between a fad demand and continuing appeal?

(c) On the basis of his own observations of the research firm's work, Mike estimates that their actual results run only about 80% correct. What is the expected value of the research under this circumstance?

BAYESIAN DECISION MODELS

20. Progress Corporation is aware that its profits are highly dependent on development of a constant stream of new and improved products. Consequently, it uses every available source of new ideas, funnelling them to a New Products Screening Committee of high officials which gives serious initial consideration to any idea presented. This committee makes an initial evaluation of the fit of the probable product to the firm's own objectives, skills, and interests, and also considers the business prospects of the idea as developed by simple research of secondary materials by the research department. About half of the ideas suggested are discarded as incompatible with the firm, and half of those remaining are discarded as having insufficient potential. The surviving fourth may be assigned a developmental budget immediately, or may be turned over to Research for concept research.

Concept research investigates the attractiveness, to the presumed target market segment, of a possible set of product performance specifications, assuming a product can be built to so perform. Typically, it works with relatively modest samples and averages $2000 per test. Generally, too, it results in something more than mere screening. The findings tend to sharpen the specifications and modify them, often appreciably, thus lending some guidance to R & D. Even if a product can be built to meet the findings, however, concept research is not infallible. Progress has found about 20% of those reaching market still fail. This is an improvement over the 50% of those not so tested initially. Concept testing passes 75% of those tested.

Concept research has no effect on the success of R & D in perfecting the product itself, however. Only about half of products sent to R & D emerge successful from the process. An average of $50,000 is spent on such work, whether or not it succeeds.

Developed products are turned over to pilot production and market or use testing of some sort. This is more expensive, typically costing an additional $200,000 per product. Half of those reaching this stage do not survive. Sometimes, the market test will be skipped as not meaningful, and a simple consumer panel test substituted. The latter requires only $100,000 but is only 80% as efficient as the market test. Half of those market or use tested pass.

Degree of success differs to some degree, but we can simplify and divide products into two categories of real success and failure. Looked at this way, the value of a successful product can be capitalized, on the average, at $5,000,000. The average full commercial introduction costs $1,000,000.

Sketch the decision tree and decision path values for the Progress Corporation's new product process.

21. Trying to decide on a best bid on the basis of past experience with the four known competitors, we estimate that each is equally likely to enter a bid at a profit level of 10 % or more: p = .20 for each one, for such a bid.

(a) What is the probability that we will win with a bid which will yield 10% on an estimated cost of $16,000,000?

(b) What is the profit position value for such a bid?

(c) What is our estimated actual profit?

22. We have a complete past record for Competitor A. We judge that 9 of these bid objectives are relevant to the current effort, ranking as follows:

-.035, -2, 0, .01, .02, .04, .0425, .07, .09

What is the initially estimated probability that A will make a break-even bid or higher on this next job?

23. The inventory model manifestly requires some estimate of the cost of shortages. Making such an estimate is much like giving an estimate of what price we would pay for something we have never bought. Direct answers to such questions have never proved very reliable. Similarly, an executive can frequently make no meaningful direct statement of what he thinks the cost value of a shortage is. What device might be used to arrive at a limiting estimate ("at least $_____") indirectly?

24. One of the early and still most practical uses of linear programming has been the so-called diet or blending model--the calculation of the least-cost mixture of ingredients to produce a given animal feed or fertilizer specification, or the most profitable mix of store merchandise or of refinery oil products. One simple mixed feeds example would be that of a farmer with corn worth \$2.40/100 lb. who wishes to turn it into the lowest cost balanced mixed feed by adding soybean meal @ \$3.60/100 lb. or meat scraps @ \$4.20/100 lb. The corn contains 14% protein, the soybean meal, 44%, and meat scraps 50%. For proper nutrition, the mix must have at least a 20% protein content.

(a) Calculating the proper proportions of a 2-item mix is simple algebra. Write the formula for the solution of the number of pounds of soybean meal in the soy-corn mix. (Note that the number of pounds of corn in a 100 lb. mix is the difference between 100 and the weight of the meal.)

(b) What is the cost of the corn-soy mix?

(c) Calculate the proportions in and the cost of the corn-meat mix. Which is the cheaper: soybean meal or meat scraps?

(d) If meat scraps drop to \$3.60/100, which mix is cheaper?

(e) Assume that soybean meal is an imperfect substitute for meat scraps, so that the extra soy protein supplied must be no more than half the extra protein. Graph the linear program space defined by previous calculations and these new conditions. What are the possible solution points? What is now the best solution, at the original prices?

25. The staffing of a school or training program requires estimates of the number of students to be handled at each level of the program. The usual method of controlling this number is at the initial input level. However, there is always some attrition during the life of the program, and some possible accessions transferred from other programs at higher levels. Normally, only the initial entrance is fully controllable. Transferees meeting the same requirements as those in the advanced classes must usually be accepted. However, for purposes of problem formulation, all entrants can be considered part of the same outside pool of potentials and as deductions from the attrition. The underlying attrition and accession rates form a relatively stable set of

transitional probabilities, hence we can represent the rates as a typical Markov matrix. Since attrition is an absorbing state, we have a limited absorbing chain--limited, that is, by the number of stages or classes.

For example, consider Prairie State University's evening MBA program. The staff consists of full-time professors with assigned loads of 6 credits a term. Classes are aimed at 25-30, with a ceiling of 40 students. The total program requires 36 hours of academic credit. The maximum credit load per student is 6 hours per semester, but some take only 3, and some drop out for a term, then re-enter. Courses differ at each level, and are divided into 4 subject fields with little substitutability. Recent experience shows the following matrix. It contains 2 absorbing states: drop-outs (0) and completions (6, 7).

		Status following term							
		0	1	2	3	4	5	6	7
	0	0	1.0	0	0	0	0	0	0
Status at the beginning of the term	1	.2	.2	.6	0	0	0	0	0
	2	.2	0	.2	.6	0	0	0	0
	3	.3	0	0	.2	.5	0	0	0
	4	.2	0	0	0	.2	.6	0	0
	5	.1	0	0	0	0	.1	.8	0
	6	.1	0	0	0	0	0	.1	.8

(a) Using ordinary empirical methods, calculate the load at each term level if a constant 100 students are admitted each year.

(b) How many degrees will be granted each year?

CRITICAL PATH NETWORKS

26. Most of us learn to parallel our simpler routine tasks without drawing critical path networks. One simple routine which concerned housewives of a previous generation was periodic washing of clothes with a wringer-type electric washing machine. Since it was seldom wise to mix white clothes and colored clothes, dirty clothes were normally accumulated until a

washer-load of each was ready, necessitating at least two loads in the machine. If there were men in the family, socks were usually put through a separate load yet. Shirt collars and cuffs were usually starched with a solution made by dissolving laundry starch in a small pan of water and bringing it to a boil.

Operations on each load of clothes usually consisted of the following tasks , in the order listed:

Presoak clothes (10 minutes, min.)
Wring into washer (or basket if machine is busy) (Min. 2 minutes)
Wash (12 minutes)
Wring into hot rinse and stir (3 minutes)
Wring into cold rinse and stir (3 minutes)
Wring into basket, putting shirts aside for starching (2 minutes)
Starch shirt collars and cuffs (2 minutes)
Hang up to dry (10 minutes)

Starch was usually prepared at some point early in the program.

The wringer could be used on clothes outside the tub while the washer was cleaning those inside. Stockings did not have to be soaked more than 2 minutes.

Draw the network which minimizes total elapsed time and total waiting time, assuming 3 loads: white, colored, and socks.

USE AND INTERPRETATION OF CHARTS, RATES, PERCENTAGES AND AVERAGES

27. Below are the gross annual birth rates in the U.S. from 1910 to 1967:

1910	30.1	1941	21.0	1950	24.1	1959	24.3
1915	29.5	1942	22.3	1951	25.0	1960	23.7
1920	27.7	1943	22.5	1952	25.2	1961	23.3
1925	25.1	1944	21.1	1953	25.2	1962	22.4
1930	21.3	1945	20.4	1954	25.5	1963	21.7
1935	18.7	1946	20.5	1955	24.1	1964	21.0
1940	19.4	1947	26.5	1956	25.5	1965	19.4
		1948	25.0	1957	25.5	1966	18.4
		1949	24.3	1958	24.7	1967	17.8

(a) Plot the graph and project the apparent long run trend. What is the latter?

(b) How would you determine whether or not this apparent long-run trend is likely to continue?

28. The PXQ Corp. has developed and proven a new high precision instrument whose initial tests in actual use have attracted wide scientific recognition as a noticeable improvement on those currently available. However, in general, the $6,000 price charged by two major competitors for their apparatus, even with a customary 10% increase to $6,600 for the improvement, will not leave any profit margin. The shop complains that the metallurgy and machining were more difficult than any previous equipment required, so that cost targets were not met. The sales department does not believe that it can sell many for more than $6,600, and points out that the profit on the $30,000 worth of accessory equipment is $1,800, more than offsetting any loss.

Are there other principles with quantitative cost implications which might justify expectations of any greater profit at the suggested price?

29. (a) Plot the following data on the daily consumption of cigarettes, male smokers, U.S.A. (When plotting grouped data, be sure to proportion your bars to the width of the class value. For an open-end class like 41 or more, you have to approximate, "41-70" is probably close enough.

Cigarettes/day		Millions of smokers
1 - 10		4.5
11 - 20		12.8
21 - 40		9.0
41 or more		2.0
	TOTAL	28.3

(b) Using the conventional approximation of the average as the midpoint of the group, estimate the total consumption by each group above.

(c) What type of smoker is the most important, from the standpoint of the sellers of cigarettes?

30. (a) Plot graphs showing the following data for one of the industries below, indicating the number of corporations in selected industries submitting income tax returns, the value of their assets, and their total cash receipts, U.S.A. 1965.

	Asset-Size Class of Firm (Millions of dollars)						
Industry	Under 0.1	0.1-0.9	1 - 24	25 - 49	50 - 99	100-249	250 and over
All Industries							
Number (thous.)	846	491	81	2.9	1.5	1.1	0.8
Total assets ($bil.)	28	143	321	99	104	165	862
Total receipts ($bil.)	76	259	290	54	55	86	374
Mining							
Number (thous.)	7463	4502	1228	49	14	18	11
Total assets ($mil.)	239	1493	4686	1775	1050	2691	4612
Total receipts ($mil.)	552	1822		937	551	1783	3606
Manufacturing							
Number (thous.)	87	78		0.6	0.3	0.2	0.2
Total assets ($bil.)	3.1	25		20	22	36	197
Total receipts ($bil.)	13	60		28	30	49	219
Wholesale and Retail Trade							
Number (thous.)	267	159		0.16	0.06	0.04	0.03
Total assets ($bil.)	9.7	44		5.4	4.1	6.4	18
Total receipts ($bil.)	37	140		14	11	15	39

(b) What do these distributions imply as to the concentration of the market for those selling industrial and commercial items?

(c) What do they imply as to the nature of the distributive mechanisms needed to reach the whole of any market?

31. What do figures like those in Question 29 and Question 30 signify with respect to attempts to design products to fit the desires of "most buyers" or "a majority of customers"?

ANSWERS TO REVIEW EXERCISES

THE MEANING OF FIGURES

1. (a) That all depends on what purpose you have in mind when you use the word "largest". If your purpose refers to total people in any way, then New York City is the largest by almost any measure you would use: city population, metropolitan area population, size of consumer market (except for automobile and gasoline dealers), etc. But if land area is the measure, Los Angeles is first whether the area of the city proper or of its metropolitan area.

   (b) Judged solely by official statistics on population Chicago was somewhat larger, both as city and metropolis in 1960. But inclusion of the arbitrarily separated Orange County area (Anaheim, et al.) would indicate Los Angeles as slightly larger, and this Orange County area is clearly part of the economic and population base of the area.

   (c) As a political municipality, measured by the people able to vote for its government, Houston was the 7th largest city in 1960, and Boston down in the 13th position. But in terms of its economic base and the metropolis it served, Boston was seventh and Houston a mere 17th.

   (d) "Importance" is related to whatever is of subjective top interest to the individual, and figures can give us an answer only when we know what that individual finds to be important. If the questioner is a real estate investor, perhaps the combination of rapid growth and size make Houston or Washington, D. C. first choice. Washington is certainly the most important to anyone who is primarily a seller to the Defense establishment or who must depend on federal regulatory action of any kind. To someone with ambitions in the worlds of the stage or of advertising, Houston and Washington would have a low rating, and New York would be close to the top. If the interest is in skiing, no listed city is likely to qualify, and perhaps Aspen, Colorado may be most important. If the question of home and job comes first, the odds are about 40 per cent that an area much smaller than any of those listed should be named.

EQUATIONS AND INEQUALITIES

2. Let t = temperature, then $-5 < t < 92$

3. Let d = distance from New York City to Elgin, Ill. Then $d > 84$

4. If m = Mary's age, then $m < 35$

5. This can be expressed in one equation in all detail, but would usually be separated, as it is on the return, into a summary and some detailed calculations. The latter is easiest to handle.

Let T = total income
W = wages, salaries, tips, etc.
D = taxable dividends
I = interest
P = receipt of pensions, annuities, rents, etc.
B = net business gain or loss
C = reportable capital gains from sale and exchange of property
C_S = short term gains
C_L = long term gains
E = expenses on property
D = depreciation on property
X = personal exemptions

Then $T = W + D + I + (P - E - D) + B + C$

If C is positive, then $C = C_S + \frac{C_L}{2}$

If C is negative, then $\$1000 > C < (T - X)$

MEASUREMENT

6. In terms of realization on liquidation, the building is worthless or worse--something which would cost money to tear down. As a usable facility, the building is currently worth whatever it would cost to provide similar facilities of equal efficiency for its current use.

7. Classifying any item into linear grades of quality (such as "good", "better", "best", or, as in eggs, AA, A, B, C, etc.) can be done only when a single attribute is associated with quality, and near universal agreement holds as to what that attribute is. The attribute must also be measureable, directly or indirectly. In eggs, that attribute is freshness, and is correlated with the size of the air cell, observable in candling. In beefsteak, it is tender-

ness, in raw cotton, the length of the staple, in wheat, milling and baking quality, etc.

However, the desirability of most important consumer goods cannot be classified on the basis of a single attribute, and thus cannot be quality-graded on some linear scale. The automobile is a case in point. Some buyers desire high acceleration, attainable only with a high power/weight ratio and at the expense of heavier fuel consumption which others find unacceptable. Some buyers prefer a soft ride, others the controllability made possible by a stiffer suspension. Some desire large size, others the maneuverability and sensitivity of a small car. What is design virtue for some is vice for others. There can thus be no "grade A" car which is, for most of the market, better than a grade B. Nor can there be a grade A ball gown for every woman's taste.

8. For any purpose of political or market planning, "under 25" is probably the most meaningless classification of people possible, grouping together newborn babies with no decision powers of any kind with, at the other extreme, young adults who usually must decide for themselves. It spans the whole of the critical period from helpless infancy to the full powers of adulthood. No other similar span of years covers individuals with as diverse a range of interests and ability to act independently. It is a spurious classification, but only the most extreme of those which many people use (such as "all Chinese," "all women," etc.). Actually, the effective market decision makers in those under 25 are always well under 2/5 of the total, and the really important 20-25-year-olds less than 1/5.

9. All three figures are expressed to exactly the same 4-significant-figure level.

10. The tape measure would permit expression to roughly 3 significant figures. (It can be read directly to 8 x 70 = 560 parts, and an estimate of fractions of an eighth-inch can be estimated from the tape, or something better than 1 part in 5000.) However, any height measurement expressed closer than an inch is meaningless, so that the proper number is two significant figures ($2 \times 70 = 140 \pm 0.5$).

11. Since the original number is barely correct to three significant figures, the correlation study is no better. However, a correlation coefficient is a square root calculation, which reduces the number of significant figures by half. The second significant figure in the correlation result is therefore a rough approximation.

12. Obviously, the usual practice of expressing GNP to 3 significant figures is going beyond the precision of the measurements. So many approximations are involved that our measure could not possibly be accurate to 1 part in 1000. The best appraisal is that the error is of the order of 3 per cent or more, signifying that even the second significant figure, as an absolute, is an approximation. Fortunately, measurement of changes in figures of this nature are more precise than the absolute, and all annual changes are expressible in billions of dollars to two significant figures.

13. A little thought shows that no standard composition average would reflect market action accurately since weights of the included stocks would have to change with the relative volume of their trading. Since stocks sell at widely different prices, a mere shift in interest from one stock to another would change the index even in a static market. Thus those who follow the trends must, like those who are interested in any price series, be content with a mere index.

14. These are excellent examples of the effects of time on perceived value. In terms of 1969 incomes, a 50¢ steak dinner and a nickel transit fare looked inviting. But in terms of the effort needed to earn these prices, at the time they were in effect, they are far from attractive. For large numbers of workers, a round-trip transit ride cost 15 minutes of work, or the equivalent of 90 cents in terms of assembly-line wages in 1969. A pound of sirloin steak at 25 cents would be equivalent in wages earned to steak at $1.40 per pound in 1969. The only correct way to make such consumption item cost comparisons is in terms of relative effort needed to earn the price.

15. (a) Any forecast within 11 degrees of 32 degrees would require precautions.

(b) An error of 9 degrees on the downside would be tolerable, since the temperature would probably still be short of freezing in any part of the area.

16. (a) 68% probability that the true percentage is at least 50 1/2%, (1σ)

95% probability that it is at least 50% (2σ)

(b) If $3 \frac{5}{\sqrt{n}} = 1$, $\sqrt{n} = 15$ $n = 225$

17. (a) It omits all newcomers and newly formed families of the previous year.

(b) Baby foods, since a large part of the market for these is composed of newly-formed families, who will be missing. The large market for soft drinks is the teen-ager, and the sample is unlikely to be strongly biased against or for families containing these.

18. He would want to take into account factors of personal physique and of family history which would be related to his own possible longevity. A consistent history of long life in his ancestors, for example, would lead him to estimate that he is likely to live longer than the rates indicate.

19. (a) 0.9 x \$34,600 = \$31,050

0.1 x (\$100,000 + \$40,000 - \$10,000) = \$13,000

Then the payoff matrix is:

	Product demand is Faddish (p = 0.9)	Stable (p = 0.1)
Invest	- \$31,050	\$13,000
Do not invest	\$34,600	\$34,600

Clearly, with no more information than this, the rational decision is "do not invest."

(b) The pay-off may be visualized by the following decision tree:

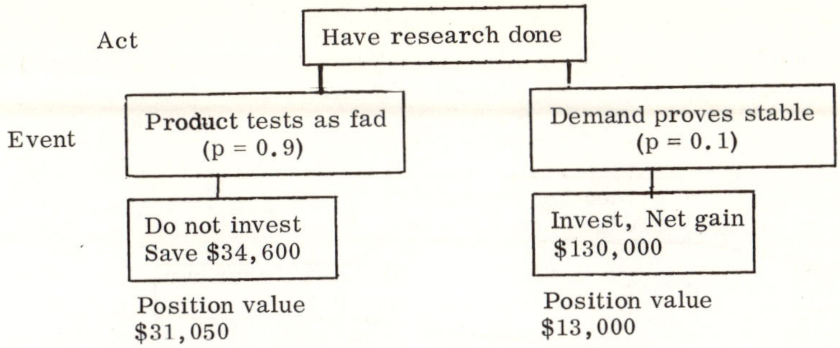

Total position value for research = $43,050

Net incremental value = ($43,050 - $34,600) = ($8,450)

(c) This more realistic situation creates a more complicated tree:

(P. V. = position value)

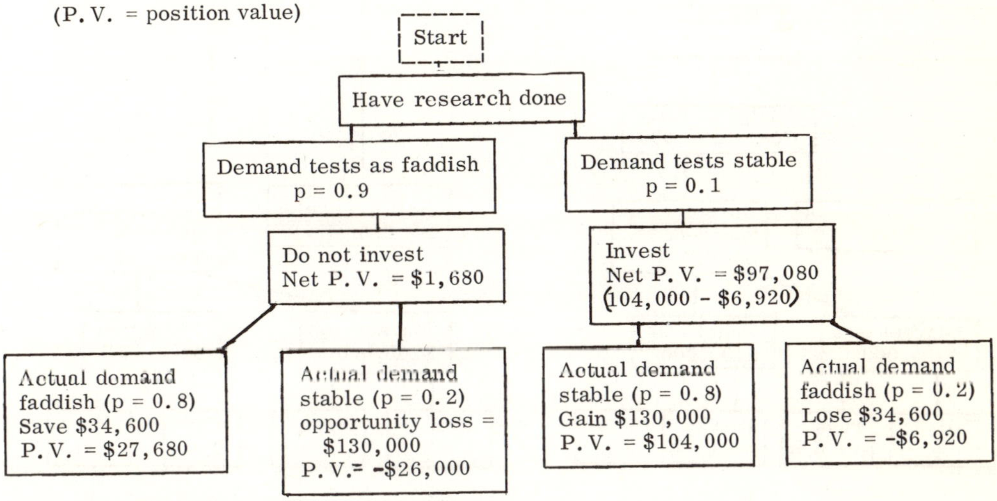

Position Value of research = (0.9 x $1,680) + (0.1 x $97,080)

= $1512 + $9,708

= $10,220

Incremental value of research = $10,220 - $34,600

= -$24,380

(Since without it the decision "not to invest" will give a certain pay-off of $34,600.)

20.

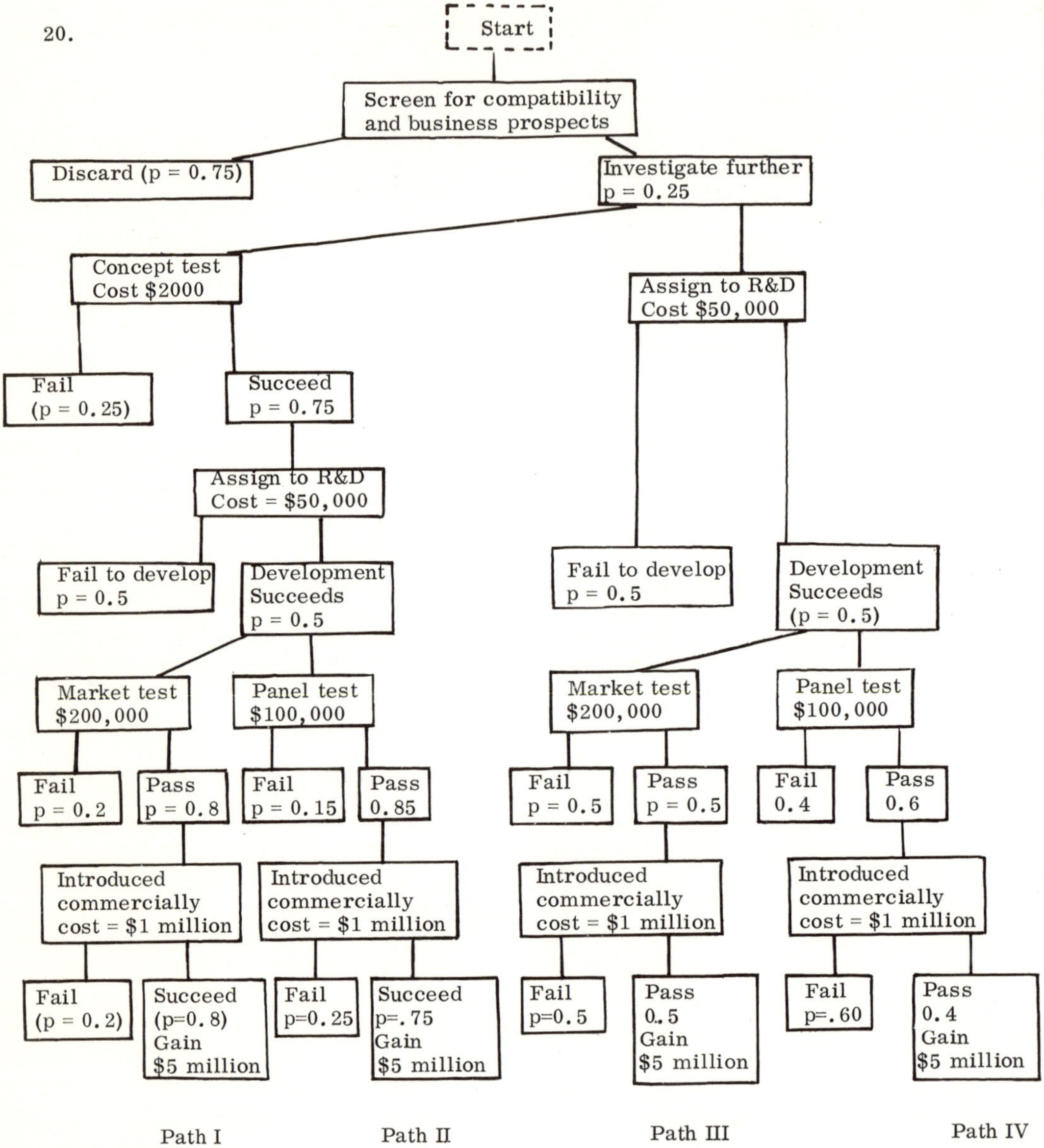
Start
Screen for compatibility and business prospects
Discard (p = 0.75)
Investigate further p = 0.25
Concept test Cost $2000
Assign to R&D Cost $50,000
Fail (p = 0.25)
Succeed p = 0.75
Assign to R&D Cost = $50,000
Fail to develop p = 0.5
Development Succeeds p = 0.5
Fail to develop p = 0.5
Development Succeeds (p = 0.5)
Market test $200,000
Panel test $100,000
Market test $200,000
Panel test $100,000
Fail p = 0.2
Pass p = 0.8
Fail p = 0.15
Pass 0.85
Fail p = 0.5
Pass p = 0.5
Fail 0.4
Pass 0.6
Introduced commercially cost = $1 million
Introduced commercially cost = $1 million
Introduced commercially cost = $1 million
Introduced commercially cost = $1 million
Fail (p = 0.2)
Succeed (p=0.8) Gain $5 million
Fail p=0.25
Succeed p=.75 Gain $5 million
Fail p=0.5
Pass 0.5 Gain $5 million
Fail p=.60
Pass 0.4 Gain $5 million
Path I
Path II
Path III
Path IV

20. (continued) Position values of the four decision paths. (Remember: start at the end and work backwards)

<u>Path I</u> (Concept-test ideas, market test developed ideas)

(0.8 x \$5,000,000) - \$1,000,000 = \$4,000,000 - \$1,000,000 = \$3,000,000

(0.8 x \$3,000,000) - \$200,000 = \$2,400,000 - \$200,000 = \$2,200,000

(0.5 x \$2,200,000) - \$50,000 = \$1,100,000 - \$50,000 = \$1,050,000

(.75 x \$1,050,000) - \$2,000 = \$787,500 - \$2,000 = <u>\$785,500</u>

<u>Path II</u> (Concept-test ideas, panel-test developed products)

(0.75 x \$5,000,000) - \$1,000,000 = \$3,750,000 - \$1,000,000 = \$2,750,000

(0.85 x \$2,750,000) - \$100,000 = \$2,337,500 - \$100,000 = \$2,237,500

(0.5 x \$2,237,500) - \$50 = \$1,118,750 - \$50,000 = \$1,068,750

(0.75 x \$1,068,750) - \$2,000 = \$801,563 - \$2,000 = <u>\$799,863</u>

<u>Path III</u> (No concept test, market-test developed products)

(0.5 x \$5,000,000) - \$1,000,000 = \$2,500,000 - \$1,000,000 = \$1,500,000

(0.5 x \$1,150,000) - \$200,000 = \$575,000 - \$200,000 = \$375,000

(0.5 x \$375,000) - \$50,000 = \$187,500 - \$50,000 = <u>\$137,500</u>

<u>Path IV</u> (No concept test, panel-test developed ideas)

(0.4 x \$5,000,000) - \$1,000,000 = \$2,000,000 - \$1,000,000 = \$1,000,000

(0.6 x \$1,000,000) - \$100,000 = \$600,000 - \$100,000 = \$500,000

(0.5 x \$500,000) - \$50,000 = \$250,000 - \$50,000 = <u>\$200,000</u>

21. (a) 0.2 x 0.2 x 0.2 x 0.2 = .0016 (The fact that they are equal does not alter the fact that they are independent.)
    (b) .0016 x \$1,600,000 = \$2,560
    (c) \$1,600,000

22. p = 0.65 (Since n = 9, each bid represents the center of $\frac{1}{9+1}$ th part of the total probability of 1.0. A bid for 0% profit is thus the center of the 7th fractile from the top.)

23. We can estimate the shortage cost corresponding to several alternative (Q, R) inventory policies and then ask if the cost of being out of stock one less time is worth at least the costs of maintaining the inventory at a level which will prevent it.

24. (a) Let C = no. of pounds of corn in 100 lb. of mix

S = no. of pounds of soybean meal in 100 lb. of mix

M = no. of pounds of meat scraps in 100 lb. of mix

Then $.14C + .44S = .20\,(100) = 20$ (Since 100 lb. has 20 lb. protein)

$.14\,(100 - S) + .44S = 14 - .14S + .44S = 20$

$$.30S = 20 - 14 = 6$$

$$S = \frac{6}{0.3} = 20$$

(b) $(.80 \times \$2.40) + (.20 \times \$3.60) = \$1.92 + \$.72 = \$2.64/100\#$

(c) $.5M + .14\,(100 - M) = 20$

$$.36M = 20 - 14 = 6$$

$$M = \frac{6}{.36} = 16.67$$

$(.1667 \times \$4.20) + (.8333 \times \$2.40) = \$.70 + \$2.00 = \$2.70/100\#$

At these prices, the corn-soy mix is cheaper by $.06/100#.

(d) If meat scraps drop to $3.60/100 lb., the cost of corn-meat mix becomes $(.1667 \times \$3.60) + (.8333 \times \$2.40) = \$.60 + \$2.00 = \$2.60/100\#$

Then the meat-corn mix will be cheaper by $.04/100#.

(e)

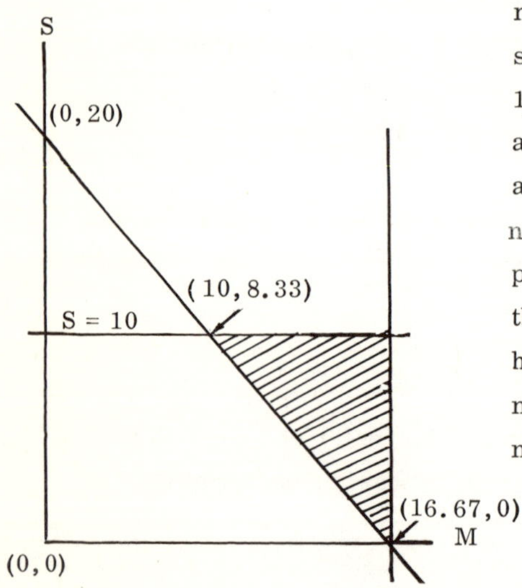

Calculations in (a) above show that the minimum protein requirements can be satisfied with either 20# of soy meal of 16.67# of meat scraps in 100#. Thus any proportionate mix of meat scraps and soy meal on the straight line connecting (0, 20) and (16.67, 0) gives the protein minimum. The added condition that soy meal constitute no more than one-half the supplement means that 100# must contain no more than 10# of soy meal, indicated by the horizontal line S = 10. Since there is no limit on the proportion of meat scraps, any mix containing 16.67 pounds of scraps will satisfy both conditions, as indicated by the vertical at M = 16.67. All solutions thus lie in the shaded area, and the most economical somewhere on the diagonal bordering it--just where depending on the relative price of meat scraps and soy meal.

25. (a)

1	120	(100 entrants plus 20 holdovers)	Lose	24
2	115	(96 from previous level plus 19 holdovers)	Lose	19
3	115	(96 from previous level plus 19 holdovers)	Lose	29
4	103	(86 from previous level plus 17 holdovers)	Lose	21
5	90	(82 from previous level plus 8 holdovers)	Lose	8
6	90	(82 from previous level plus 8 holdovers)	Lose	8

(b) Grant 72 degrees

26. The most common procedure in use usually diagrammed as shown in the accompanying chart.

27. (a) BIRTH RATE, PER 1,000 POPULATION 1910-1967, U.S.A.

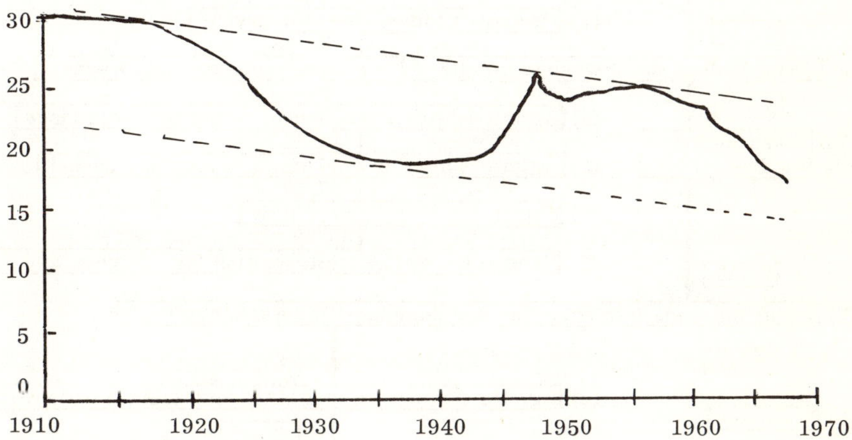

The long-run trend of the general rate appears to be down. Neither the temporary sharp demobilization rise of 1947 nor the baby boom peak of 1957 reached the 1910 level, and the 1967 level had already gone below the depression level.

(b) Judgment on the likelihood that the trend may be fundamental would depend on looking for the relationship of specific birth rates to population factors which seem likely not to be reversed in time--the relationship of birth rates to urbanization, education of women, rising occupational class of families, housewives working outside of the home. In fact, all of these trends are clearly associated with declining birth rates (see discussion in Wasson & McConaughy, Buying Behavior and Marketing Decisions, Appleton-Century-Crofts, 1968, pp. 181-184).

26. A COMMON WRINGING WASHING MACHINE WASHDAY NETWORK

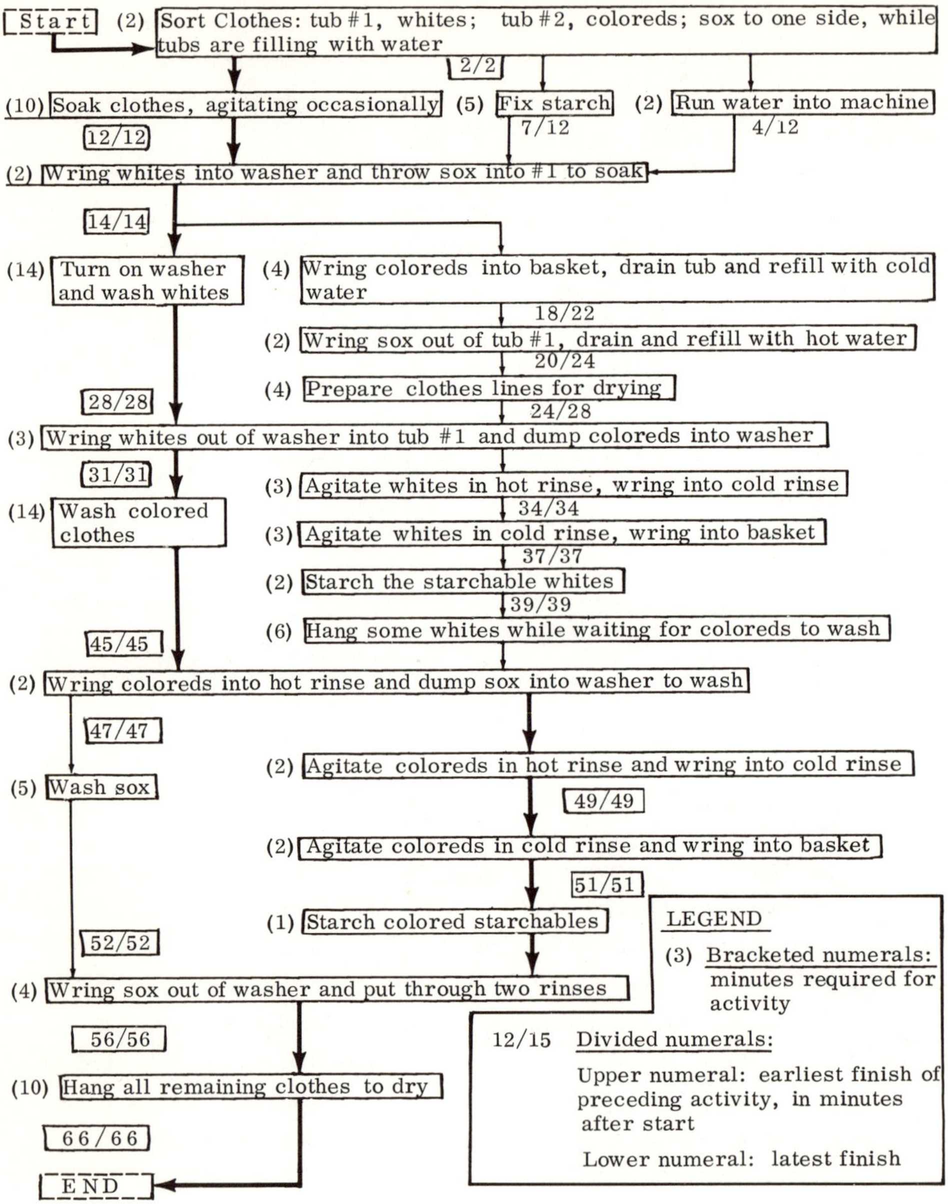

28. The fact that the process is both complex and unfamiliar renders it almost certain that the cost estimate developed on the basis of the initial production run is highly inflated. As the aircraft industry has learned, the learning curve effect is bound to decrease costs with time. The first Boeing 707 airliner built cost $12,000,000, but a price of $5,000,000 each proved very profitable.

29. (a) Your graph should look something like the following:

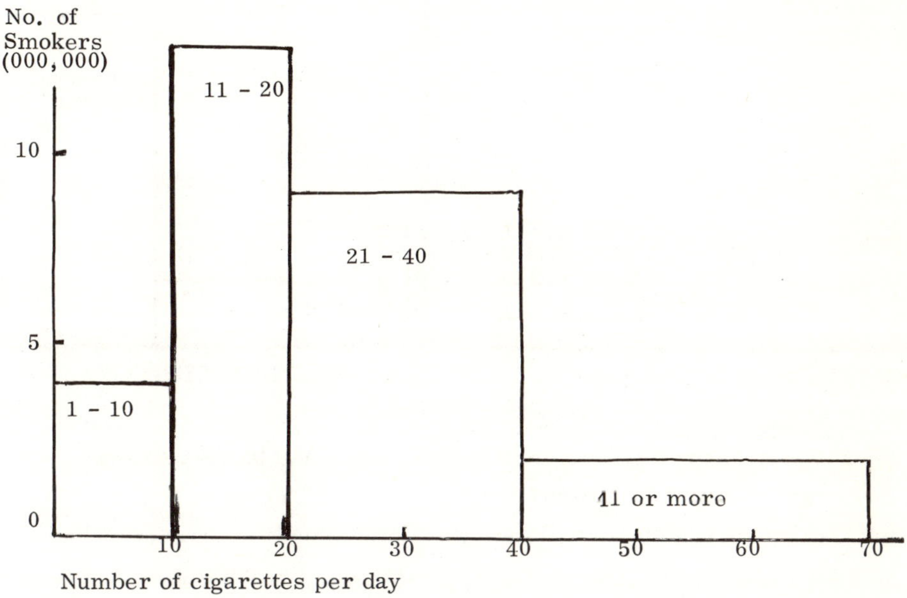

(b)

Cigarettes/day	Smokers		Cigarettes/day	
	Millions	%	Millions	%
Total	28.3	100	594	100
1 - 10	4.5	16	22.5	4
11 - 20	12.8	45	192	32
21 - 40	9.0	32	270	45
40 or more	2.0	7	110	19

(c) Quite clearly, those who smoke more than a pack a day, and probably those who exceed a pack-and-a-half a day. Indeed, while those smoking more than 2 packs a day constitute only 7 percent of the market, they burn up about one-fifth of all cigarettes consumed.

30. You should have a series of plots looking somewhat like the following 2 for "all industries":

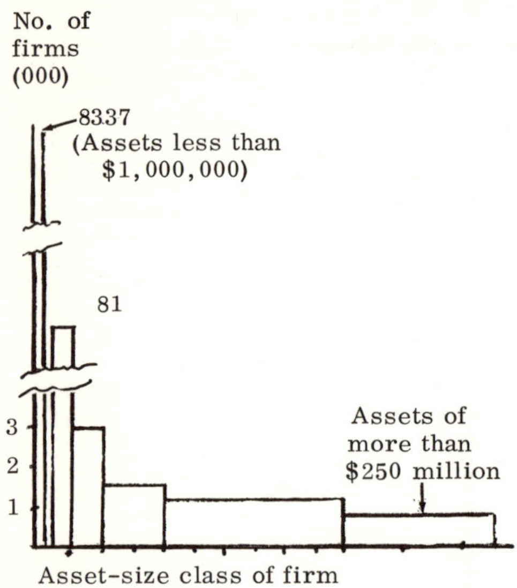

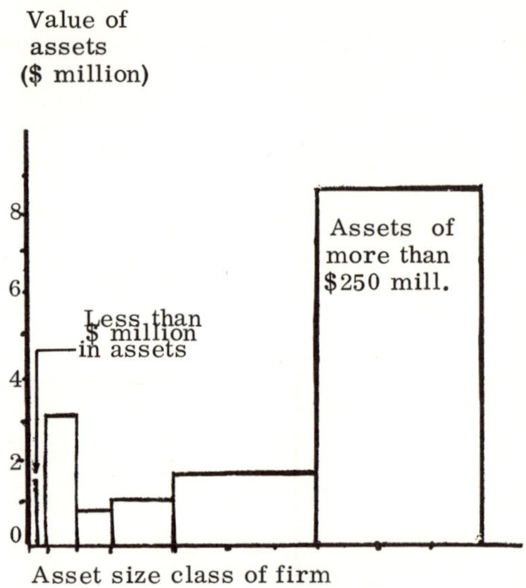

(b) For any one product, a mere handful of firms will be the customer for the great bulk of the product.

(c) The few big customers will have such large requirements, they will be most economically sold and serviced directly. By contrast the great majority of buyers will make such small purchases that they will have to be serviced by some intermediary set of distributive organizations.

31. "The majority" are not the principle market for any important product. The heavy users are a definite minority, but they buy the greatest part of the product. Generally speaking, the most profitable design is usually one which appeals to this heavy-user minority--they use most of it, and are sold easiest. Of course, if one competitor has this market "sewed-up," then the vulnerable part consists of some light-user segment, but the firm which follows this strategy will seldom be better than Number Two. The important percentage figure is not of numbers of customers, but of volume of use.

INDEX